D1643893

DAVID
CRAIG
NATIVE
STONES

ALSO BY DAVID CRAIG

POETRY
Latest News (with Ken Sprague)
Homing
Against Looting

FICTION
The Rebels and the Hostage (with Nigel Gray)

NON-FICTION
Scottish Literature and the Scottish People 1680–1830
The Real Foundations
Extreme Situations (with Michael Egan)

DAVID CRAIG

NATIVE STONES

A Book About Climbing

Secker and Warburg

LONDON

First published in England 1987 by
Martin Secker & Warburg Limited
54 Poland Street, London W1V 3DF

Copyright © 1987 by David Craig

British Library Cataloguing in Publication Data
Craig, David, 1932–
  Native stones : a book about climbing
  1. Rock climbing
  I. Title
  796.5'223'0924   GV200.2

ISBN 0-436-11350-3

Typeset in 10½/13½pt Bembo by
Hewer Text Composition Services, Edinburgh
Printed in Great Britain by
Redwood Burn Ltd, Trowbridge

To the veterans

Acknowledgements

Several parts of this book first appeared in different forms in the following magazines, to whose editors the usual acknowledgements are due: *Climber, Climber and Rambler, Giant Steps, High, London Review of Books, Poetry Wales.*

My thanks are also due to the following for permission to quote from the titles mentioned: W. B. Yeats, 'An Irish Airman Foresees His Death', from *The Collected Poems of W. B. Yeats*, A. P. Watt Ltd on behalf of Michael B. Yeats and Macmillan London Ltd; Hugh MacDiarmid, 'The War With England', Martin Brian & O'Keefe Ltd; Rev. Christopher Idle, *John Wesley's Journal*, Lion Publishing; T. S. Eliot, 'East Coker' and 'Ash Wednesday' from *Collected Poems 1909–1962*, Ted Hughes, 'Prometheus on His Crag (11)' from *Moortown*, Ezra Pound, 'Pisan Cantos' from *The Cantos of Ezra Pound*, all published by Faber & Faber Ltd; Samuel Coleridge, *Collected Letters*, Keith Douglas, *From Alamein to Zem Zem*, Gerard Manley Hopkins, 'The Wreck of the Deutschland', William Wordsworth, *The Prelude*, all published by Oxford University Press; Ed Drummond, *Hard Rock*, ed. Ken Wilson, Grafton, a division of the Collins Publishing Group; Lewis Mumford, *The Condition of Man* © 1944, 1972, Harcourt Brace Jovanovich Inc; Donald MacAuley, 'Comharra Stiùiridh', Gairm Publications; Geoffrey Moorhouse, *The Fearful Void*, A. P. Watt Ltd on behalf of Geoffrey Moorhouse; Plekhanov, *Unaddressed Letters*, Lawrence & Wishart Ltd; *The Mountain Spirit*, ed. Charles Tobias and Harold Drasdo, Victor Gollancz Ltd; Michael Roberts, 'The Poetry and Humour of Mountaineering', Janet Adam Smith.

List of Illustrations

As a young man Moore preferred to use native stones, believing that as an Englishman he should understand them. His choice of brown Hornton stone from Edgehill in Oxfordshire for the Leeds *Reclining Figure*, a material with fossil remains, pronounced veins of iron ore and colours varying from light brown to greenish blue, enabled him to express his idea of figure sculpture as landscape. The extremities are treated like sunlit hills with a valley in shadow between them and veins like contours on a map.

Henry Moore: Sculpture in the Making,
Leeds City Art Gallery, 1985

1

The crags act on us as the moon does on the seas, inert mineral masses exerting their force, leading us to their poles. People, birds, goats, sheep – we are drawn along the ledges, up the gullies, out onto the buttresses and pinnacles. In front of the spires of the Dolomites the swallows, swifts and martins whirl in an insect-dance, like migrants swarming round a phalanx of lighthouses. Beneath most crags in the Lake District a sheep lies smashed, the bones and fleece rendering down into the scree, the meat gone to the foxes and the hoodie crows. People make tracks each year for Lundy Island, its pier of granite jutting four hundred feet out of the Bristol Channel, to find intricate routes up the three miles of ramparts on its western coast or to ring and weigh its birds of passage, the goldcrests and the flycatchers. On Brimham moor above Nidderdale the gritstone masses, great rough-cut gems, are disposed among pines and birches and shaggy heather, like masterworks in a sculpture park. We humans pass to and fro between them, playing hide-and-seek with our children or performing the gymnastic movements of our cult on the facets of the rocks.

All sorts frequent the crags. Ravens wing high above: at one time, on our way up to a crag, if a single raven's black cross was printed on the blue I would say, 'Raven, seek thy brother,' an Arab saying to ward off ill-luck. But the ravens are benign, barking and tumbling in the lifelong mating play. The peregrines are deadly purposeful, trim-forged arrow-heads shooting in a straight line into sight above the skyline of the cliff or perching on a vantage-point and grating out their warnings for an hour on end. In France or the Dolomites, alpine swifts scamper frantically across and across the air a few feet out from the limestone massif, never alighting, seeming to follow some invisible wirewalk rigged along the face. On rock terraces in Cumbria you meet Herdwick sheep who have nibbled their way along a narrowing pasture to a point of no return and stare at you out of their obstinate eyes, determined not to be rescued.

On the crag itself the old, the young, and the middle-aged cross their purposes and even their ropes at times. Grizzled men, who remember when these places were nearly deserted, climb routes where the rock has taken on a patina from two or three generations of sweaty use, they wear shabby anoraks and use protection nuts whose metal shoulders are rounded like stones ground to shingle. While out on the sheerest faces sun-tanned boys in their teens, in gymnasts' shorts, festooned like Christmas trees with the latest vivid gear, manoeuvre up lines marked by little dabs of powder-white where the Extreme climbers have put 'chalk' (magnesium carbonate) on their fingerends to absorb sweat and maximise the friction.

Here you can achieve an exhilaration where the most concentrated thoughts and the most draining exertion of your body fuse in a using, an expressing and deploying, of your self that can be compared with only one other thing – making love. You can balance and dance and brachiate so limberly from point to point – up glinting granite with waves white as gannets bursting a hundred feet beneath – that it takes an effort not to breast off into the air and let the updraught carry you like a seagull. Or you can quail in the face of a stride or a stretch too frightening to be contemplated – back off and surrender the lead to your mate (if he'll take it), and then the memory of having capitulated turns your self-respect as pulpy as a fruit that is rotting from the stone outwards.

It all happens at a pace that can be remembered: as deliberately as a work of art shaping under your pen or brush or mallet; as lengthily as a night when one dream dissolves into the next and none of them are forgotten; as concentratedly as a spell of watching to see an animal. The gradual, trudging hours peak into an instant of revelation – there it is (the roedeer, the eagle) – the lovely image manifests itself – your mind snaps it for good – then nature lapses back into its immense quietude. So it is with climbing: the hours of the long walk in; the upward plod under loads that bow us till we look like a file of prisoners in the exercise yard; the brilliant minutes when that fusion of thought, sensation, and bodily movement happens yet again, as though a flare had exploded and shown you the features of your earth as you had never seen them before. On a great route (Gimmer Crack in Great Langdale or A Dream of White Horses on Anglesey) this happens continuously until you feel as though you have been swimming for hours as fluently as a dolphin in its halcyon element.

You can do it anywhere, almost. 'Why don't they do it in the road?' sang the Beatles, and so they do. Dave Cook, one of the funniest and most political of our climbing writers, described in *High* (April 1985) how some Londoners climb on a long brick wall three hundred yards from Clapham North tube station. The local boys call them 'spiders' and fling hockey balls at them to try and knock them off into the dog shit down below. In the Peak district they seem to revel in climbing immediately above the ragged tin roofs and oily concrete of old goods yards, above trunk roads and chimney pots, and the whole place is reft by workings: the vertebrae of the region's limestone spine have been shattered as much by gelignite as by the Ice Ages. I sometimes climb there to humour my Sheffield friends but all the time I want to be away, to fly as straight as a spring migrant northwards to the Cairngorm corries, or at least to some back dale in Cumbria, perhaps to Swindale abreast of Shap, where most days you will see not even a walker. As you look out from a stance level with the peregrine's well-limed perch, nothing is happening below except, perhaps, a hay-baler chugging along the lines of tossed June hay or some cattle suddenly deciding to go and stand knee-deep in the shallows of the beck. Here nothing gets between me and the steeps themselves, Gouther Crag and Fang Buttress. So few feet tread the paths that they are still green between the unwinding croziers of the bracken. Human use of the land is changing at a pace that seems more evolutionary than historical. The stone dykes look as permanent as the crags, though even these are far from eternal: since 1983 a ten-foot pendent fang has dropped off a fine steep route called Sostenuto and made its start much harder. But frost and spate and drought are to be expected. When you climb in such a place, you are working with the grain of nature, immersed in its atmosphere, and your very heartbeat feels eased into more inevitable, less forced rhythms.

I have climbed for only thirteen seasons, never in the Alps, never in America, never been to the great limestone cliffs of the Verdon, never been above eight thousand feet, never climbed above E2 or led above 5b. I am a middling sort of club climber at the flickering age of fifty-four, who has been to the Dolomites a couple of times and has helped to put up a dozen routes. So what is the justification for offering my experiences as having any significance in any age, least of all one in which climbers can scale six thousand-foot faces in the Andes, or spend three weeks on one route in Yosemite that overhangs all the way, sleeping in bags suspended above nine hundred feet of air, or climb Nanga Parbat or Everest solo, without oxygen or (in the end) a tent?

Climbing literature, naturally, has shone its strongest light on the leaders and heroes of the sport, whose feats are enough to make the armchair public gasp with awe or horror. The climbing writers whose work has lasted have nearly all been in the forefront of the sport in their time: O. G. Jones at the start of intensive rock-climbing in the Lake District, H. W. Tilman in the Himalayas in the Thirties, Menlove Edwards, chief pioneer of hard rock-climbing in Snowdonia just before and during the

War, W. H. Murray in the first heyday of severe Scottish ice-climbing, Peter Boardman among post-War specialists in 24,000-foot mountains, and now Ed Drummond and Jim Perrin in this latest phase when rock-climbing has attained its highest profile in the evolution of special skills, training methods, equipment, and also in literary sophistication.

My own approach lies in what are now the back dales and easier-angled crags. I am most at home on the routes of the last generation because those of the present one are too steep for me and the holds too small. My climbing grew late out of a lifelong fascination with nature, consciously escapist and very much concerned with the secretion of poetry and expressive prose.

> The social scene could be little
> But confusion and loss to me,
> And, Scotland, better than all your towns
> Was a bed of moss to me . . .
>
> I was better with the sounds of the sea
> Than with the voices of men
> And in desolate and desert places
> I found myself again . . .

Probably nobody who says that (whether Hugh MacDiarmid writing it or myself invoking it) ever quite means it. We are that much more sociable than our more romantically beleaguered self-images imply. Yet nature has enthralled me since I first staggered about waist-deep in the heather hills of Aberdeenshire. I wanted always to immerse myself in the wilderness, the beyond-the-civilised, the steep slopes and the blue or grey skylines angling up beyond the suburbs and beyond the farm-lands. Nature was the lovely element, the countryside was where we went whenever we were free, and this was renewed when our children had come into the world and needed the nourishment of getting to know whatever lay outside our own city limits.

We walked the green trods through the dales of Yorkshire, we climbed the mountains and combed the beaches of Wester Ross and the Hebrides, and then the whole thing leafed again, renewed and refocused itself, by taking to the steepest, least frequented parts of the country – the crags. It was as though I had grown another pair of eyes, or a special limb – one that reached up compulsively, curled round edges, fitted itself onto the rough, far-out ends of things.

Even if you walk out into the wilderness there is still a layer of artefact between yourself and nature – the sole of your boot. But to climb is to be intimate with the very stuff of our habitat, to smell its minerals (the struck-match odour of split rock or rock in a heatwave), to imitate the lie of it in the twisting and flexing of your muscles, to relish its most durable elements through the nerves of your fingerends. One of Engels's most fundamental insights has always been for me the motto I would choose if I was allowed just one. 'Practically,' he said about Lancashire work-people who had dispensed with religion, 'they live for this world and strive to make themselves at home in it.' We can't actually make ourselves at home on the crags (although a friend of mine spent three weeks on the North America Wall of El Capitan, writing his novel in the morning and climbing in the afternoon). But when I sit on a six-inch ledge with my feet dangling above a two hundred-foot drop, the hart's-tongue fern and dwarf hawthorn a few inches from my eyes, the air smelling of moss, wood-pigeons clattering out of the tree-tops down below, then at least for a time I have grafted myself back into nature, and the sense of rightness achieved, or regained, is unmistakable.

2
————

Into Rock

He stretched to fit the rock
He crouched and eeled to fit the rock
Thinned and flexed to fit it
Spreadeagled on its smelted plates
Feeling his fingers hone to claws

6
————

He chimneyed up the gigantic split
Sitting in air like an ejecting pilot
While the sky out there
Blazed at him and the granite ground his spine
Then surfaced from the fissure like a mole

Bearing the chimney's pressure in his hunch
Its rising in his springing tendons
Its darkness in the gleam behind his eyes

Bearing the face's crystals in his fingerprints
Its cracking torsions in his wrists
Its drop in the air beneath his insteps

It moulded him. He was its casting.
His clay was kneaded to its bas-relief.
His brain infolded, mimicking its strata.
And when he called, and the echo heard his note,
It parodied his language.

3

The first rocks that I remember (who knows what dark rough shapes were there on the horizon, or in the foreground, before my conscious memory began?) were the Three Kings, at the west end of the beach at Cullen, on the Banffshire coast of the Moray Firth. They set a bound to our summer holiday playground. On this side were tin buckets with cartoon pictures on their sides, yellow and cherry-red and blue, chortling faces, pop-eyes, fat bathers dancing on one foot with an orange crab clinging to the big toe of the other; spades with wooden handles whose blades buckled at mid-point if you shovelled too vigorously; white-legged fathers in blue swimming-costumes with shoulderstraps; mothers in rubber bathingcaps, long fringed towels shawled round their shoulders . . . Beyond the Three Kings? Nothing. That I knew of. Or was curious about, even. This smoothed yellowish-white stretch was all we needed, my brother and I, the grains of it prickling between our toes, its dry drifts mining and collapsing under our footsoles.

The Three Kings stood up out of the wave-planed beach, earth-brown, shaggy with their own secret atmosphere. Kings? The word resonated obscurely. Heads of grass which time had grazed and roughened like statues buried in rubble. Kings – robes tattered by hardship in exile. Kings – three of them – the biggest was the strongest, the other two diminished in perspective, Rock the First, Rock the Second, Rock the Third – a line of rulers, ruins, castles, derelict keeps . . . Such were the images that lurked in the density of those three crags, thirty-foot hulks of Old Red Sandstone, which I last saw fifty years ago and have never dwelt on again till now.

They occupied the foreshore like the Welsh rocks in John Blakemore's photograph, standing for durance (see plate 1). The dictionary says this word is obsolete. Then we had better revive it, for what else means continuance and hardness and the further connotation of imprisonment? The rock is trapped, it will 'always' be there. How ever it churned and bounced and grated in its earlier days, it lost momentum long ago. Although it is confined 'forever' to this site, there is chagrin under the pity we feel for its simplicity and the respect we have for its hardihood, because we know it will outlast us. In itself it is innocent of meanings. It is so real yet so unalive. It is as present, in Blakemore's portrait, as the two thousand-year-old bogman exhumed from the Danish peat, skin tough and blackened as the hardwood of a ju-ju mask, yet the pores still show and the hairs that grew for a little after the rawhide strangled him at the moment of the sacrifice . . .

But this rock never lived, never changed by its own actions, never inched along the floors of lukewarm oceans or opened and closed little mouths as the tide filled and drained until the flesh died and the ooze packed each shell, moulding a cast that outlasted the dinosaurs and may outlast the mammals. This rock seemed as autonomous as an animal only when it welled or spurted in the torrents of magma from the volcanic furnaces where the planet smelts itself, outpouring material for the forges up above. It is azoic; it never housed the tunnellings and wormings of the spirifers. For a thousand million years it was a particle in the Archaean shield which the world bared to the sun's tempering. It plunged to the bottom of a Cambrian gorge, the Ordovician ocean sluiced above its head until a volcano opened under it, tossed it clear into the only seconds' sunshine it would know for thirty million years until it fell back onto the Cambrian seabed and waited for the Caledonian mountains to shoulder out of the welter of waters and boulders. It baked in desert heat, howling sandstorms buffed it, it chilled to the core as the Carboniferous seas rose round it, it could not feel the fingerings of seaweeds and bivalves that lodged in the grain of it where the sheer armouring of the bedding-planes had parted under stress . . .

Or so it would fantasise, if rock was minded, and wanted to write itself back into history with a human vanity, lusting to be an immortal individual, to save the self from dying backwards and forwards into the flux of material. Traumas of fusing and melting and crystallising into unrecognisable identities have gone from Rock's awareness, overlaid in Rock's impregnable ego-fortress. 'I am, therefore I think,' he boasts, but nobody hears him, he is inaudible (actually he is mute), and in this he is consistent, he is the same all through. There was never a toad at the heart of a stone or a diamond in the head of a toad. Inflexible crystals, pulpy tissues – the two cannot merge unless the one dissolves or the other dies: a kidney-stone's fine daggers are the worst of torments. Rock is everything we are not, the hardest thing to be. We have to approach it knowing it is unyielding and that our fantasies steam back off it, making as little impression on the thing itself as a wind-flaw dappling and vanishing on a field of barley.

4

My first climb now seems more like a memoir than a memory, like pages from someone else's book with pieces missing, eaten away by damp and pests, by careless use and the blowing of some wind that covers up our past. It is still 'there', cells of my brain must be secreting it, but they are clogged and overlaid by other things too much . . .

Lochnagar in Aberdeenshire, pure Cairngorm in its physique but separated from the main range by the River Dee. October 1952: a louring sky like swathes of dirty fleece. Buttresses of granite dimming in and out of focus – out of sight – sharpening into view again. In the huge scoop of the corrie, boulders litter like herds of shaggy bison; in their shelter I had found oversized blaeberries on a hill walk with Jill that summer, or maybe the summer before . . . Above and to the right a fearsome entrance funnels upwards between the tall, cracked strakes of the corrie face. This is Black Spout . . . Sharp shingle and gravel slippery underfoot. Unappetising sandwiches, the first I ever made for myself, white bread cut thick, Echo margarine plastered on in sickly yellow scabs, tomatoes whose sliced flesh drops coldly into my stomach as we perch beneath the left-hand branch of the Spout and make ourselves eat . . .

It has been a long but gradual slog up past Fox's Well from Allt-na-giubhsaich in the upper reaches of Glen Muick. My companions (how did they find out that I wanted to climb?) are Ian MacPhail, a learned elf, aquiline nose and humorous eyes, and Gavin Alexander, a very Aberdonian person of the old school, round-lensed glasses, moustache like a small bundle of hay stuck in beneath his probing scholar's nose. My maternal uncle, archaeologist and librarian, must have looked just like this thirty years before. Both of them (I think) wore massive boots shod with Tricounis – climbing nails studded round the welts, each one with a row of blunt points, like elephants' molars.

I scarcely knew them, had never been out with them before, and I never saw Gavin Alexander again. Gavin and Ian, I hope you are both alive and well. You gave me a start on this utterly exhilarating and absorbing pursuit, the climbing of steep rock.

From the débris of memoir three highlights still shine out. As we approached the foot of the Spout, a voice hailed me from the air above our heads: 'Hiya, Davie! Fancy seeing you here!' (or words to that effect). It was Bill Brooker, clinging onto an overhang. He had been at school with me for thirteen years (from 1937). His tall stories enthralled and amused us in kindergarten: his father had lived in India and Bill told us calmly that tigers prowled in the streets of Calcutta. Once the War broke out, Bill of course had several bombs in his garden. Presently his knees became ornamented with red and purple scars. He was forever climbing, up the highest trees, along ivied walls with apple trees on the far side. At seventeen he was a fearless rugby forward in the 1st XV whose high-kneed, dodging charges smashed straight through the pack behind which (in the 2nd XV) I scurried about as a rather light and vulnerable scrum-half. Now, at university, I was immersed in studying and writing while Bill was busy doing something or other 'up in the hills'. It was more than twenty years before I learned that he had become a leader in the elite of Cairngorm climbers and that his winter pioneering on those thousand-foot cliffs, climbing usually between three and four thousand feet above sea level, had earned him eleven mentions in the *Mountain* list of 'British Climbing since the War'. And it was not until August 1985 that I was able to find out, as we walked up to climb Pinnacle Face on Lochnagar, that on that day in October 1952 he was roped up with Tom Patey, doing the first ascent of a route called The Stack.

Ian, Gavin and I were aiming for a route on Black Spout Pinnacle which peaked for me in two further highlights. To escape from the left-hand branch of the Spout and reach the crag itself, we squirmed through a hole. Moist rocks resisted us, forced us into the cavers' experience where ribs and lungs feel crushed inwards not by actual pressure but by the duress of darkness and the sheer obduracy of rock. You become a lower animal, jerking and scrabbling like an armadillo, working more by the contraction and expansion of an earthworm than by the higher techniques of anthropoid limbs and digits.

Somewhere up above I had my first taste of exposure – not in the medical but the climbers' sense – the experience of precariously occupying a perch above a drop, with minimal supports. For the next hour this mined at me continuously, instilling a sense of weakness, powerlessness, and fear (fear of falling, hurting, failing). But I was not powerless. As Ian (or Gavin) took in the rope above me and I clawed and inched up a slabby wall with a great gulf between my heels and the scree and the metallic loch-water five hundred feet below, fear alchemised into thrill, or nearly. The negative (demoralised) feelings still predominated but the awareness of upward movement achieved by one's own muscle and daring against the subversion of gravity was extremely delicious. At one point (the scraps of memoir are hard to decipher here) I felt my feet pedalling helplessly on the granite. I'd time to think, 'That gulf is waiting for me – I can't manage this.' But no fall occurred. Did I manage? Or did Ian or Gavin give me the aid I would come to know much later as the indignity of a tight rope?

I hope I managed.

I climbed once more that autumn, in still gloomier mists, on the Mitre Ridge of Garbh Choire, Beinn a Buird, in the main range of the Cairngorms, along with Ian and his brother Malcolm – a short broad man with a kilt and handsomely moulded calves.

I never climbed again for twenty-one years, or on Lochnagar for thirty-three.

5

Where does the climbing impulse spring from? How conditioned is it, and how inborn? At the cold dry Easter of 1966, Jill and I drove over from Aberdeen to Torridon with our youngest son,

Neil. He was showing lively signs of evolving into a toddler, hauling himself up by the legs of brothers and sister, tables and piano, but relaxed too and content to locomote around by a method he had just invented – jerking rapidly backwards in a sitting position by drawing up his legs then shooting them out again. (It was much quicker on vinyl floors than on carpet or grass.) Where the Gairloch road forks off to Badachro between aboriginal oaks and alders and thickly mossed outcrops, we paused for fresh air, dressed Neil in his red jumpsuit, and leaned him against a little rockface that rose out of the fescue grass beside the road. He looked quietly gratified at the sensation of balancing and surveying the world from two and a half feet up – slowly turned – explored the bumps and ledges of the rock with inquisitive fingers – reached for an edge at the extremity of his grasp – pulled a little – raised his foot and toed a hold experimentally . . . We didn't stop him. He just, apparently, found it unmanageable and came back down, looking thoughtful and unworried . . . He had not been imitating anybody; I hadn't climbed on rock for almost fourteen years and the others didn't begin for another eight.

Presumably what Neil did that day was equivalent to the behaviour of the weeks-old babies who hang contentedly by their hands from crossbars if someone places them in that position. It's a standard illustration in pediatric textbooks. The instinctive power of brachiating like an ape or monkey surfaces from the matrix where it has been latent for hundreds of generations. Yet people say 'But *why* do you climb?' with a strange emphasis, unbelieving or derisive or querulous, as though they were trying to understand (or not to understand) the impulse behind a sex-change or a rubber fetish. We should simply answer, 'Because it's natural – because we can.' Swimming never attracts the Incredulous Question syndrome yet it too is latent in the depths of our natures and it too is something babies can do readily, before they have learned to fear.

This incomprehension on the part of some non-climbers is then reflected in our own compulsion to find reasons for what we do. Mallory's wonderfully cool, even teasing 'Because it's there' sounds like his pukka-sahib way of holding at arm's length this boring or silly ferretting after motives. True, it is as natural for adults to analyse themselves as it is for infants to climb or swim, but as we analyse we should be remembering that at bottom we do this thing – we clamber and swing and reach and balance – because we can. Our limbs and digits reach up for the next vantage-point with an urge as inevitable as a seedling's when it erects itself towards the light. We can see it in time-lapse film: the quivering of the plumule's sinuous little stem, its nosing this way and that between the crumbs of the earth, its lithe extension upwards. And we have seen this also in a natural-time film, made by Border Television and nationally networked in 1985: the slow stretching by Dave Armstrong as he tried to clip a karabiner into the piton on the third pitch of a new Extreme climb, Incantations, on the east wall of the Napes in Wasdale – his persuading of his arm to untelescope itself just one inch more – his fingers' effort to grip at their very furthest reach without any clutching that might jerk his body out of balance.

Neil next climbed when he was nine – quite a lag. Usual in our society when so many physical powers slumber or else flow into the more organised sports whose tortuous rules lend themselves to the full civilised treatment, coaching, competitions, even exam papers . . . But we clambered about – onto the roof for tennis balls lodged in gutters, up sycamores or alders with ladders of branches overhanging the rivers of Roeburndale and Dent. If there was a way up the smooth lower bole of a tree, up I went: the ape in me was at least that much liberated. And Neil had his flying start: when he was just nine, his elder siblings were fourteen or so and beginning to go climbing in the Lake District.

In the summer of 1974, in Torridon, we rowed across from Diabaig to Araid, a deserted crofting village whose last two people, Maggy and Flora, had come to live in the old schoolhouse near our camp. Only a footpath led to Araid, overgrown with jungly heather where lizards flickered and black water rose through the peat. The crofts had occupied a grassy saddle between one sea-loch and another. Bog-cotton had invaded the township's peat cuttings and bracken rose thickly inside the dry-stone dykes surrounding the few apple trees. A single rowan stood on a rocky islet beside the landing-place, its cluster of red berries shining like a leading-light. Civilisation had made this beach-head on the narrow arable isthmus, and then (in the third quarter of the twentieth century) it had retreated finally to easier places. Maggy and Flora were growing too old and confused to pasture their sheep there for much longer, although Flora the sharp-eyed still asked you how many sheep you had counted if she had seen you rowing across.

When we explored the place each thing stood out as meaningful, a trace of a culture, because the surroundings were so wild. In the house, whose roof-tree blew off the gable-ends at last, a Ready Reckoner with stained and yellowed pages which must have been used at a hundred lamb sales. Amongst the bracken a single antler, its one tine chewed white by animals, reminding us of the first palaeolithic ploughs. On the south shore of the isthmus, lying waterlogged inside a fish-trap made by building a semi-circular dyke out into the sea, a tea chest whose walls had become home for the biggest buckies (or winkles) that we ever boiled and ate. Such were our gleanings over the years.

In 1974 one more feature of Araid came into focus: a shaggy outcrop of Lewisian gneiss, sixty feet high, which half-divided the northen crofts of the township from the southern. By now any rock whatsoever was a magnetic pole of possibilities, we stared up at every flaking, waterworn face, with its tattered heather and its birches twisting backwards to maintain root-hold on the brittle ledges, and wondered 'Will it go?'. A slant led up this face, six inches wide, apparently continuous. 'Let's have a look at that,' I said to Neil, not wanting to be always leaving him out of the new climbing sorties, and I started up it, coaxing him after me, suggesting footholds, reassuring him when the drop got to him and he turned a little tremulous. The climbing was about Mild Severe in guidebook terms, ninety feet of unroped rising traverse, feeling our way along and up to a dubious exit through trailing heather and honeysuckle and rotting birch debris. I am not proud of having inveigled an innocent youngster along so narrow an edge between safety and injury.

15

At the time my second son Donald (aged twelve and a half) ran along below us, his face red and his eyes aghast at his father's wicked recklessness, yelling at us to come down. I suppose he was right, although I at least put no nasty pressures on Neil, he set off happily up the climb, by the time the gangway had narrowed awkwardly it would have been as difficult to edge backwards as to carry on, and I never for a moment threatened or scoffed or bullied.

The relationship between parents and offspring on a climb (on whichever side the advantage lies in skill and strength) has a poignancy implicit in it. All the mutuality and dependence of family ties, all the shifting ratios of maturity between members of the group, are whetted to a fine edge. The following February I set off up the most toilsome path in the Lake District, the Band, above Stool End in Langdale, to climb Bow Fell Buttress with Chris and my daughter Marian. A low cloud-ceiling loured and dripped and we huddled into our swaddling jerseys and anoraks. But a temperature inversion had taken place; at a thousand feet we climbed through that dingy roof to find its upper side as goose-feather white as a cloud seen from a high-flying jet. Shirtsleeve weather. In the shadow at the foot of the Buttress a snowdrift brought winter back to us and on its white slope a climber's figure-of-eight descendeur was lying intact, as finite a sign of someone else's life as Man Friday's footprint on the beach. The cold enveloped us again and the loom of the crag became formidable. The route is 'only' Hard Difficult but 'the climb quickly becomes much harder when damp'. It faces east, its dark joints secreting moisture for weeks after rain, and by the time you've forced your way up the one nearly vertical crack at two hundred feet, fighting the rock like a terrier burrowing into a cairn, you're committed to staying balanced on this 350-foot trunk of rock with little comfort or possibility of escape in the wrinkled faces and blind grooves to either side. The climb never taxed me, its lovely soaring stature gives time for my middle-aged oil to warm up to a good working heat. But there did come to me, as I led leftwards up the dank slabs on pitch six, this sense of poignant paradox: we spend our best efforts bringing our

16

children into the world, bringing them up defended against all harm, only to connive at their being lured onto these slippery heights where only ravens and peregrines are truly at home. It was just a chilly undertow in my thoughts. Soon Marian's blue Joe Brown helmet was bobbing up towards me like a balloon at a party, and we went on to do some excellent things together – most airily and memorably Crackstone Rib on Carreg Wastad in the Pass of Llanberis. But the undertow still ran beneath my thoughts and it surfaced with a vengeance in Wester Ross two and a half years later.

On the sandstone sea-cliffs below our camp at Diabaig, exploring in a free and easy mood one August afternoon, we found a small stack and climbed it, naming it Cream Crackers after the shape and solidity of the rock. Then we quested along without our gear, combing the cliff for climbable lines, for a place, at least, where the best holds could not be lifted out of their sockets like Lego bricks. It was no good, the roseate rock with its handsome, blocky architecture had been sapped to pieces by the waters leaching through from the moor above. As a quick way back to base we decided to climb out of a deep little geo by a natural staircase sixty or seventy feet high. I worked my way upwards, hammering possible holds with my fist to test for looseness (as I had learned from Blackshaw's *Mountaineering* and as Marian had no doubt been taught on school outings to the Lakeland crags). Some indefinite sound – a gasp, a mutter – made me turn at the rim of the cliff and look back down. Marian was lying on her back among boulders and shingle, arms angled away from her sides. Perfectly still. Face white. Dead? I downclimbed urgently, stiff with horror – wanting to fly – yet forced to take the utmost care. At the mouth of the geo, bluish-grey waves slapped sharply as the tide flowed in. She felt a deadweight as I boosted her up the stones, away from the water's edge. Then she was groaning and mouthing nonsense as she came up through concussion into semi-consciousness. I made sure that she was safe, her limbs not twisted, explained things to her, climbed round the shelves at the geo mouth and pelted off along the shore, up to the road end near our camp, down to the village for help.

Bruce Wallace and Alan Brown, who had rescued climbers from a nearby crag before, came in a small boat with an outboard, lifted her onto a stretcher, brought her along to the harbour, from which she went by car and ambulance to the hospital at Inverness.

Both her wrists were broken and they troubled her for several years after. She has never blamed me – has explicitly not blamed me – and it is true that she had had more systematic training in climbing skills than I. We exorcised the dangers of the steep places on her one and only return to the crags, four years later, when we climbed the long, rough slopes of Steeple Buttress in Ennerdale. But it still feels like a breach of parenthood that it should have happened at all. The parents give the lead, don't they? They know the dangers, have experienced them already on their own skin, the children learn fear partly by seeing what we flinch from. But suppose the generations are learning together? going forward together into new sorts of difficulty?

The morning after writing those last sentences, an hour before sitting down to go on with this passage, I read in the *Guardian* for February 11 1986 that a father and son were climbing in Glencoe. The son, aged fourteen, saw his father fall two hundred feet to his death. Then he had to perch for two hours on a ledge giving Mayday signals with his torch to attract rescuers.

Nevertheless we go on together into the difficult places, believing that we can manage this thing, this winning of fierce pleasure from nature's less accommodating fastnesses. Neil's climbing with me, especially in the seasons of 1977–79, was a prime thing that helped me to weather the wrenching pains of leaving home and going through a divorce. In the course of it we evolved from the father/son relationship to friendship, and he grew from boyhood to young manhood. The way is marked by standing stones: Overbeck on Yewbarrow, Wasdale; the Main Face at Bosigran, north of Land's End; the Punta della Disperazione and the Dente del Rifugio above the Val Canali in the Pala Dolomites; Pavey Ark and the North-west Face of Gimmer; the Devil's Slide on Lundy; and the Castle Rock of Triermain near Thirlmere. In the early summer of 1979, camping with my partner Anne and her son Rob in an anti-cyclonic gale that sent the sandgrains hissing Sahara-style between the dunes at Haverigg, we climbed The Gargoyle on Overbeck. It was still assumed that I did the leading. On the top pitch I needed most of my nerve and strength to balance up to, then surge over the crowning overhang. When Neil's fingers appeared on the edge, the red of his Joe Brown helmet, his blue eyes wide with effort, relief boiled in me mingling with delight at his growing: the same mixture of emotions any parent feels when the child makes it unaided across the living-room floor, or gets through the song or the musical piece without a stumble.

A year later, at Easter, we camped at Hollows in Borrowdale under iron skies. When the season's lambs came into the world a few days later, they would have to shelter on their mother's lee side against the searing easterlies that seemed to polish both the holds and our fingers, minimising friction. In January a dog had slashed the middle finger on my right hand and infection had reached the bone before a cocktail of antibiotics scotched it. I had to climb with a leather fingerstall, so Neil did most of the leading. As I pulled over the jutting brow of Mandrake on Quayfoot Buttress I sensed that I would have been pushed to lead this – that I was relieved I had had a medical excuse to let me out of this scary piece of work. It was a faintly pulpy feeling, a sleepy patch on the firm flesh of the pear.

In the early summer Neil was still a boy when he got into difficulties on the crux of Assegai, on a hundred-foot limestone wall in Trowbarrow Quarry near Silverdale. Spreadeagled above the traverse, trying desperately to fit the keys of his fingers into the subtle wards of the cracks, he urgently shouted 'Dad!' before he fell. I held him, then led the pitch. He was never again dependent, the hard-pressed junior crying out for advice or help, on any route we climbed together; and soon he was calling me 'Dave' instead of 'Dad'. In August, in the Val Canali, a few miles east of San Martino di Castrozza, he led the Grade VI crux of the hardest route on 'Desperation Buttress', a 'route sufficiently beautiful with difficulty greatly sustained', passing below a 'roof with a grand boulder (not too secure)' – disconcerting phrases from a guidebook that called sound rock 'excellent' (*ottima*) and dubious rock 'good' (*buona*). The crux moves crossed a vertical face below the roof, heading for an arête. Below us gaped a few hundred feet of thinnish air (the crag starts at about six thousand feet above sea level). Later, Anne told us that the guide and hut *gestore*, Renzo Timillero, who had put up the route eight years before, was watching us climb through his binoculars and made approving noises when he saw this fresh-faced lad in his early teens move steadily over the dizzy moves. If he kept his glasses on me, he will have seen me wrap my hand round the sling which Neil had clipped into the wedge Timillero had hammered in under the roof and swing in safety along the face before reaching back to take the sling off and clip it onto my harness. I still regret that little failure, that spot of tarnish on the pure zest of climbing unaided. But I had been feeling like a parachutist who sees the miniature trees and riverbeds thousands of feet below and thinks, 'Will my 'chute open? will it? will it?'

So the father depended almost entirely on the son, who had done the venturing up to his own limit, hung on to arrange the protection, and now held the ropes. In this way climbing can obliterate seniority and rank, a salutary experience which has happened to me in my teaching and writing when I have had to realise that one of my students argues more cogently or writes more originally than I can. And this should be so, otherwise the elders can never be displaced and then, as Marx said, 'The tradition of all the dead generations weighs like a nightmare on the brain of the living.'

The worst thing would be to take pique when this junior being, to whom you have taught everything he knows (the use of his legs, a pencil, a pen, the alphabet, a map), surges skywards past you. Did I feel this and manage to repress it? or had I the sanity not to feel it at all? The following July (by which time we had done some fine hard things together – Carnage at Malham, Cascade on Pavey Ark, Praying Mantis on Goat Crag, Borrowdale, The Mortician across the dale on Black Crag) what exactly was I feeling when I shouted out shrilly, between petulance and alarm, on the water-filmed slabs of Arcturus on Pavey Ark? We had already climbed another route by Allan Austin, the wily rock-master from Ilkley – Poker Face, above Jack's Rake, where I had struggled with all my will and balance to stay clung into the groove where the sun-tanned face of Golden Slipper, with its beautifully granular rock like hardened clinker, turns round the arête into black east-facing verticals and I knew I was almost beyond my depth as surely as a swimmer who sees the seawater below him darken into opacity. Neil was pushing out beyond me now, wanting to extend himself, describing middle-grade climbing as 'not refreshing enough, like drinking Tizer'. So, no cruise up some Forties classic. In spite of the trickling and welling moisture below the Rake, we must go for Arcturus. Those slabs are what I call 'holdless' – only tenuous cracks and lips for the very ends of the fingers and coated with peaty ooze. I felt as deserted by my element, cast into another mortifying one, as a crab on the foreshore at low tide with nothing to hide under. I know I called up, as I suctioned precariously and fiddled the krab out from the protection peg, 'I told you I didn't want to do this!' Bad faith, because I could have said no as we sat and ate mint cake and conferred back at the rucksacks. I was just making something or somebody – Neil, the slippery slope, the walls and corners rearing above us – into scapegoats for my own inability. Never again. Adrenalin dissolved my ill-humour and we climbed with mounting delight up the two remaining pitches where the rock was steeper but rough as pinetree bark with that special gnarled and pocketed Pavey quality.

Next month, when I failed to climb the tilted shield on Carnage Left Hand at Malham and had to ask Neil to lower me off, I was at ease in the acknowledgement of my own limitation. Honour and self-esteem can be like overbred beasts, turning sickly or vicious at the least setback. If I can never lead beyond 5a or second beyond 5c, it only means that there are those specific places where I can never go, and there is much else that is superbly fine. With Neil's help, or Pete's, I can still move up the burnished faces of North-west Gimmer by the finger's-breadth ledges of Gimmer String or the hanging groove of The Poacher, or cling my way like a garden snail up the planed slabs of The Brackenclock on Pavey, where Neil wordlessly lowered me his chalkbag and I wordlessly, for once, accepted it, or set the edges of my rock-boots on the fossilised stems of the marine water-lilies on Trowbarrow Main Wall and make upward progress of a sheerness which, left to myself, I would have called 'impossible'. Seconding Cracked Actor on that wall, I pulled up without compunction on Pete's protection nut when my own wells of finger-strength and equilibrium had run out – when it was beyond my ingenuity even to conceive of moves to fit the shapes and angles of the rock. On Springbank on Gimmer Crag, when my arms felt as powerless as gossamer to pull me up the overlap, I asked my patient son to winch me up the few feet and felt no humiliation at all. Having worked my way unaided up the amazingly blank and high-angled slab below, why let false pride spoil a venture which seemed to have set us treading the cleaving, plunging, mounting planes of the air itself? After The Brackenclock in May 1984, and after finishing that evening by climbing Red Groove round on the East Face in three-quarters darkness, we scree-slid down to Stickle Tarn, then stepping-stoned the boulder ruckle of the ruined path down Mill Ghyll while the moon rolled up the sky like a cheese set on edge and the sweatdrops sprang out of our hair. We had been as one in our savouring of bold moves, our rhapsodisings at the great hollow-ings and overleanings of these highlands that are free for our delight.

6

Sometimes, on hearing my poems about climbing, people have said (with that enlightened anxiety which marks the intelligentsia in our time), 'I wonder if it isn't a little dangerous to be too close to your offspring? Mustn't we let them go their own way?' Well yes, undoubtedly, but what if their way and mine both lead up rock? Pete and Neil are extraordinarily like me physically and they are the two who climb. Marian and Don can do it but they don't revel in it; they also look much less like me. When Pete was a baby, I used to look at him sleeping in his cot and feel a weird choking, as though a membrane was closing round me, as though I was being clad in the skin of a child. He looked so like me that I was touched by twinges of fantasy that I was an adult shrunk back into, and therefore imprisoned in, the body of an infant. When he was two hours old he lay on a sheet, just after noon on a dry-season day in Ceylon, with his feet and hands fidgeting gently, curling and opening, constantly moving in a hypermobile way that characterised him for years. The first stirrings of agility. Of course many different physiques can take naturally to climbing, but that toe- and fingertip mobility was surely one of them. When the genes transmit such a tendency, it would be to my mind a wilful severance from nature not to carry it on in harmonious activity together.

I can see now that such considerations were flickering round the horizons of our awareness as Pete and I set out, in August 1977, to walk up the River Lair from Achnashellach in Wester Ross, making our way into the heart of the mountains between Strath Carron and Torridon. It is a large and peaceful country, seamed by glens that twist back on themselves, hiding both goal and starting-point, and then rise up to passes which suddenly display promised lands beyond – deer pastures and lochans glittering darkly. The summits stride along at the 3,000-foot level, shapely cones, blunt towers, Beinn Liath Mhòr and Sgòrr Ruadh and Fuar Tholl, the big grey hill and the russet peak and the cold hole. 'Huge inarticulate Sphinxes,' Leslie Stephen calls them in *The Playgrounds of Europe* (1895), that suggest 'problems as to the growth of the world, the barest statement of which affected the scientific imagination with a sense of overpowering sublimity.'

In this country, if a broad-winged bird planes at two thousand feet or rises out of a corrie on the slow twist of a thermal, it is a golden eagle, not a buzzard. Its wings are still, it is noiseless. The spaces between the mountains brim with the quietude that follows after the groaning and cracking as the ice-sheets recede and before people come with their rifles and 12-bores, their bulldozers and jet engines. And Pete and I walked in silence, partly because we were too used to the routine of a climbing day to need many words, partly because family troubles (the break-up of marriage and household) underlay and subdued our spirits. It was to be the last of our family holidays.

Our goal was the Mainreachan Buttress. *Happy Hamish's Bumper Book of Lies* – our nickname for MacInnes's *Scottish Climbs*, volume 2 (1976) – had turned us on with its talk of the 'wonderful' Mainreachan Buttress. Wonderful compared with what? We'd been caught out two years before, on Harris, by Norman Tennent's climbing guide to *The Islands of Scotland* (1971). His account of the north-east face of Sgurr Scaladale, with its airy phrases about 'obvious steep black walls' and 'sound and clean rock' (all of it? on a seven hundred-foot climb?), had lured us onto a sort of Scottish Roraima where we plunged crazily upwards via filthy chimneys and overhanging heather with stems like razor-wire, our eyes stinging with anti-midge cream, our hands greasy with cream and squashed midges, hordes of the insects levitating beside us on sultry currents of convection. But MacInnes's photos of Mainreachan were convincing and therefore appetising: tall stretches of bare rock, the rectangular profile of the Buttress with one dwarf climber (Martin Boysen or Dave Alcock) perched above space like a figure in some myth about ascending a giant's tower to Heaven.

After two hours of steaming slog we were surrounded by mountains with massive terraced faces. The great scale of them (after England) was simultaneously daunting and inspiring. As the path eased around 1,300 feet, we stared up at the shaggy flanks, trying to match them to the one-inch map. And there at last it is, jutting out between the northern spurs of Fuar Tholl like a colossal stone tongue rooted in the throat of the corrie. We enter the amphitheatre and start comparing the Buttress with the book, trying to pick out the major ramps and chimneys which should signpost our route, Snoopy, and mark it off from its neighbours, Investigator and Sherlock, to say nothing of Sleuth round on the north face. But only the main grain of the strata can be identified for sure. The Buttress is too big, too riddled with features of all kinds – deep black chimneys, massive ribs, hanging gardens of rain-fed weeds – for it to be decoded yet. All we can make out is a gallery of wet gangways that zig-zag upwards from the base of the west face where the roots of the Buttress are deeply buried in a million chunks of rock swept down from the mountain.

To save time we carry the ropes up the first hundred feet without uncoiling or tying on. We pad over beds of sopping plants, reluctant to wet our soles, not feeling too secure as we move out onto the cliff and our fingers grovel on the water-worn slabs beside us, which are coated with primitive rust-coloured plant life. As the gangway zigs back rightwards and rears more steeply, we look for a belay. Pete will lead the first pitch. I'm always slow to gear my nerves for steepness and anyway he's spied a plum pitch from the book description and has clearly been working out which series of earlier leads will put him in place to lead the plum. I'm resigned to being out-manoeuvred by youth, flair and skill.

After two false starts Pete pulls up a little mossy wall and disappears. The ropes begin to run out almost uncomfortably fast – he must be waltzing up the next stage of the gangway. No comments come echoing down. The pitch must be too easy to merit either the ravings of the happy climber: 'Gemsville! Lovely stuff! You'll like this' (usually sarcastic), or the grunted remarks a leader makes to vent his tension. Twenty-five feet of rope left, fifteen, ten. I give him a call: 'Ten feet to go.' No reply. I call again. He shouts 'Okay' but the ropes still pay out and start to drag at the knots in front of my harness. 'Pete!' (irritably). 'Pete! That's me!' He pauses, shouts (irritably), 'No belays in this fucking place,' and moves upwards more slowly. I untie at top speed, telling myself he'd never slip on rock so easy. He stops, feeling the impossible rope-drag, and presently the ropes are taken in and a wordless shout urges me to get moving. I pull up steeply, with the usual feeling of ineptitude on the first exposed and awkward moves of the day. And as usual it goes well enough and limbs become supple as the old lubricant warms up.

I join Pete on his little landing up on the second storey and find him absentmindedly taking in coils of rope while he eyes the next few moves. It's up to me to lead through and I fancy, maybe too suspiciously, that Pete is working out whether this will definitely put him in line for the tracts of clean rock that wait for us above our heads. I finish the remaining simple climbing and find some sharp-edged vertical cracks for nuts to belay on. The only trouble is that the rock on the right or outer side of the cracks is not solidly part of the mother crag, it's a poised pillar cracked through at its base. The rock parts slightly as I wedge in a nut. The Buttress is starting to show its rotten teeth. None of the homely solidity of Lakeland rock, sound, gardened, and tidied by thousands of climbers. This particular high, damp, north-facing chunk of the Scottish Highlands is so rarely climbed, so constantly prised by long-lasting winter ice, that it's one monumental ruin, ready to fall apart.

The gangway reaches a dead end. The grain of the rock has changed. Above us hang overlaps, slabs, and nearly vertical walls, dozens of them, like scales on a huge stone dragon. Lines are not obvious, though three fine routes, Investigator, Sherlock, and our own Snoopy, are supposed to converge here. The book points us at an 'obvious black corner'. We've learned to dread that word 'obvious'. There are approximately two hundred black corners, all of them no doubt obvious from one angle or another. No wonder the pioneers thought up those detective names. All we can do is keep moving upwards – the serrated vertical blades round to our right do not invite an exploratory traverse. Pete, now purged of his ill humour at the messy start to the climb, pulls up into a shallow groove, helped by cracked blocks on either side, and moves deliberately, without bafflement but with much care, up a thirty-foot wall immediately above us, pausing often, at his ease on very small footholds, to put in small nuts on wire. It looks quite technical. As usual I try to memorise the moves, as usual they scramble in my head, and I remind myself that it's more fun working it out for yourself anyway. He moves unexpectedly right off the wall onto a series of airy little shoulders, moves back left using features too small to make out from below, pulls over onto a ledge, and then spends so long fixing the belay that I know it must be exposed up there. Clearly the marvels of the Buttress have begun to show themselves.

In a minute or two I move up, admiring the lead. The system of tensions and balances I'm having to use, side-pulls on narrow cracks, feet edging on little flakes, often feels improbable but it isn't hard to climb smoothly on the security of the top rope. I join Pete to find him looking along the crag in a surmising way. As we face inwards, the stance ends on our left in a drop with a blank face above it. Just above us are more off-putting dragon-scales with no hint of helpful cracks or spikes, just evil little greenish slopes ready to throw us back down. To the right is a precarious pile of spurs – fingers and bones of rock jammed into each other like off-cuts in a timber yard. A ledge leads towards this. It would go. But the looseness! Pete says, 'This is pure gannet shit' (a phrase from our daft ploy on Harris), and looks witheringly at the waste of stony rubbish that towers and falls around us, dwarfing us. On a bad day, if it was cold, late, or otherwise ill-starred, the feeling might well begin to niggle: 'This is no place to be.' But the Buttress is so handsome, the vistas of the Torridon mountains so tremendously sculpted, and I am so ready to lose my bothered self in physical grapple with the wilderness that nothing can baffle our momentum.

I set the inside edge of my right foot on the ledge and ease myself along it, curling my fingers round various spikes and letting go again when they rattle about like old door handles. I could now drop, not throw, a stone three hundred feet straight down onto the scree that washes the right-hand (west) face of the Buttress. Have I led a whole pitch? If so, this must be a stance. My feet are as much on air as on rock, only my left hand is on anything sizeable or solid, and when I push a wired nut into the only crack available, like a dentist probing a bad mouth wondering what to fill and what to extract, I realise I'm only comforting, not safeguarding, myself because it's another Mainreachan Special. The right-hand jamb of the crack is formed by an undercut block that would knock off with one swing of a sledgehammer.

I call to Pete, 'I can't stop here.' Do I mean I want to reverse the last twenty-five feet? Or that I expect him miraculously to reassure me that this perch is indeed a stance? He calls back, 'What's it like round the corner?' I lean out from my good left-hand hold and peer round the shattered rib to my right. It's like a badly bombed cathedral, stubs of flying buttresses far below, cracked walls angling out of sight at eye-level, broken gutters spilling débris onto us from above. Twenty feet below there are little ledges with some grass. But it would take Extreme, maybe impossible, climbing to reach them. The arête above me which runs down to the shattered rib might go but it would be desperate to start, and who knows what's up there? It's a perfect case of the devil you know. A ragged crack-line leads off on a traverse at our level. It makes sense to at least set out across the twenty-five-foot bay of nearly vertical rock between my corner and its counterpart across the way. I shout to Pete, 'I'll try and traverse,' and set off, wishing I was leaving an anchor more convincing than that wee wire in the shaky rock. If I fall, Pete will hold me, but if the corner collapses it could cut the ropes . . . It is now so necessary to move, in the teeth of whatever risks, that the risks themselves shrink into finite factors. Each one is no less but no more real than the things we have going for us. The climb has been climbed before, by Boysen and Alcock (but which line exactly?). We have plenty of gear and we know how to use it. Above all, the flow of momentum draws us upwards, magnetised by the grand size and shaping of this scarp that towers into the blue summer sky, powered from below by memories of how often we've set off upwards and usually made it.

I still can't believe this looseness. The crack-line continues but the holds it links are mostly loosely-wedged spikes far gone in some long process of parting from the crag and rattling down onto the spoil-heap below. They're also far apart. I have to move by stretching my right foot as far as I can stride, lodging it on a spike that moves a little, gripping another such thing in my right hand, and balancing along the wall. Never before have I entertained for a moment the idea of trusting my weight to stuff like this. There is nothing else to do. The route is here to be followed, the crag to be climbed, and we're marooned in the middle of it. Each precarious move is no more thinkable, no more possible, than the last. Each is thought of and then done. Instability becomes normal, like settling down to live on ground being shaken and broken by an earthquake.

No point in putting in nuts: the only lodgements are next to the creaking spike-holds, and when my weight came on them, the nuts would pop out like peas from a split pod. In these conditions you can so distribute your weight that no one wobbly hold is taking the whole stress. Or so you tell yourself. This needs such concentration that I can feel my brain starting to flag. And the fear is eating in, although touch and muscle-power go on functioning smoothly – they have to. I even manage to pause, crucified on nails of creaking rock, to spy out the remaining feet of traverse. I *hate* this insecurity. The position is so exposed, the holds so unconvincing, that the great space of air behind and below me has begun to seem more real and near than the rockface. It's more like hang-gliding than climbing! But six feet above, the rock now looks better. There's a stratum of pocked and bubbly material like a slab of Aero two-foot thick. Friable or solid? Pulling up more than I like on yet another loose spike, I lodge the fingers of my right hand in the strange rock and tug hard at it. Solid as can be. Much less for the fingers to grip but secure, secure. I pull up some more, at last get two points of firmness, continue to do the splits along the wall, but now I'm hanging from this solid stuff above my head, the danger is waning, I make it to the far corner, to a little platform with room for a pair of feet, and anchor thankfully on a secure nut.

I shout 'Taking in' and pull rope along the face until I'm ankle-deep in it, not daring to drop the slack in case it jams in the crevices below. Sweat runs down my brow from below my helmet and stings my eyes. A shout from Pete: 'That's me.' I check the belay and shout back, 'Climb when you're ready.' A couple of minutes and his face peers round the shattered rib. He scans the traverse and smiles a weird smile. 'Killer, eh?' he says.

'All good stuff,' I say. He plucks the wire out of the crack, racks it, and steps round onto the Wall of Horrors (but that is a climb in Yorkshire, and perfectly solid). He doesn't move fast, and when he reaches the last little section he makes to move downwards before seeing the impasse and trending upwards towards the bubbly stratum. Has this pitch been climbed before? It doesn't match the book too well, but how would you define 620 feet of rock like this in six lines of unambiguous prose? If not the route, is it a hard variation? A new line? Have we strayed off Snoopy on to Investigator? (It doesn't match it either.) We say little as Pete joins me on the stance. All thought has to be for the tidy managing of the ropes and the picking of some line up the bulging array of dragon-scales above us. Pete leads a sixty-foot pitch that turns out more sustained and technical than its forerunner two pitches ago – bridging with holds for the left foot but the right relying on hope and friction, laying away sideways from sharp but shallow cracks, finding it hard but sensing that the climb is about to yield its last defences.

When I follow, I feel so tired in my head that I don't mind asking for advice on a few of the moves. In any case the previous five hundred feet of climbing has served as a whole weekend's work-out forced into three hours and my limbs now feel as if they could find their own way up anything. The belay is a solid ledge which actually gives us room to stretch a bit and wiggle our bruised toes. Above us are heaps of scree ready to spill off the summit edges like slates off a roof. To the right, prows like gargoyles jut out from the last eave of the Buttress. Normally the situation would still be awesome but there's a limit to how many qualms you can feel in one day. I diagonal quickly upwards towards the gargoyles, loving the feel of sound, sun-dried rock as though it were newly-baked bread. My arms and back are tired – how many pull-ups could I do now? But strength is reflected back into them by the adamant quality of this last rock, by the sunshine we're climbing into out of the corrie's shadow. We monkey along and up those final overhangs, not bothering about protection, as though we had made it back into the primate world we evolved from, and lie down on the parched moss of the summit. Above us clouds drift past and normality flows in on us like water into thirsty soil.

During the day Chris Culshaw had walked from Torridon by the Bealach na Lice and the Bealach Ban to meet us and take some photos. As we were conferring on the fifth stance, his voice hailed us and we saw him on the saddle just west of Fuar Toll summit. Before we finished he had gone off over the mountain to Achnashellach while we scree-slid back down to the rucksacks and then retraced our path of the morning. Pete took that homeward journey like a fell runner and I jogged as quickly as I could, a hundred yards behind him, two hundred yards . . . My eldest son, pulling steadily away from me . . . The day's intense comradeship was not going to well up into words, not yet at any rate. By the following year he had outgrown me as a regular climbing partner, although fulfilling days in the Avon and Cheddar Gorges, on Lochnagar and the Castle Rock of Triermain, still lay ahead, and still do.

Some time during the following year I was with him and some friends in Trowbarrow Quarry and as we stood among our little heaps of gear, looking up at the hundred sheer feet of the main wall and deciding what to do, I saw that Pete had started up Jean Jeannie, the Very Severe crack that splits the centre of the wall. As you pull up it, you feel very small, especially when you realise there is no resting-place. Sharp, tilted blocks litter the floor beneath it. A fall from twenty feet or more might mean a fracture or crushed vertebrae and from forty feet or more, most probably death. Now Pete was climbing it solo. It seemed the sheerest madness and I was horrified enough to shout out, among that gaggle of blasé teenagers, 'Pete! If you fall, who'll push the wheelchair the rest of your life?' He said nothing. Everybody else said nothing. He pulled easily up the climb and in five minutes was back down among us. Not another word was uttered, then or since, whether to congratulate or reproach.

Even at the time, before he had reached the crumbling earthy rim of the quarry, I was realising that he was now going away from me into his own free life. He was dispensing with the red

31

rope that had linked us so often up till then as decisively as he had been separated from the umbilical cord a little over seventeen years before.

7

———

It is by chance that my rope is red, red with tiny glints of blue: one hundred and fifty feet of white nylon sleeved in scarlet by the method called kernmantel, made by Edelrid. After a season or two of constant use your rope is as familiar as a favourite animal who shares your home. Between outings it lies there coiled, warm with readiness, sinuous with potential. Between climbs it is secured by tying one end round and round the twenty or more strands of the main coil as though putting a whipping on the handle of a knife or a metal mug. This spare end sprouts from the whipping, looking ready to unfasten itself and spring off up the rockface, finding its own way along the crannies. This rope should not be mine at all. It belonged, till January 1977, to Dave Steed, a good friend and climbing partner of Pete's and mine. Soon after New Year he did a long snow-and-ice climb in Coire Leis on Ben Nevis with two friends from Morecambe who often climbed with us. They relaxed on the summit plateau full of the day's exertions, took photos, sorted gear. A moment later Dave had fallen a thousand feet to the cliff's foot. Nobody knows why. It was simply as though a hole had opened in the world.

Several days later a few of us crossed Loch Linnhe by the ferry at Corran and set off on a circular walk through Ardgour, sleeping in bothies, following threads of paths through knee-deep moors and fertile glens, all perfectly deserted. The only remnants of civilisation the oblongs made of boulders that survived from the streets and houses of the villages wiped out by Cumberland's search-and-destroy raids after Culloden. I looked

32
———

back across the loch at the Ben, its great snowed mass rounding against the dead-fish-grey of a windless winter sky, and I wanted to howl and chant my grief for Dave. In the poem I made up as I walked and wrote down a little later, 'One Thousand Feet of Shadow', I couldn't help blaming the mountain:

> . . . The corrie gaped its whale jaws,
> The great gut constricted,
> A cold draught came from the depths,
> Stiffening rapidly the torn skin,
> Coagulating blood, limbs out of true,
> And my friend's face transfixed
> In the tearing gasp of his last breath.

So the red of the rope means his blood as well as the life of those it has held in safety since.

The rope has grown dirty very slowly and looks a different colour now from Peter Greenwood's identical rope which he and I began to use in 1985 as we set out to repeat his routes of the early Fifties. It has taken on some of the brown of the earth where it has had to score through layers of peaty turf at the lip of various crags and I don't dare wash it too often in case it loses its fine inherent suppleness. It should be eleven millimetres in diameter, now it seems more like twelve: a middle-age spread that makes it a little hard to push through the slot in the Sticht plate when I'm belaying somebody. But it has developed none of the kinkiness which bedevils some of its kind; the fibres still feel textured, not wiry. It has also avoided the fate of our first kernmantel rope, a lovely purple item bought at Fort William on the way to Harris. The following year, in camp at Diabaig, a fish-hook became embedded in it. When I found this out on the way through dense and mossy forest near Achnashellach, en route for Mainreachan, I tried to twist the hook free and snapped it at the shank, leaving the barb in there somewhere. We should not have climbed on it again but we needed double ropes to thread the vertical labyrinth of Snoopy and to climb many hundreds of feet of hard and virgin rock near Torridon on that same holiday. Nothing went wrong, no steely remnant stung our fingers. Soon after, the purple rope was put out to grass (and finally cut in two) for bouldering on the gritstone outcrops when Pete went to live in Leeds.

The red rope lives on – too old now, in its thirteenth season, to meet strict safety standards, but my comparative lack of courage has kept me from getting into too many positions where a long leader fall is likely. I have given it that worst kind of shock only twice and then the falls were not free enough to inflict much shock-load: once climbing with Dave on Rectangular Slab on Pavey Ark and once in the middle of winter, on a frosty limestone edge called Oxenber near Settle, when I fell out of the moist and polished bottom pitch of Bullroar. But the rope is all right, it seems to be stiffening no faster than my own tendons and may well outlast them in crag-credibility.

How different it is from our first rope, a hundred and twenty feet of plain white nylon, which already counts as an artifact from a much earlier climbing epoch. Now, cut in half, it travels as a tow-rope in the tailgate of my car. When we bought it in 1974, it shone with promise, and it did not let us down (although occasionally we let ourselves down by it). When it was wet, it grew nearly stiff enough to stand up in the manner of the Indian rope trick and this led us, by Monty Python logic, to dub it the Broccoli Rope. I learned the art of coiling on it, giving a half-turn on each coil to avoid the corkscrewing effect, and I performed my first big pendule on it on my first Hard Very Severe (Kipling Groove on Gimmer). On damp days it sat on our shoulders about as flexibly as a horse-collar on a Clydesdale, but in its time it was the best, less likely to snap than the old hawser-laid hemp which Bill Peascod and I used just once, by way of historical experiment, on Buckstone How.

Pete and I made our own first ludicrous experiment with hemp rope at the very start of our climbing, before we knew many more terms than 'handhold', and 'crack' and 'chimney'. We found a length of clumsy, sodden hemp, cast off from some fishing boat, on the shore at Diabaig and flung it over an oak on a little cliff to try out the technique called 'laybacking'. In climbing terms we were still at the epoch before the invention of the wheel and we thought that what you had to do was lay, or lie, back,

34

grasping the rope in both hands, then plant your footsoles against the rockface and haul upwards. We tugged and tugged like demented bellringers, breathed in gasps, swung about helplessly as old barndoors in a breeze, pawed the rock with our feet, and once or twice finished up lying *right* back on the shingle below the cliff. To layback actually means to grasp a vertical or near-vertical edge, plant your feet on the adjoining facet of the crag, and pull, which causes you to rise in a way that at first feels miraculous. And of course nobody climbs by hauling up on a dangling rope – it can't be done. A few years later, I gathered from the memoirs of veteran climbers such as Brown and Whillans, and from the conversation of Peter Moffat of Seascale, who has been climbing since before the War, that in those days everyone went through this phase when they climbed with an old piece of sash-cord, their mother's washing-line, or the like. A real fall would have snapped them like string but they gave the beginner the grand feeling of doing it right. Paul Ross, leading Borrowdale climber in the Fifties, told me that when he first climbed, in his teens, he and his friends soloed up Brown Slabs on Shepherd's Crag, found a ten-foot length of old hemp rope, tied it on, and climbed back down so that they could take photos of each other, with a Kodak Box Brownie, in imitation of the famous images they had seen in the shop-window of Abrahams the photographers in Keswick. But that was in 1952. It was fairly silly of us to live through this archaic stage all over again in 1974, but then, experiment (the intellectual counterpart of exploration) is the soul of climbing, isn't it? And it is certainly a far less forgettable form of learning than following instructions in a book.

Dave Steed's parents gave Dave's rope to Pete and let me have his protection gear at a nominal price. In a way they were perpetuating the youth of their dead son. There are few things I have respected more than the unflinching friendliness with which they put that bundle of metal nuts and perlon and karabiners into my hands, a few months after his death. Here is the natural process whereby we accumulate our trusted life-support kits – some of it from the shops, some of it passed on by comrades, some of it found jammed or forgotten in nooks of crags. Most days when I go out climbing I find a placement for Dave's smallest hexagonal nut, a No. 3 made by Chouinard, on its loop of dowdy greyish perlon, or clip the red rope into his heavy Bonaiti krab whose orange paint is nearly worn away. Both could be replaced by rather lighter and more adaptable things, but my climbing is not so amazingly expert or near the frontier of the possible that I need the very best equipment. To use Dave's things is like sitting in your father's old chair, or handing down a sampler through generations of family. He is as present as the dead can be, his surprised grin like a happy cartoon hare's as he looks down a route he's just led for the first time up Trowbarrow Main Wall, his fair hair bleaching and his blond skin flushing in the heatwave of 1976 as we grilled on the griddle-face of Pavey till the corners of our big toes bled in the tight-fitting Ellis Brigham rock-boots.

It was not the fault of the Ben, Dave, that you fell down its height. In some way we'll never know it must have been your own fault. But you climbed with zest whenever we were on a rope together for those two awakening years and the rest of us are lucky that our mistakes have left us so much less scathed.

8

Would I ever have let the climber in me out of the two decades' hibernation had not my children taken up climbing as a school-based Outdoor Pursuit? Impossible to be sure about such a change but their activity was certainly the cause of it happening for me when it did. At Morecambe High School the headmaster, Jim Foster, was a climber who had put up some routes in Scotland and has recently, in early retirement, finally reached the top of all 277 Munros. His policy seemed to be to appoint climbers to the staff (other things being equal) so that they could take parties to the Lakes in the school minibus and train them to canoe and climb and find their way by map and compass in the mountains. By the spring of 1974 Marian and Pete were constantly away at 'Shepherd's' and 'Raven', whatever these were. The Lake District was ceasing to be a collection of blue-and-green landscapes on the calendars and biscuit tins or a place to drive through. As a family we had taken ourselves more often to less-frequented areas, where we could find our own hidden dales and pools free from the almost overbearing cult of 'Wordsworth country' and the fashery of congested carparks. But now there was this new way of perceiving 'the Lake District': it was rich in sources of a special excitement, so it seemed, which stirred up my curiosity and made Aberdeenshire images turn over in the silt of the twenty-five-year memory-layers. At Whitsun I drove Marian and Pete to a school camp on the close-cropped meadows beside Coniston Water with a vague premonition of trying out these rocks myself. The lake was shimmering in windless sunlight. Chris Culshaw drove me over to Lower Scout Crag in Great Langdale, an outcrop I soon learned to identify in all weathers and seasons by the dangling queues of lads and lasses in orange dayglo anoraks learning to clamber up it and abseil down again. Chris took me up the Slab and the cracked wall to its left, I didn't fall off, and a delicious sense of rubbery power began to steal into my tendons, through my forearms and shoulders. To feel upwards, to pull strongly, smoothly, to rise and keep on rising – here was one of the best states in the world!

Chris is so fascinated by the ways in which we find language for new perceptions as we learn things that he makes an ideal teacher, and in his work as a teacher of Remedial English he has had to be a kind of specialised parent or intelligent uncle to hundreds of children whose unhappiness and lack of security has made it hard for them to use or understand words as precisely as they would need if they were to think for themselves. Nobody could have been better fitted to get me on to the rockfaces of Cumbria. Scout Crag had been a *bonne bouche*, a summer evening's-worth. Dow Crag, the next day, was dwarfingly huge – an entire mountainside, facing the Old Man of Coniston across the high cold tarn of Goats Water, its eastern front mined by cavernous gullies, spurred with buttresses. Their strangely systematic names, 'A', 'B', 'C', and 'D', were themselves an initiation into this special world where someone or other, evidently quite some time ago, had come here to explore and classify. Gordon and Craig had been here, for example, in the autumn of 1909, and had found a tortuous line through the undercut bulges and slanting galleries of 'A' Buttress. We started on Giant's Crawl, which had first been climbed by two hyphenated gentlemen that same year, and there on 'B' Buttress at the stance between pitches five and six of the Crawl was an unmistakable crux (I didn't yet know this term) – clearly impossible, clearly requiring to be done.

A roomy ledge ends at an overhanging corner, a black slit pointing at the sky. It is an impasse and it stares back at me impassively. Chris reaches up one of his telescopic arms (he is six foot two), pulls up, perches briefly in silhouette, breathes deeply and pulls some more. Gone. I am alone. The rope runs slowly out between my hands, pauses, and runs out again. In a few minutes, before I am mentally prepared for it, Chris's voice comes down out of the sky: 'Climb when you're ready.' I don't want to, Chris! It daunts me wholly. I move towards it as though locked in a dream. I set my hands on a steeply angled edge, wedge my big black Austrian climbing-boot into the big black slit, pull, clamber, balance myself, no problem at all, the daunt melts and then mutates into pure delight.

The transition from fear to exhilaration had felt as distinct as the moment when heat runs through a gas-mantle and the dead-white of it glows vermilion.

At such a moment on a climb adrenalin is secreted in an abnormal flow to aid the extra effort. Primal well-being results, pervading your whole self. And from that moment you are addicted (literally), and want it more and more.

By the end of that day on Dow we had climbed seven hundred feet of rock and I had come to feel at home on the mountain. We could look across at terraces and pinnacles where we had been a few hours before and know that the inaccessible had turned into the possible, even the welcoming. I had also had time to tread some way into the peculiar loneliness of climbing. It is true that you and your mate meet frequently, you co-operate in the management of the rope and the protection gear, you compare notes on what has just happened and admit to clumsiness here and fear there, you savour the meaty exertions and the subtle gymnastics. At the top of Gordon and Craig's Chris and I sat for a good hour, talking closely about fatherhood (he and Julie had not yet had a child), about possible ways of writing climbing poetry. However between these togethernesses stretch the bleaker passages where you are more purely on your own than at most other points in your life because here you depend so much on your own powers to get you out of it again.

I felt this almost overpoweringly on the long ledge two hundred feet up Gordon and Craig's. Chris had disappeared upwards. No other climbers were in sight except a few packing up their rucksacks down at the toe of 'B' Buttress beside the Mountain Rescue Box. The escape from this ledge looks quite hard. What am I doing here, I achingly wonder. Why have I chosen to impale myself on this cross? That raven sailing freely past, for it there is nothing problematic here, it is in its element. But I? In some peculiar way I am looking at myself and sensing my own features with salutary clarity, my forehead gathered into a mesh of crumples above my nose, my eyes darkened with boding, my mouth tight and drawn down at the corners . . . I am in a very small room and one wall is all mirror, reflecting me from head to foot. There I am, such as I am. These hands and arms, these thighs and toes, this brain armoured in a red plastic climbing helmet – such is the sum of my wherewithal and *nothing else* will get me out of here. And it can, it can – I *can* apply these powers to that hard squeeze and that dizzy fulcrum, I can unlock this mountain.

> I had to lie on the hills and watch
> The founts that to keep their tryst
> Had found their way through the wards of the rock
> Slower than the second coming of Christ
> To know how my task was priced . . .

MacDiarmid in one of his loneliest poems, from 'The War With England'. And another snatch also began to reverberate in my head that day and has come back to me hundreds of times, whenever I have been on a stance by myself waiting to climb, looking up the tall, intricate face and wondering 'Will it go?' It is from Yeats's 'An Irish Airman Foresees His Death' and it must sound absurdly grandiloquent in this context:

> I know that I will meet my fate
> Somewhere among the clouds above . . .
> A lonely impulse of delight
> Drove to this tumult in the clouds;
> I balanced all, brought all to mind,
> The years to come seemed waste of breath,
> A waste of breath the years behind,
> In balance with this life, this death.

Does this make too much of a carefree outdoor sport? Such are the burdens of overconsciousness. I climb with my feet on solid rock and my head in a dense cloud of thoughts. It might have been less so if I had started as one should, in childhood, and the fundamental patterns of balance, effort, and self-reliance had been imprinted so deeply that they could hold fast with the strength of a yew against all the minings and crumblings of self-doubt. Such strength is needed far more when you're leading the climb, on what is called the sharp end of the rope, when no tensile lifeline leads in all its lovely security from your waist to the unshakable and fatherly figure up above.

Next day we drove over the mountainous ridge between Coniston and Dunnerdale to find a crag called Wallowbarrow – barely two hundred feet high yet this was enough to create a little wilderness of its own. Weathered grey faces sheer upwards to heathery ledges camouflaged by oaks, their roots grasping in mid-air like exposed muscles. The uppermost rim looked no more accessible than the summit of a cloud seen from the window of a plane. Only two days before, that same top of a little hill, in a dale cosy with hawthorn hedges and coppiced ashtrees and seventeenth-century farmhouses, would have been something to amble round at our ease, bird-watching and taking snaps. Now we set off up Trinity Slabs, a comfortable route whose wooded ledges are suitable for conversation and happy rhapsodies about the scenery. But Chris, I now see, has educative plans for me. I'm not to be allowed to dawdle onwards in a middle-aged way. On the third pitch I find myself (as they say) in the lead. Abruptly I feel as exposed as a survivor on a ship that has turned turtle, leaving him clawing at the sheer steel plates. As soon as I move upwards a bottomless chaos is sucking at my heels – up is the only thing for it – can I will myself to that when each hold is so absurdly small? I claw my fingers and pull upwards on a little edge where a stratum, tilted vertically, has chipped off. What next, for godsake? In mid-pull I turn the hauling movement into a downward press on the outer edges of my hands, and that was my first mantelshelf move, discovered in the experimental not the textbook fashion. In a few minutes the landing-place is smiling down at me, bowered in green oak leaves with their scalloped edges and jointy black oak limbs, the very embodiment of security. I reach up, my fingers slither on sandy gravel, horrors! the edge of the ledge isn't squared at all but rounded, and that was my first lesson in the impossibility of assessing a hold without actually using it. No way up. Unthinkable to downclimb safely. Set the fingers on that repulsive edge again, pull, pull! The will refuses to translate into action, the sense of safety is stronger than the urge upwards – but this is not safety, it's using up the last pints of strength in my reserve tank. Fifty feet below Chris is shouting 'Fight the rock!' and this is the boost I need. I pull for real; with every second the friction increases as my weight comes onto my hands and gives rise to better leverage, the edge 'improves', I'm lurching happily onto the stance, whooping and gasping down to Chris. The thing can be done, I can surmount the rock and I can also quell the inhibiting fears inside myself.

After this abrupt thawing-out of a kind of personal Ice Age, a torrent of activity came seething through the gap. Soon I was leading more than seconding, and often climbing so avidly that I scarcely paused to put on runners. Bill Peascod recalls a similar stage when he was told off by the President of the Fell and Rock Climbing Club for climbing too fast, but he was nineteen then, at what he calls 'the first faint opening of the flood gates' (*Journey After Dawn*, 1985, p 22), whereas I was forty-two. I was climbing like a boy and usually with a boy, Pete, aged fourteen and a half. I couldn't wait to get to the crag, I drove fast, I walked uphill at speeds which my then state of fitness could barely sustain. My wife said, 'You're a driven man,' but I was not being driven. My own drives were powering me as twenty missing years craved to be lived at last, while there was still time.

Four years later, after Pete had come of age and climbed much more often with the strongest and most skilled members of our club (the Lancaster Mountaineering Club), we teamed up again for a day on the consistently steepest crag in the Lakes, the Castle Rock of Triermain. A rope let down from the lip of the cliff reaches the ground ten or fifteen feet from its base and the overhang is such that the face often stays dry in a downpour. Pete led me up my second Extreme, the North Crag Eliminate, and a very steep route of Peter Greenwood's called Angels' Highway which has no resting-place for over a hundred feet. It was a revelation to see him at work: perfectly poised on verticals with slender holds for the fingertips, bringing his arms up in arcs out to each side because the verticality brought the rock so near his chest, fitting his fingers deliberately into the efficient positions, as though by now he knew the seven hundred and ninety-five possible adjustments and could infallibly find the right one. A very good climber looks like a praying mantis, with that uncanny quality whereby the machinery of joints and digits seems to be working on its own, separated from personality or emotion.

There could not have been a more graphic display of your own offspring coming to adulthood, his inborn physical nature flowing into the moulds of acquired skills, his habits firming up and elaborating themselves, his behaviour imprinted more than skin-deep by the sub-culture he had become a member of. Ever since 1975, when he had held me as I fell off Kipling Groove, he had been overtaking me in technique and strength with the unstoppable impetus of a motor vessel overtaking a sailing ship.

And I had never resented it, and scarcely envied it, partly because I was enjoying myself to the top of my own bent and partly because his (and soon Neil's) greater powers made possible for me tremendous days on rock which I had not the hardihood to get for myself. In its way it prefigures the much later stage when an aged parent becomes dependent on his children for much more basic supports, but it is a benign and positive form of it. After all, we can both get up the routes and, after all, the second climber is necessary to the leader, if only as an anchor.

9

The attitude of my own parents had been vastly different. It embodied the worst of an earlier age. The sitting-room of our home in Aberdeen, on evenings when I was nerving myself to tell my father that I planned a trip to the mountains, used to turn into a chamber two or three times its already ample size, the light dimmed, red mahogany loomed as dark as sherry, the tall plum velvet curtains reared up to the ceiling like trees whose upper branches were webbed with gloom. I sat there, trying to read my book, wanting (to bursting-point) to say, 'Daddy, we're thinking of going hostelling to Inverey, hill-walking in the Cairngorms.' I practised the words, decided on the diplomatically tentative 'thinking' although the plan was already firm, didn't specify who 'we' were (it was transparent anyway), rehearsed counters to his disapprovals, promised myself to speak after a count of twenty, delayed the start of the count.

Does he know I'm about to make my proposal? Behind the *Scotsman* his eyes flicker – by chance? or under the stress of his awareness of my stress? My head is now encased in a special atmosphere which makes my ears sing slightly. My chair is a pinnacle, on whose top I roost in a clench of apprehensiveness, hazy unplumbed depths far far below and all around. In the fireplace consumed coals fall inwards with a clink. The pulse of the clock on the mantelpiece beats hurriedly.

The pressure grows unbearable. 'Daddy,' I hear my voice saying, 'we're thinking of going hostelling . . . in the Cairngorms . . . at Easter . . .'

You, the reader, are presuming that I was fourteen or fifteen at the time. But the date was 1952, and I was twenty.

My father shakes his newspaper to keep it upright. He lets me sweat for some seconds. 'Won't it be very cold?' he finally asks, not looking at me. This is the first of a series of questions, most of them negative. 'Will you be able to carry enough food for a week? Isn't it a bit early in the year? Will the Estate let you have a key?' (to the long moor road to Derry Lodge, which we'd like to cycle). 'What does Mrs Stephenson say?' (my girlfriend's mother, my mother-in-law-to-be). Really these questions are a series of tactical moves that lead up to the final strategic blockade – the warning pronounced with the whole force of his prestige as the leading children's physician in Scotland (on call for the royal children when they were at Balmoral): 'Remember what I said about your back.'

Was there anything wrong with my back? (It's still in quite good fettle – aching sometimes but serviceable). The fact was that I had had iridocyclitis of my left eye in the late spring of 1950. The story was that I would have lost the sight of it had not my father been able to use his position to contact a doctor in America, who had been stationed near Aberdeen during the War, and ask him to send over by plane a supply of the then brand-new drug called adreno-cortico-tropine hormone, ACTH, a cortisone. My eyeball had turned green, the lens muscle was paralysed and I couldn't focus. I was seeing double as I played in a trial for the 1st XI at the start of the season. It was the last game of cricket that I played for twenty years. After some weeks in a hospital bed and a series of injections in the buttock I was pronounced cured. My leg muscles recovered their tone after three weeks' complete disuse, and I spent my last weeks at school wearing a pair of dark glasses with turquoise plastic frames, an eccentricity that gratified me no end, especially when I stepped up onto the platform at Assembly and read out choice passages from arcane parts of the Old Testament (Zephaniah or Amos) which I had chosen to air their superb language and irritate the headmaster.

The eye condition is considered minor nowadays. The feeling allowed to permeate the family at that time was that it was dreadfully serious, it had been a near thing, and my father made a connection (validly, no doubt) with our hereditary tendency to arthritis. 'If you go on playing cricket,' he said grimly when I began to chafe at the long lay-off from games, 'your back could go as stiff as a poker – and *stay like that*.' I gave up cricket. Three months later, although I'd been an ardent rugby player, I bowed to his ban on playing for the 3rd XV of the Former Pupils' Club. Golf was all right, a still-ball game played at a walking pace, retired ministers in their seventies could play it, so I went round and round the superb links course of Balgownie just north of Aberdeen, wearing my green-framed shades, until one day, as I hit a drive off the seventeenth tee, an arm of the glasses snapped and I finished the round blinking in the bright marine sunshine. (Two of the old ministers, members of a regular foursome, died on the course not long afterwards.)

Other bans now slid into place under cover of my recent illness. If I 'overdid it' and got very wet or sweaty, the rheumatic tendency might be potentiated. I must be very careful about cold winds or grit in the eyes in case the iritis recrudesced. The fact was that the hellish consequences of 'overdoing it' had overcast our lives for years. In those days it was dangerous to sit on the grass in case you 'caught your death of cold'. If you got 'overheated', the demon pneumonia would seize his chance and get you. My father had only just been saved from what was a killing disease in 1936 by the brand-new May & Baker drugs and 'M&B 693' still rang in our ears like a charm.

So the chains were draped over my shoulders, over my wrists, my legs – lined with the velvet of fatherly concern, forged by the hammer-blows of medical knowledge, weighted extra-heavy by the fact that my elder brother had gone down with rheumatic fever in his eighteenth year, his knees were swollen and useless, his university career cut through in its bright bud. Now he was in bed upstairs and if I went to the mountains I was deserting him, the feckless selfish younger son (and remaining hope of the family) putting *his* health in jeopardy while leaving his worried and saddened parents 'alone' with their ill offspring.

This was my construct. My parents did not put it on me (not in so many words). 'Mind-forg'd manacles' – we compound our own unfreedoms by letting the phobias of others into our selves. An offspring with more hardihood (moral, not physical: I never flinched from the shocks and bruisings of the games field) would have steeled himself to break through those parental binds. Some of my contemporaries did it all the time. Bill Brooker told me recently how he always had to promise his mother, when he started going off to climb on Lochnagar in his early teens, that he would 'not go near Black Spout'. The very name of the huge scree funnel must have sounded infernal to Aberdonian mothers at a time when the rockfaces of that corrie had not been climbed and safety gear was minimal. Bill and his friends had to swear that they would only be going up Red Spout, an easy-angled chute of warm-coloured gravel which can be walked up and down in all conditions. Presently, Bill says, he became an experienced go-between, interceding with other worried parents to let their sons go off to climb in the Cairngorms. But love had nearly smothered me by then. I walked the mountains in summer – in the company of my family. I can still see my father's eyes widen to show the whites, his mouth pursed to draw in a hissing breath, as he warned us against steep drops or deep pools in the burns by simulating the sounds and faces people make when actual danger has just missed them. So I was twenty years old before I was first benighted and slept in a bothy (Corrour in the Lairig Ghru between Deeside and Speyside), before I first skited off down a re-frozen snow slope (on Cairn Toul above the Lairig) and was only saved by my girlfriend sticking in our single ice-axe (ex-War Department) and holding me when I fetched up against her. I was twenty-four before I first bivouacked under the night sky (beside the Spey on the way to the Pass of Corrieyairack) with the embers of a cooking fire pulsing red among the river shingle nearby (and on this occasion my father allowed me to see and hear his disappointment that I was leaving my brother 'alone' and gadding off through the Highlands).

But I did, in the autumn of 1952, go up to Lochnagar and Beinn a Bhuird for those two rock-climbs. And I can remember no utterly sinking warnings or disapprovals (but plenty of apprehensiveness) when they were mooted. Something else was needed to intensify the deterrence to its crushing maximum. I now believe it was that other, even more inhibiting ban – the taboo that parents seek (or sought) to put upon the girlfriend. Bill Brooker and his friends, the first great wave of rock-and-ice climbers in the Cairngorms, Graham Nicol and Kenny Grassick and Gordon Lillie and the rest – all from my university, mostly from my school – climbed in all-male company. Girls were for necking sessions and hops. Whereas I assumed that whatever I did, I did it with my girlfriend Jill. Therefore to plan a time away in the hills was to propose a time alone with her – in youth hostels or bothies – and what parent was sure of the sleeping arrangements there? When a great friend of mine, precocious in his personal life, arranged to go to the south of France with his girlfriend and I mentioned this choice piece of news to my father, he said with a full dark look into my eyes, '*I* would not have *trusted* myself when *I* was his age.' Sex before marriage was wicked. Sex of any kind was unmentionable. My mother never said someone was pregnant, she used the word *enceinte*. When I brought home the unexpurgated edition of *Lady Chatterley's Lover* (published in Sweden), hidden in a road map to hoodwink the Customs at Dover, my father got hold of it and pronounced, after a short inspection, 'Some things should not be written about.' The facts of life were studiously ignored – at the age of seventeen I had no idea how intercourse took place – and this kind of ban gave rise to a whole comedy of concealments. My father always had his bath behind a locked door and the only time I ever went into the bathroom while he was in the water, he sat bolt upright and covered his genitals with his facecloth.

How did we survive? Deformed, is the answer, curtailed and crippled, and especially so if, like me, you let the phobias of your elders invade your head and body. I grew up so shy of women that it felt like a disease and for many years I blushed feverishly when I had to relate to them. The trouble was worse because the bans put on us were not outright prohibitions, enforced with physical punishment or threat of it, which could then have been resisted outright with heroic and self-confirming bloodyminded-ness. Instead they were solemn pleas, appeals to 'our own' consciences, displays of wounded or affronted love. When my brother and I (intellectually precocious) first defied our father by refusing to go to church at the age of ten or so on atheist grounds, he said with a heavy, tragic face, 'I'm not angry; I'm just disappointed.' I was standing near our playroom window and I remember how the granite windowsill outside grew greyer, the lime tree branches drooped lower. How could we disappoint our father, who loved us so dearly? Presently his own Christian belief failed, although he had been an elder of the Kirk, and the religious issue lost its sting. But the important matters lurked in the future: would I grow up to be independently and happily sexual? would I let my agility and daring, my tree-climbing and adoration of wild uplands, carry me up onto the rockfaces? or would the fearfulness I had inherited from my parents compound inside me with the fears they now expressed on my behalf and hold me back and down?

Kafka has the wisdom of the matter, in 'Letter to my Father', when he writes that they were both 'entirely blameless' in what passed (and failed to pass) between them:

> I'm not going to say, of course, that I have become what I am only as a result of your influence. That would be very much exaggerated (and I am indeed inclined to this exaggeration). It is indeed quite possible that even if I had grown up entirely free from your influence . . . I should probably have still become a weakly, timid, hesitant, restless person . . .
>
> Courage, resolution, confidence, delight in this and that, did not endure to the end when you were against whatever it was or even if your opposition was merely to be assumed . . .
>
> 'Do whatever you like. So far as I'm concerned you have a free hand. You're of age, I've no advice to give you,' and all this with that frightful hoarse undertone of anger . . .

I was too docile, I became completely dumb, cringed away from you, hid from you, and only dared to stir when I was so far from you that your power could no longer reach me, at any rate directly . . .

[Mother] loved you too much and was too devoted and loyal to you to have been able to constitute an independent spiritual force, in the long run, in the child's struggle.

– *Wedding Preparations in the Country*, 1954, pp 159–83

I can only wince with admiration at the unsparing lucidity with which this defines my own case. All it lacks is a more modern, genetically-based definition of how the family binds are double: parents frightened of physical danger or sex or nakedness or illness tend to produce offspring whose hereditary excess of frailty or qualm is then re-instilled by the parents' worrying on their behalf ('for their sake').

There is no way out of these twisted bonds except by clarity, of both will and mind. I as a parent must be clear with myself which of my fears are bogeys – projections of my own phobias, not accurate images of dangers in the real world. If I am afraid of heights, and take my children to some beauty spot, Pavey Ark in the Lakes or Malham Cove in the Yorkshire Dales, and spend the afternoon hissing at them, '*Don't* go near that *edge*!', then I am protecting them against a possible fall at the cost of stopping them from using their own perception of space and drop in order to choose their own footholds rationally. Animals do not readily plunge to their deaths. It is true that one-eighth of gibbons in the wild have healed fractures of a limb but they are at risk all the time as they move through the trees. Sheep fall from the crags but they are driven onto irreversibly narrow ledges by over-grazing on scanty hill pastures and further disadvantaged by being bred for wool, which makes them top-heavy and upsets their natural goat-like agility. My own dog, a yellow Labrador, has come to the crags with me hundreds of times and I have never held him back or shouted at him to 'save' him from a drop, not even when he trotted to the very end of the ledge below the climb called Sundance Wall, three hundred feet up the Cove at Malham. At the tapered end he looked down and then backed eight or nine paces until he was able to turn in his own length (to the horror of my companion, who has no pet) and trotted surefootedly along to safety. I have also never held back or shouted deterrently at my children. We left them to see the manifest dangers for themselves. Even when they played cricket hour after hour in a lane sloping down to a main road, I never cautioned them against rushing after the ball when it bounced out into the traffic. And every time they chased it, they paused at the kerb and looked before running out to retrieve it. They were impulsive enough – cannoning into stone dykes when they went downhill too fast on new bikes, injuring knees in headlong rugby tackles. But they were allowed to build up their own working sense of what was too broad a gap to jump, too dark a pool to wade, too sheer a face to climb.

Whenever parents say to their offspring 'Be careful', instead of leaving them to discover for themselves that a drop or a depth is dangerous and must be explored with care, they cut at the offspring's sense of balance, their fine control of muscle and digit, their self-reliance, their ability to estimate risk. It is analogous to amputation, or leucotomy. The psychological tendons, the driving-belts between mind and limb, are threatened with severance. You start to look elsewhere rather than into yourself for the faculties that will enable you to survive.

In my own case I was so unnerved by my father's forebodings – or to put it less partially, was unduly frail in myself and therefore shrank from the stress of facing up to his disapprovals – that I went into the mountains far less than I might have done. When I did I was so tense, so ill-at-ease that sometimes my stomach would accept no food all day and I finished up retching with emptiness. And even if I had forced the issue and gone out climbing as much as my contemporaries, would I have been able to find in myself the well-tempered mix of flair and will that climbing calls upon? From seeing my sons at the very thresholds of their climbing lives I would say that to embark on unknown, steep rock demands a certain blithe dash, an unimpaired animal assumption that the thing can be done and you are up to it. I never had that. The baby-reins of upbringing had grown into my tendons, stiffening and holding back – not entirely, or I could not have set off onto the steeps again at the age of forty-one; but I can't climb with a mental poise equal to my muscular capacities. On the hardest rock I can climb physically I need a leader. Hundreds of hours of the keenest and most fundamental comradeship have come of this, and at least one epiphany of tragi-comic realisation. This occurred on one of Cumbria's most famous climbs, Kipling Groove on Gimmer Crag. The western shoulder of the mountain, visible from our garden thirty miles away as a steeply angled edge, juts towards the big boys across the way, Bow Fell with Sca Fell behind it, as though to say, 'You're bigger than me but I'm as hard as you.' A climber from Bradford called Arthur Dolphin, in the spring of 1948, managed to climb a line here which for years had been focusing the attention of the best local climbers. He called it Kipling Groove because it was 'ruddy 'ard'. Ever since it has been a burning point on the horizon, making us try it, exacting our best efforts.

We first went for it, Pete and I, on a brilliant, breezy June day in 1975. I had climbed nothing of that grade before (Hard Very Severe). Pete's eagerness used to set him off up coveted routes even when other climbers were already on them. This time we were just behind a rope of three men in their early thirties, all of them doctors who, we gathered from their echoing conversations, had had some years' lay-off to graduate, start work, get married, and the like. They were 'rusty', they kept telling each other, and as they clambered rustily upwards Pete had to pause in mid-pitch and wait until the chimney stance (before the severest difficulties) cleared of at least some of the doctors and made room for him. Sixty feet away, in a shirt and squashy tennis pumps, I shivered in the whipping wind, then nodded off to sleep – an escape from fear? After an hour's doldrum Pete went up to the stance, I joined him there, and he climbed out onto the burnished, airy front of Gimmer in his boyishly speedy style. The crux was up there, out in space. On the third ascent, in 1951, Joe Brown had hammered in a piton for protection because the run-out was so long and exposed. The Lancashire climber Mick Burke (later killed on Everest) had made eight attempts before he got past that point. I was well deterred already. When distant shouts signalled to me to move, I climbed up and outwards from the narrowing cleft above the stance feeling as though I was stepping onto an invisible ladder in the midst of the blue air itself. I made three efforts at a high step onto a frighteningly small notch on the arête before shouting up to Pete, 'I've done the crux!'

Shout from above: 'That wasn't the crux.'

With energy fading (more mentally than physically) I stretched way past the rusting stub of Brown's peg – what in hell's the handhold? That smooth-lipped incut far away (a few feet away) to the right? Can't reach that – try and get the palms of my hands on the shelf just above me and mantel upwards – scrabble and press – stretch upwards like a telescope – too far, it's too far – the muscles round my nose squirm with the last spasms of exertion, my feet skid backwards off their little edge, I'm off on a pendulum-swing that faces me outwards – Wrynose Fell, Pike of Blisco, Crinkle Crags, Bow Fell swim past in a slow-motion arc – crunch as my right hip hits rock and the arc reverses itself, majestic, as exhilarating as flying, the best way to see the Lake District . . .

Pete held me manfully (aged fifteen), I recovered grip on the rock and finished the climb, but I hadn't really climbed it because I had swung Tarzan-style past the main difficulty. Five years later, when Neil was fifteen and felt ready to lead it, I was of course minutely aware of what to do. Too aware. A kind of absurd negative charge, a barrier of fear, had gathered round the pole of that crux and it scattered my mental clarity. When I tried the mantelshelf move again and again found it too hard to get my weight above my hands, instead of traversing a few yards rightwards with my hands first on the shelf and then on the incut I made another scrabbling effort to palm myself upwards, fell off, and dangled about . . . This time I collected myself a little more coolly and when the pendule had stopped I duly made the hand-traverse rightwards, with a little help from the rope held taut above me. But Neil knew and I knew that Kipling had defeated me again. As I pulled up the last few feet towards him, he gave me a pawky smile and uttered the most final sentence ever addressed to me: 'Tough luck, Dad – you've run out of sons.'

10

I had first perceived the fear barrier on my first Very Severe – the Barbican on the Castle Rock of Triermain. As you drive towards Keswick from the south, a lumpy formation comes into sight on your right, a kind of squat grey-green tower like an eroded Stilton cheese. Dark faces appear, it's rockier than you'd thought, and then as you come abreast of it its massive front lifts into sight as though a mastodon had risen to its feet and stooped its great forehead at you. Four of us, using two ropes, set off up this monster on a damp March day in 1975. The big black boots; the stiffish nylon rope; not much experience, on my part. The guidebook's relentless phrases had shelved themselves in a shadowed layer of my brain. 'Exposed and sensational in the upper part,' I would rather not have known that, 'particularly for the last man' – I couldn't understand this, which made it the more disconcerting. Presently we were huddled beside an ash tree above the seeping vegetable life of the lower pitches, staring at a corner which bent round into space. It was undercut and it looked holdless. Below there was nothing but the crowns of tall trees and the backs of flying wood-pigeons. Pete led off round the corner, fingers on invisible holds, toes on derisory edges, moving fluently. Later he told us he had been in a state of 'blind fear'. Julie, an experienced climber but years out of practice, leaned her head against the rock beside the ash with her eyes shut. When I followed Pete, it felt like treading a wire-thin line of rock stretched in mid-air. At the corner the fear barrier appeared, a zone of menace, of impossibility. As I neared it, it shrank, became transparent, turned out to be impalpable. I rounded the corner and there it was again, part of the way along the seemingly unclimbable wall. As though in a dream, pulled by the magnet of sheer necessity, pushed by the unthinkability of going back, I kept fitting the hefty Vibrams to the little edges, advancing on the barrier – until it disappeared, and we both felt fully human again, tethered to a rusty but solid peg and starting to glow with the realisation that the barrier could be nullified.

But the fear still lurked, ready to materialise on any crag, and for me it still has the character of that great wall on Castle Rock, a character made of the hollow drop below an overhang, the vacancy that yawns behind you as you climb only just in balance, the silent obdurate resistance of any big steep mass of stone. There it was again on the crux of Kipling Groove; on Timillero's route on the Punta della Disperazione, where I only made it vanish by deciding beforehand to pull my way along on Neil's sling; at the apex of the flake on the traverse of Haste Not, Jim Birkett's most spectacular route on White Ghyll in Langdale, where you cling on with strained forearms and frictioning toes trying to drape a sling (see plate 2); on the traverse pitch of Anvil Chorus at Bosigran, where I exorcised it after ten minutes' swithering by a magical charm, saying to Rob, 'If I fall, I fall,' which made the whole thing seem fated and therefore beyond personal worriting. The barrier is an invisible obstacle – the point where your arms and your nerve will buckle and fail – the divide where impossibility begins, where everything is too much, the steepness, the sheerness, the not-yet-known – a kind of break in the world, a spacewarp, where the laws favouring your survival will stop applying and pure gravity will take over.

In that same March, when the mist verged on drizzle, we went to White Ghyll Chimney, my first effort at a Severe lead. Where you leave the sheltering security of the corner and step out onto a wall which is all bare ribs and fingery edges, I met the fear barrier when I wasn't expecting it, I felt suddenly club-footed, all friction seemed to cease, the rock turned blank and dark, the mental steps afforded by protection nuts ran out and I perched there fearfully, face to face with the barrier, willing it to vanish – it didn't – calling out excuses to the other two in the party, but they said nothing. The barrier consists also of loneliness: you are on your own, as helplessly solitary as though you were hovering in mid-air, trying to invent the glider or evolve wings. But with help from equipment and from people, and with experience, the

1. 'Rocks and Tide' by John Blakemore

2. DC and Bill Peascod climbing Haste Not, White Ghyll, Great
Langdale, August 1982, by Chris Culshaw

barrier does lose power. In May we went back to White Ghyll Chimney, I in squashy pumps, and of course I swarmed across and up that wall, and as Chris joined me at the top he said, 'Loony tunesville! You failed on that six weeks ago – in proper footgear!' his quaint name for hulking boots. Six weeks later again I made my hash of Kipling, feeling the pumps splurge and wobble on the little notches and rims, but by the autumn I had graduated to PA's, rock-boots with high-friction soles, and my feet felt elegant as an okapi's, unerring as an orang's. But the fear barrier hadn't lost its power, it had only moved, to a perhaps diminishing but still vast number of locations on the crags of the world.

Perhaps it has lost some power in one respect, that I usually notice it much less when I'm seconding. If you fall as a second, you can usually swing about airily, like some clumsy trapeze artist, and the wild free arcing through air helps to make up for the ignominy of failing to surmount the crag by your own powers. Such a failure is itself a thing to fear, which may be why some of the usual symptoms still flicker: the sinking gut as the impossible move looms just beyond you, the inefficient scrabbling with fingers that just aren't up to it, the slow relaxing of braced limbs as you sag back downwards and prepare to fall. But all this is much less of a body-blow than the barrier as the leader meets it: the zone of pure ill-being or unbeing where your imagination balks, across which it can't throw any Bailey bridge of conceivable moves, into which it implodes like matter in a black hole.

At times the fear barrier locks itself onto a piece of rock and stays there with all the illusory deadliness of the Bermuda Triangle: the only way to prove it doesn't exist is to fly through it and come out alive and well at the other side. For me it was locked for six years (until June 19 1984) onto the overhung corner and rib on Castle Rock where Triermain Eliminate, a Brown and Whillans route, goes straight up, and Harlot Face, a Birkett route, veers out onto the rib, then round and up it out of sight. The book promises 'a good resting place', but you can't see it, and this invisibility helps the fear barrier to form out of the overhung steepness all around. On the Eliminate, in 1978, I tried to follow Pete up the corner, got past the *in situ* nut, and faced with more overhang and diminishing help from the crack in the joint before I could even reach the high step onto the doubtful perch on the downward-sloping block, the scale of everything and the colossal outward shove of the mammoth's forehead overcame me. I had reached the fear barrier – it had continued to exert power invisibly, like negative magnetism, and I had to downclimb rapidly (to put it politely) and abseil off the ash on the first stance.

I hadn't even tried the crucial move and failed. Pathetic. And this mental failure is what potentiates the fear barrier like nothing else. In this case it made it spread until it permeated the crux stride out of the corner onto the rib of Harlot Face. Like a fool I let this move become a rite of passage. It was the great thing I must do to prove my courage, out of the thousands of other commitment-points that I might as well have made into The One. On a day of cold rushing wind early in June 1983, after retreating off the Raven Traverse on the mountain opposite because we were too numb and shuddering to climb, Neil and I went over to the Castle for my first epic tilt at the barrier on The One. Seconding it would be worse than useless. The One must be led. I climbed up to the ash tree ledge much too quickly, putting on no runners, and belayed to the tree with my guts feeling thin and quaky like watery porridge.

Neil settles himself down for the siege. I put on a nut absurdly low down, where it would do no good at all, and pull clumsily up the corner towards a blur or two of chalk left by previous climbers. The crack takes a second nut and as my forearms tire I eye the fateful step, the tiny abyss, one stride through air to fix my right foot on the side of the rib and then . . . The moment I make as if to move, the fear barrier rears – almost visible, almost palpable – a kind of tough formation of the air which my will and imagination can't win through. No, not my imagination, I can conceive of the move all right: find the best lodgement for the left foot on the pockety wall – right hand onto the first small sweat-blackened spike on the rib – swing out – go for the fine flake three feet up – transfer the left hand – but how? It's feet away, clung on by its fingerends to a little saw-edged pocket, and if I can't bring it across double-quick to some sharp hold or other on the rib or a jam in the corner-crack . . . The half-chances and fantasy-moves flick through almost subliminally like frames in a thriller. My faith in myself has now been sucked into the black hole and I half-lower off the second nut, feeling witless and craven and defeated.

Five or six minutes on the ledge, shaking out the arms and hands to restore muscle-tone, analysing the moves to Neil – over-analysing them, letting the mental tension build far beyond the point of a useful surge. Neil is phlegmatic, sceptical. He has a motto for this situation now: 'You're your own worst enemy, Dave.' He adds helpfully, 'It's just one move,' a well-known climbers' nostrum, like 'Good holds arrive'. I now have a plan – climb higher up the corner. From there I can launch across to a point where the rib is less steep. It turns out that this takes me too high to use the black spike, to reach the good flake I'd have to fly or something, and anyway at that height the corner impends, demolishing my strength. I slither back down from nut to nut and stand on the ledge speechless with chagrin, fingertips numb, then starting to throb. Three more deranged efforts make no impression on the Harlot, or on the fear barrier, which remains in place. During the final one I find myself absurdly crouched ten feet up the corner, like a slug impaled on a cactus, craning rightwards, eyeing the gap and that taunting rib beyond it, urging my inner self to go for it, feeling my inner self quail as the fear barrier toughens into a thick glass presence against which my mind scrabbles and fizzes like a trapped bee.

Then I spent a year re-screening the moves.

The barrier was never more precise: six inches out from the rib. At that point the exact grasping of the fingers must begin, the centre of gravity shift smoothly across, the feet pick the perfect friction points, the will remain intact. At the barrier the will may crumple like plastic in a fire or it may hold and then the barrier is a nothing.

Over the winter I do the climb most weeks, in my head. In a bad week six or seven times. Maybe I should do more on snow and ice, to reduce the pressure of brooding, since it hardens and thickens the fear barrier still more.

Just after the anniversary of the epic siege we are up there again.

A fine drizzle has made the Castle the obvious place to go: it overhangs so much that the face stays dry, at least until the rainfall soaked up by the ground above begins to seep out of the rock at its dark little mouths. Neil has designs on an Extreme route of Paul Ross's called Rigor Mortis, whose second pitch he fell off several times when he was sixteen. For me, of course, it has to be The One. 'Here it comes at last, the great grey distinguished thing,' as Henry James said on his death-bed, and nobody knew whether he meant death or the Order of Merit. Such banter makes me forget the fear barrier, for a minute or two. And then we're up there again, Neil steady on the ledge, amused at me but helpful, while I stare at the corner and run my eye across the void to the rib. Move up, put on nut, move up, lean out, sketch a sally with the right foot through space, downclimb in good order, five minutes to let the fingertips recover, back up to put in a nut higher up and take a last reconnaissance. I lean way out, bridging to the utmost, get my right hand on the black spike – then the fear barrier repels my right foot. The lodgement for it under the rib is useless, a mere greenish slip of cracked rock. I change hands and reach for the good flake with my right but the barrier is still on full power. The flake top runs out, how could I use so poor a hold to haul my full weight up at an angle beyond the vertical? Again I retreat, as deliberately as a projectionist winding back a film (after all, I've done it six or seven times).

'This time,' I tell Neil, 'I'll go for it – no more waste of glycogen. If I fall, I fall.' He puts up both thumbs and blows out lips and cheeks in his inimitable mime of jollying and confirming. And as I swing across this time the barrier shatters and scatters around me. It almost takes me with it, I don't climb well. 'I can't *do* this, Neil!' I remember squawking, as my left fingers just clenched my weight inwards and my right just curled hard enough over the flake-top to power me round up into that resting-place I have been trying to visualise for six years. That which has become for me *the* embodiment of whatever lies beyond the fear barrier. It's a flat ledge about the size of a large dinner-mat and as I stand on it for several minutes, breathing hard and matching small nuts to the crack above, I feel as ensconced in mid-air as a kestrel or a helicopter.

When we finished the hard pitch, we were so pleased with ourselves that instead of obeying the guidebook and moving left, we went up a fine steep groove which turned out to be the natural continuation of the dreaded corner down below. The last thing that had ever occurred to me was that one day I would be able to add a Direct Finish to a famous route by Jim Birkett, the greatest of Cumbrian climbers between 1937 and 1954. No doubt, when he made his route in 1949, he surmounted those crux moves at his first attempt. His balance was superb and his hands, toughened by his work as a quarryman, were very strong. 'When I got my fingers over something, the rest of me generally followed,' was his sublime motto. The fear barrier will have been so much less hard and deep for him, and locked onto fewer places, although (according to his son) he clearly saw it one winter, climbing Engineer's Chimney on the north face of Great Gable in nailed boots with one long-shafted ice-axe. Len Muscroft (his second also on Harlot Face) heard him give a short rasping cough as he moved across the steep wall coated with verglas: 'When he did this I knew it was going to be desperate.' (Bill Birkett, *Lakeland's Greatest Pioneers*, 1983, p 122)

I now see that the image of a barrier which is there, as though finite, is not true enough. The fear barrier is a zone of nothing, where you cannot be. As you move up closer to it, it may enter into you – *you* become nothing, your strength is cancelled, weakness hollows out your arms, your feet can't be trusted, your brain ceases to screen clear images, your balance shakes out of true, your imagination can't conceive of a way beyond. But if the fear barrier fails to invade you, it cancels itself, and you remain yourself, strong, limber, and collected, in a fit state to savour the lovely jubilation that floods through you as you move on and up, unscathed.

To what extent are such things felt by the 'hard men', as leading climbers were called in the recent golden age of machismo? After all, at their own level they spend as much time operating at the limit of their powers as the rest of us in respect of our lesser ones. Remarkable athletes have time and again used kindred metaphors to evoke whatever is uttermost for them. Daley Thompson, the decathlon champion, during the 1984 Olympics said, about the threshold of his crucial event, 'This is the moment to look over the goddam cliff and face whatever is there.' Joe Simpson, the Sheffield climber who fell at 24,000 feet on one of the biggest unclimbed faces in Peru and crawled down the mountain for three days, alone, with a broken leg, describes himself as having had to 'get through whatever wall had been in my way'. *(High*, October 1985) This connects with a remarkable passage in Norman Mailer's book about Muhammad Ali's fight with George Foreman in Zaire in which the novelist, at the ring-side, observes Ali between rounds, perfectly still and absorbed. He imagines that he is looking into the deepest, darkest well of himself and estimating how much of his essence is still left in reserve. The barrier, after all, is not a thing, it is a mental construct in which your perceptions of your own shortcomings and of the objective difficulties you're facing merge into one.

It is not easy to say how commonly climbers experience such states of mind because to express them calls for specially considered, even creative uses of language and there is still some he-man taboo on this. Expedition books have been notorious for being little more than workmanlike reports. On television climbs the leading climbers tend to be studiously monosyllabic, like subalterns from the heyday of the stiff upper lip. This high imperial and military style had evolved in the public schools and the army barracks as a way of not owning up to 'funk', the need being to keep yourself intact not only against the terrifying menaces of whatever Dervishes, Kurds, or Zulus were surrounding you at the time but also against the jeers of 'cissy' or 'softy' or 'mummy's boy' from your fellows. Eric Shipton, greatest of English big-mountain explorers, was an imperial civil servant, a consul, and I recall a passage from a lecture he gave in Aberdeen thirty-five years ago which, quite unaffectedly on his part, came out like a parody of the nonchalant sahib behaving 'like a brick'. On a Himalyan snow-ridge, climbing roped but with no belays, his companion fell down one side, above a huge drop, and Shipton had to decide to jump off on the other side as a counterweight. Looking at us from his lean height, out of scooped eye-sockets, he said in his extremely slow, quiet, stainless-steel voice, 'It was . . . quite an . . . alarming . . . moment.' Such was his only phrase for what must have been one of the most mortally unsettling experiences of his life.

Nowadays, being neither imperial nor military, we tend to 'let it all hang out' and the language of mountaineering has become more candid. Peter Boardman, describing the gale that nearly blew his party off Kangchenjunga in 1979, is willing to admit to a state of 'caged terror', 'hating the predicament, and then hating climbing, utterly and in general'. (*Sacred Summits*, 1982) Another member of the party, Georges Bettembourg, says that 'Tempers were flaring and nerves were on end.' (*The White Death*, 1981) Joe Brown says in his autobiography, about a crisis moment when trying a new route on Clogwyn du'r Arddu in Snowdonia, 'My position was perilous; I was sweating profusely and my throat was bone-dry' – a counter to the foolish legend that he is a 'climbing machine'. Describing his first ascent of Cemetery Gates on Dinas y Gromlech in the Pass of Llanberis he writes, 'The position on the face was very sensational and frightening. I brought up Don [Whillans] and he was flabbergasted. "Christ, this is a gripping place," he muttered hoarsely.' (*The Hard Years*, 1967, pp 69, 73) When I asked Whillans last year if he recognised the fear barrier, he said at once, 'Oh aye, and it's bloody near the ground, because if I fell from there I'd damage meself.' This is a wonderfully rational observation, and shows up my own neurosis, since I perceive the barrier even if a fall would leave me safely dangling, but even Brown and Whillans were not wholly consistent here since Cemetery Gates was so steep that a fall from it would have been 'through space' (in Brown's own phrase). The fact is that sure contact with terra-firma is so ingrained in us from infancy onwards that any loosening of it begins to undermine us and the resulting qualms have to be repressed, or else freely admitted to if the repressing would use up psychic energy needed for the climbing itself.

I saw this vividly in action in the scorching June of 1976, amongst fells whose pasture was already parched as blond as savannah grass by weeks of anti-cyclone. We were about to climb on Goat Crag in Borrowdale. A few yards away Ron Fawcett, who is still setting new standards for the hardest climbing in England, America, and the Continent, was tackling what was then the hardest crux on Cumbrian rock, the overhangs on a route called Footless Crow. It is one hundred and ninety feet of rock, often past the vertical, with no resting-place, and had only been climbed by pulling up on bolts and pitons until Pete Livesey climbed it free on April 19 1974. As we stood at its base it looked unclimbable, a sequence of awkward planes with no visible cracks or flakes, towering up to a brow of yellowish overhangs. Fawcett had been going round the New Dungeon Ghyll the night before trying to borrow a two hundred-foot rope in place of the usual one hundred and fifty. Now his second, Chris Gibb, was sitting at the foot of the crag and belaying in a most individual style. He had his back to the rock and was looking straight out over the luminous green woodlands with a fixed scowl of uninterest, smoke from a weedy roll-up fuming into his eyes as he controlled the ropes wholly by feel and ignored the little crowd that had gathered. Fawcett moved up a few feet just under the brow, inserted a small wired nut, clipped its karabiner onto one of the ropes, and climbed back down a foot or two to 'rest'. Presently someone shouted up, 'What's it like?' and he called down, 'A 'orrendous place – Ah'm scared out of me wits', leaning way back on his fingerends and relaxing as comfortably as a sloth under a branch.

So in some sense he was afraid (unless his remark was a piece of false modesty, and people agree that he is a most candid and unaffected person). But whatever the level of his fear, he was coping with it solidly, the place was not getting to him, his self was intact. In bodily terms, he was not building up an unuseful tension which would have wasted glycogen on keeping muscle-fibres excessively taut – the condition that makes less poised climbers tremble violently from the knee down. In cultural terms, consider that Fawcett was coping solidly with a place which would have been too much for even Brown and Whillans – although his inborn powers will have been no greater than theirs.

The difference lies in one main thing, tradition which is a mental ladder of possibilities. In each age the pioneer finds himself so many rungs above zero, he comes of age on the highest rung achieved by his predecessors and can then spend his (or her) energy on pushing up still further, having probably repeated those lower stages with youthful unconcern. So the fear barrier exists for a generation as well as for an individual. The American mountaineer Galen Rowell argues this from his own experience in his essay 'Storming a Myth':

Climbing big walls was serious business in 1966. On the way to the base of the climb I didn't look up. I was too scared. Several times before, I'd walked in the pre-dawn darkness with big-name climbers who looked up for a few moments too long. They lost their nerve and made up an excuse to retreat: a telltale cloud, a runny nose, a worn haul bag, a missing piton – things that wouldn't give a moment's hesitation to the wall climbers of the seventies who have broken so far through the fear threshold they aren't even aware it once existed. In 1966 we had no helicopters buzzing in the back of our consciousness; if we were in trouble, we were on our own.
– *The Mountain Spirit*, ed. Michael Charles Tobias and Harold Drasdo, 1980, p 86

Presumably, however, each of these Seventies heroes does have his own threshold, or barrier, which he finds by soloing, by putting up new routes on previously unthinkable loose rock, or by some other means of taking it to the limit (the name of a recent Extreme route on Deer Bield Crag in Far Easedale). At whatever level our barrier lies, each of us has to face it with what Brown calls, in his list of the five main qualities a climber needs, 'the right amount of confidence' (*The Hard Years*, p 17). Not unlimited but the right amount – it isn't a matter of unalloyed dash or flair but of enjoying the risk and respecting the danger, these two near but different insights held in a fine balance together. W. H. Murray puts this classically in his story of his first climb (Slanting Ledge on Buachaille Etive Mór) after coming back from the War:

When I made the right traverse and looked up I felt as weak as a kitten – the drop, the angle, the lack of holds – frightening! but healthily frightening, and not like lying flat in a midnight cellar listening to a bomb whistling down like a grand piano, nor like going into a bare room to chat with the Gestapo – here one had chosen the route, was free to act sharply amid sunny rock and air, to rely on oneself.

— *Undiscovered Scotland*, 1951, p 13

At such a moment we accept our fear as an inseparable fibre of our experience instead of treating it like some infected foreign body. The feared thing takes on this malignant aspect when it is beyond our control. We can see this laid bare at a certain testing-point, almost a rite of passage, which seems to be standard in climbers' lives. It is the point when an ordeal surmounted brings home to them for the first time that sheer animal hardihood isn't enough. This happened to Hermann Buhl when he was sixteen. He was climbing the Kadner route in the Wetterstein Alps. Seven hundred feet up he and his mates were overtaken by a solo climber. Some time later they heard a clattering sound and ducked, expecting rockfall. 'Instead, a dark, heavy object – rather long, like a sack full of something – sailed past through thin air.' The solo climber had fallen – they heard him hit the bottom – blood splashes marked the rocks. 'For days and weeks after this fearful experience I was so shaken that I could not bear the sight of my mountaineering equipment. For a time I thought I should have to give up my climbing career, which had hardly even begun.' (*Nanga Parbat Pilgrimage*, 1982, pp 31–3) Bill Peascod underwent an exactly similar experience when he was twenty, in the first flush of his explorations among the crags of the north-west Lakes. A young solo climber was on the North Route on Pillar Rock, Ennerdale, while Bill and his mates were round on the South West Climb. They heard a flapping noise, like pigeons taking off, and thought nothing of it. A little later they saw the young man's corpse at the base of the cliff, which is a great rough tower set like a beacon on the mountainside. For a long time after that they were all 'slowed down a bit' and they 'underwent traumatic moments': 'a piece of brightly coloured litter or lost equipment or cached rucksack, would bring a start to my eyes and a jolt to my heart.' The first 'wonderful haze of confidence' had been blown away. (*Journey After Dawn*, pp 34–5)

Paul Ross, one of the most fearless climbers in Borrowdale in the Fifties, bore similar witness when he told me in 1983 how at the age of twenty-six he injured his vertebrae seriously as a result of jumping off trees from up to thirty feet to practise falling. On his return to serious climbing,

> I was struggling. I never again had the same flair until much later in the States. I was thinking about what harm might come. I had come from a good Roman Catholic family, and I wasn't afraid of *death*. I knew, you see, that that was all taken care of. If I had to go I would accept it. *At that time*, if I was gripped out of my mind, I used to say four Hail Mary's, and that saw me over the crux . . .

In each case the climber loses his innocence. Then he must live on after the fall, both literally and mythically. He is no longer in Eden where harm is unthinkable and bodily vitality rules unchallenged. That things can go badly wrong is now a truth of life and from this point on people must take their way through the wilderness in a state of complex awareness, looking before and after, protecting themselves, anticipating troubles and even (such is the seeming perversity of humans) seeking them out.

This courting of the fearful by going into conditions where the difficulties are not all within your control is graphically dealt with by Mick Fowler. He is the most expert of climbers on loose rock – the shale cliffs of the north Cornwall coast and the chalk cliffs of the south-east, which he explores using ice gear (crampons, axes, and ice-screws for protection). His writings show how well he knows the score. Describing the first ascent of Vagabond at Tintagel he says: 'the serious process of frightening oneself can start.' Again and again his key phrases touch on fear:

> Fear increasing, I searched frantically for some protection on the traverse . . . I was frightened enough for a peg runner to seem like a good idea; having admitted my weakness, it was quick work to hammer one home . . . Panic was rising and arms were failing . . . Panic took over . . . Apart from terrifying me, the removal of the grass exposed a useful crack . . . At the overhang matters took a turn for the worse, the possibilities noted from below looked frightening and at the worst thoroughly impossible, the death potential looked

excellent . . . retreat from here seemed an horrendous proposition involving the loss of many brain cells as well as much equipment.

His most self-conscious remark gives the oblique key to how he coped with all this fear: 'being a natural coward, I searched studiously but ineffectively for more runners.' ('The Battle of Tintagel': *Crags* No. 16; 'A Mountain by the Sea': *Mountain*, September/October 1980) Clearly Fowler isn't a coward in any normal sense, and he must know that. The second of these articles is about climbing a new five hundred-foot route in the rain, up a shale cliff whose collapsing ledges were heaped with rubble and a soggy paste in a state near to avalanche. There are probably only half a dozen people in the country who would dare to climb there. 'Being a natural coward' and 'the death potential looked excellent' represent a kind of laid-back wit, a pose of apparent unconcern deliberately out of keeping with the surrounding chaos, and its source must lie in the studied, technical finesse he made himself apply to the rockface even while his instinctive self screamed 'Let me outta here!' It's the same as the famous unflappable style which combatants used to keep their nerve in the Battle of Britain or the Western Desert, recorded, for example, in the memoirs of the poet Keith Douglas, who fought in a Crusader tank in Tunisia:

> 'My tank is not a dressing station,' he said in a mock-serious voice which, so carefully did he maintain it, made it clear that it was an insurance against real seriousness . . .

> 'That chap is a Jerry in a MK III,' I said. 'I should quite like to shoot him up before he sees us . . .' My stomach was turning over inside me. 'King Five,' Piccadilly Jim answered before Edward could acknowledge my message. 'Give the bugger hell,' with a kind of refined emphasis quite divorced from the words.

> The pain in my foot, which Bert had tied up very tightly to stop it bleeding, was increasing. I said to Bert: 'Don't take any notice if I moan. I like moaning,' and with this excuse began to moan in a jerky way, dependent on the bumps. It was a way of taking my mind off the foot.

> – From *Alamein to Zem Zem*, 1969, pp 23, 127–8, 140

The perversity of climbing rock that needs such cunning psychological routines to cope with it is only a seeming one because it is our whole selves that climb, not some crooked or freaky vein in our beings. The satisfaction of it is precisely that it embroils and extends our whole selves like almost nothing else. Yet it does have a strangeness whose motives root deep in our natures and follow subtle paths. Michael Roberts, poet and poetry-editor in the Thirties, explained these motives:

> To justify mountaineering in the fullest sense, we must justify the loss of life, the deliberate taking of risks. And I think the only answer is the sheer uselessness of the loss: man [*sc.* a person] can preserve his dignity only by showing that he is not afraid of anything, not even death . . . The sacrifice is not necessary: the risk brings no material gain, but it offers something – the exhilaration, the clear vision – which partly excuses the risk . . . It is a demonstration that man is not wholly tied to grubbing for his food, not wholly tied by family and social loyalties . . . sacrifices are good because they show superiority to all merely utilitarian values: they show an excess and overflow which is really a gesture of confidence and vitality.
> – 'The Poetry and Humour of Mountaineering': from *Mirrors in the Cliffs*, ed. Jim Perrin, 1983, pp 667–8

This explains very well the cultural basis of the sport but it is still a little aside from our own motives. True, people since the heyday of the Industrial Revolution have included climbing in their behavioural range because they now have energy to spare from bread-winning. But that is not my own reason for walking up to Hollow Stones on a sultry August morning to climb the Central Buttress of Sca Fell. As I do so, I'm aware that I'm spending my day on something hard and trying, as well as fiercely enjoyable, and this is a bit strange because normally, left to ourselves, we choose ease, not wear-and-tear.

The most searching analysis I have seen of this particular sort of voluntary experience is made by Geoffrey Moorhouse in his book *The Fearful Void* (1974, pp 17–18). It describes his crossing the Sahara by camel from west to east. His deepest fears, he says, had always been 'of annihilation, of being surrounded by what is hostile, of being unwanted, of loss and of being lost'. Such neuroses are not inborn, in that the child 'finds itself always in natural movements towards its fellows' until it is 'pained for the first time by an encounter with some other creature'. Here is a loss of innocence much earlier than the 'fall' I discussed a few pages ago. So, Moorhouse suggests, we shrink in on ourselves, we become tainted by 'the fear of being afraid'. Here is the dark underside of climbing experience: will I be equal to the climb? or will its cruxes find out my lack of power? Moorhouse then confirms the fear barrier model when he writes that 'if, in the face of fear, we can summon the strength and the faith to go forward', then usually 'the encounter with the thing feared demonstrates that it is by no means as laden with terrible properties as we had supposed'.

Yet why are we impelled to prove this again and again? Why is once not enough? Moorhouse found this out when he had a choice, at a place called Aguelhok, to carry on eastwards across the desert or get on a truck northwards up the trans-Sahara highway into Algeria. He had already tested himself to extremes of thirst, hunger, heat, difficulties of navigation by the stars and of socialisation among alien people:

> I now knew precisely what the most fearful thing consisted of; I had measured it, I had touched it, I had almost been destroyed by it. I had to go out to meet it anew, at once, or I would never dare look upon it again. If I turned my back upon it now, I would be pursued by it to the end of my life, always running away from the subject of my fear. And this would not be fear of death by thirst and dehydration, or fear of being lost in a wilderness of sand. It would be fear of encounter. Nothing more. Fear of encounter with a person, with a task, with anything at all intimidating that might cross my path.
>
> – p 215

No doubt a perfectly integrated person would not need to keep proving himself, he would be content to coast up climbs comfortably inside his or her limits. I can imagine such a state but I don't know it inside myself. As soon as the rock dries out, or as soon as the last climb that fired me has died down to a gentle glow, I have to be out there attempting the seemingly infinite series of routes I have been setting myself in the meantime –

whose images I have been projecting onto the blank grey screen of winter when cold fogs and rains repel us. These images are vastly various – cramped or imposing, sunlit or permanently shadowed – to be found in all the crannies of our country. A route called Zig Zag at Sennen, just north of Land's End: 'In all but perfectly dry conditions this climb is rather a tough proposition for its grade,' says Pat Littlejohn in *South-west Climbs*. Just the kind of phrase that goads me, especially when it means that the climb is near my limit as a leader. I have crouched in the little black cupboard weathered out of the granite at the top of Zig Zag, which is a mere sixty feet of impending cliff, looking down its straight clefts at a maelstrom surfing round its base, wishing for a partner who would come with me into the dank zawn floored with chunks of rock like decaying barons of beef and match our arm strength against those square-cut overhangs. Or, more imposing, the climb of Littlejohn's called Mercury, at Carn Gowla near St Agnes in north Cornwall. In Ken Wilson's tremendous photograph the climber is as dwarfed, but as strongly poised, as Sadak in the John Martin painting I discuss below, and this classic image of a person taking on the steepness, urging upwards, negotiating the rockface in the one place where it relents, is deepened when you know that to reach the foot of the route you have to abseil on two ropes knotted together and anchored onto the one possible point in the slope above – a couple of rocks, one on top of the other, whose points just meet like teeth, round which the ropes are threaded. Or again, in my own country, I hope some time to muster my powers and solo up the thousand feet of the Central Buttress of Coire Mhic Fhearchair on Beinn Eighe, backing myself to find and then have the steadiness to climb the Original Route, which takes the front of one of three giant towers, Black Country pottery kilns made out of quartzite, resting on their plinth of ancient sandstone. And in Wales I hope one day to set off up *that corner* – everybody's test-piece – Cenotaph on Dinas y Gromlech, whose walls confront you like a bare stage challenging you to remember your lines, your moves.

So many pungent courses of rock, hundreds tasted already but the series ahead will never run out. Each time you extend yourself the well-being lasts for days. Presently it cools. Geoffrey Moorhouse said about his crux, 'If I could go into the desert again to face another encounter with what I knew to be there, as exactly and clearly as if I had fashioned it myself, I could walk forwards for the rest of my life into all the deserts of my life.' A splendid hope. But that was written immediately after his journey ended, in 1973, and my guess would be that in the years since then he has found that the 'deserts' are never quelled, that he has had to rouse himself again (and again and again) to launch out across new voids. You know they are there, they lurk in the world's fastnesses, actual but also with something of a dream status – images you entertain in advance of the experience, which feel so alive that they become magnets, attracting you half-reluctantly into their reality.

11

Climbers weave their ways, in many neighbourhoods, among the wreckage of a culture that used stone directly, where we crush it, imitate it, pulverise it into cement or blacken it with tar. Rising east out of Buttermere, a quarrymen's road (track is too slight a word) builds across the slopes beneath Fleetwith Pike and Striddle Crag by a system of causeway, palisade, revetment, step, and kerb whose massiness suggests Macchu Picchu. Under the swarthy little cliffs west of Sheffield that are called edges, Froggatt and Millstone and Curbar, nearly-finished and half-finished grindstones lie abandoned like foundered moons.

The city of Bolton was born out of the north-facing quarries, Pilkington's, Brownstones, and Wilton, behind Winter Hill, a place where polar winds and the left-overs from harsh labour bring to mind the word *gulag*. The stark atmosphere gets to me and my hips and shoulders feel cramped, my fingerends stunned. The Prow at Wilton is a pier of buff sandstone. From end-on it looks like a pillar, left by the quarrymen to jut against the westerlies and challenge us with its vertical planes. Such pillars stand like totems in many quarries, and though there may have been practical reasons for leaving them, their phallic shapeliness also looks totemistic. Did the quarrymen see them as emblems of the value they set on the stuff they worked, the staff of their life? They recall the natural stacks of Scotland, at Hoy in Orkney, Stoer in Sutherland, The Storr in Skye. They are mostly called 'Old Man' and the Gaelic word for them, *bodach*, seems to mean 'cock' or 'phallus' as much as it means 'old man'. *Bod*, the word for 'penis', occurs in at least one mountain name: Devil's Point, near the south entrance of the Lairig Ghru in the Cairngorms, was originally Bod an Deamhain, and what could be more mythically potent than the Demon's Prick? Presently, of course, all this was covered up for shame and the topographical writers used to leave it blank, 'the Devil's – ', when they were obliged to mention it.

The first Old Man I climbed in England was on Mow Cop, above Biddulph on the boundary between Cheshire and Staffordshire, looking out over the green dairying country and the mesh of canals and industrial settlements which for centuries have worked the coal, the salt-mines, and the uniquely pure glacial sand used in glass-making. It's a place of pigeon-lofts and converted gritstone cottages and cindery tracks ending among bumpy, burrowed hillsides. Nearby a peacock screams from a wired hen-run. The sun lowers itself gently into the haze that blurs the highlands of north Wales and mutes the drone of motorway traffic. This hill sent grindstones as far afield as Oxfordshire at least as early as the fifteenth century. In the middle of a small deserted quarry the Old Man angles upwards, a lopsided Cubist sculpture sixty feet high. (A good name for it might be 'Staircase Ascending a Nude'.) Frost and driven moisture still hew at it, prising off blocks, leaving yellow scars and altering the routes.

On a June evening, after a day's work examining students at Alsager College, I arrived there at last to climb it with Graham Hollins, a pawky man, who seems to know every quarry and outcrop in the southern Peak as well as someone knows the stones of his own house wall. He likes to offer the lead with a teasing grin which means 'This easy-angled slab turns suddenly holdless' or 'That edge up there is much less positive than it looks'. The photo of the Old Man in Paul Nunn's *Rock Climbing in the Peak District* had been appetising me for years. Photos, of course, foreshorten and minimise. As you approach this Old Man, he rears up and starts to dominate. The easiest route, Spiral, is graded Severe but strikes a Lakeland climber as harder than that. As I snail round on to the Old Man's weathered chest, security leaks a little. I have just left a solid platform, another awaits me fifteen feet on and up, but here, just here, there is a space to bridge with only a sloping step to launch from. I stretch my left leg, my left arm, am I embracing the Old Man or being crucified on him? My footsoles lodge on a step, my weight leans and leans, my cheek rests on a pillow of air. All I have to embrace is the girth of the totem. Mother, stony mother! Give me a big hug! These are my arms around you, let me slink back into your flesh. Father! Let me lie under your chin, against your massive chest, breathing your smell of sweat and matches. I stretch, I stretch, a fingertip finds a wrinkle on the unfriendly face. I make it round and up, I perch on the fissured tip, lord of the middle air for a moment, high on achievement, chuckling like a jackdaw. Below, the hoary sides and foreheads which have passed me on look out indifferently across Cheshire.

The special quality of places like Mow Cop is that they occupy the fringe where country and city interpenetrate. From Wharncliffe Edge, west of Sheffield, the countryside as you look out from The Prow displays most of England other than its coasts. Housing estates brim up the slopes, making for the green skylines, silos show as white as lighthouses above the serried roofs, an abortive railway pushes its infilled rubble like a dry glacier between ridges tapestried densely with sycamore and birch. At a sewage farm crossed arms of piping revolve above the filter-beds. Railways, arterial roads and the earthy wound of a new highway drive between fields where square hay-bales stand in rows like dwellings. To the west, rising clear of all this urban fret, the Pennines, featureless and impassive, keep to themselves.

72

If Derbyshire climbing has a family tree, its taproot is here, where J. W. Puttrell climbed the first recorded gritstone route, in 1885, up the back of the Prow. Now as you look through the crevasse the quarrymen left between the mother-rock and their totem, the eyeline is blocked by a very functional upright, a pylon of the CEGB. From the top of Tegness Pinnacle near Froggatt you look across the vale of the Derwent to a hilltop mast that beams the news and the soaps and the ads to several million homes.

The older industrial beacons are going back into nature. To find Wharncliffe and Rivelin you have to drive along the wooded valleys between the suburbs, scanning their sides until angular black faces peer out above the fruity greenery before dodging out of sight again. To reach the Prow at Wharncliffe you follow brick-vaulted tunnels that burrow under multiple railway lines. Under your feet crudely masoned setts wet with condensed fog dripping from the sycamore leaves make a causeway between boles and ferns and lichenous gritstone reefs. Cindered trackways end in permanently padlocked gates that guard clearings floored with crushed factory tippings. Crane hooks and windlass chains massive enough to have served Brunel rust among the fireweed.

Nobody except birds and climbers has set foot on these pinnacle tops since the time when they were clad in turf and part of the level moor. As you near a top, you surface like a swimmer from deep down, draw breath, and look out to a scatter of single settlements, farms and old quarry-huts and isolated pubs moored on the green and brown expanse like a fishing-fleet at anchor. Rivelin Needle is hard to get up, a blunt bald tower, almost beyond me but I made it (see plate 3). It was my hardest lead on gritstone, fingers white as a baker's, backs of the hands bleeding. The route was called Croton Oil, which is a medicine the British Army in India used to cure the runs. I think the first ascensionist must have meant that the line involved a few of what we call brown-trouser moves. The flag-floored summit dotted with the lime of jackdaws and kestrels felt all the more hospitable, somewhere to sprawl and chat the sun down under the Pennines, after the finger-racking creep up that pitiless front where cracks don't quite open and wrinkles don't quite fold outwards into edges. But Tegness was classic, in the slimness of its shaft, in the intimate nearness of the quarried faces that enclose it for more than two hundred degrees of the circle (see plate 4). On its top you revolve slowly, the furthest horizon dipping a little, rising a little, turning its wheel round this hub. The floor forty feet below shows rocky through the turf for several yards beyond the pinnacle's outer face. Unlike Froggatt Pinnacle, whose top must always have been exposed as a tor looming through mist like the head of a couched walrus, Tegness must have been a core, the last bone in an arm of the hillside, bared as the quarrymen ate round it. They might as well have devoured it too, but no, the taboo saved it, caused it to matter more than the thousand tons of stone locked up in it, and though its value for them was grounded in needs more practical than mine, both of us have desired that it should stay standing, offering a focus. I am animate, it is not, and we endow such towering presences with life in the most primitive way: we swear at them, 'a hold, you bastard, give me a bloody hold,' venting our panic on them as scapegoats, or afterwards, 'climbed the bugger,' mixing resentment at the demands they make on us with respect for their stature. It's like the mixture of emotions that we feel towards our parents. With that seeming perversity we even choose to submit ourselves to such ordeals, impelled to justify ourselves again and again in the eyes of the elders, to measure up to them – still locked into this pattern even after they have died and become as immobile as stones.

Deeper down, beneath the superego, down into what Reich called the biologic core, the body yearns for such intimate contact. The hand sinks sideways into a dark crack, toes take the shape of the rock, nose smells moist fibre inches away as fingernails delve into earthy crevices, arms embrace a burnished yew trunk, eardrums vibrate to the hoarse hissing of jackdaw chicks three feet inside the rock . . . During one of my first hard climbs, Jim Birkett's route Haste Not, which picks its way along the clenched teeth of the overhangs on the upper crag in White Ghyll, Langdale, I had a sense of myself cladding the rock as closely as the clay applied to a sculpture to make a mould. Seven years later, in 1982, after it had been round the circuits of my brain a hundred times, this came out in the poem 'Into Rock' printed above in section two, whose crucial lines, to my mind, are

> His clay was kneaded to its bas-relief.
> His brain infolded, mimicking its strata.

Through such experience I'm moving back into the elemental immersion I left at birth – having nearly chosen (again with seeming perversity) to relinquish physical contact the more to confirm and heighten the capacity for it once it is regained. The climber is taught always to 'retain at least three points of contact with the rock': both hands and a foot, one hand and both feet. There are also some wild varieties. Bill Peascod told me that he once clenched his teeth on a nubbin of rock in a desperate effort to keep clinging on when he was climbing on an outcrop (Yew Crag near St John's in the Vale) during a high wind; and I have seen both Neil and my dog, Shep the Labrador, press their heads against the rock (limestone near Ingleborough, red sandstone at St Bees Head) to create pressure holds when their feet threatened to slip.

'Three points of contact' sounds so slender. On a precarious crux we may well crave more than mere points. We long for mother earth's big hug and curse our daftness at ever deserting her in the first place. Such is the cry of the weaned child, so often displaced into a religious form.

> . . . even among these rocks
> Sister, mother
> And spirit of the river, spirit of the sea,
> Suffer me not to be separated,

prays T. S. Eliot in the final section of 'Ash Wednesday'. The most articulated expression of this longing is Hopkins's 'The Wreck of the Deutschland' – the only poem in modern times which begins to show me what religion can be for a believer. In the fourth verse the cry for reunion (in his case with Jesus) turns

75

naturally to mountain and steepness symbolism, using specifically
the places of north Wales:

> I am soft sift
> In an hourglass – at the wall
> Fast, but mined with a motion, a drift,
> And it crowds and it combs to the fall;
> I steady as a water in a well, to a poise, to a pane,
> But roped with, always, all the way down from the tall
> Fells or flanks of the voel, a vein
> Of the gospel proffer, a pressure, a principle, Christ's gift.

Voel is both a particular mountain near St Beuno's College, in
north Wales, and a noun of feminine gender meaning 'bare hill':
the perfect word for the poet's meanings. Of course the verse
doesn't literally concern climbing (although his next poem,
'Penmaen Pool', mentions walking up Cader Idris), yet the two
states that he's evoking, being mined and falling as against
remaining steady and poised, are the twin poles of the climbing
experience, so that the word 'roped', when it comes, feels
uncannily fitting. And it connotes more than the physical tie of
the rope itself. Each time I stand below or upon the front of a fell
and my eye climbs its height by the long unbroken twisting cord
of a burn that courses down a joint between its spurs, those lines
of Hopkins surface again. The burn falls down, down, 'all the
way down'. The eyes rise against the streaming of it, tracking
up 'the tall fells or flanks'. Falling and climbing are focused
simultaneously or (if we think of the cord as umbilical) the
experience of dropping out of the mother's flanks and urging to
cleave to them again.

Now Hopkins's words have been joined by the ninth photograph in Fay Godwin's book *Land* – an image seen from Green
Gable between Wasdale and Borrowdale, across wind-combed
blond grasses, beyond a shadowed ridge (see plate 5). The fells'
faces are as gnarled as Rembrandts, scored by runnels, their grain
picked out by slant sunbeams. In a seam of the fell a ghyll shows,
exquisitely fine and white, drawn from a thread to a rope to a
thread again as its ply changes with the twist of its course,

transparent essence of the mountain, quick where it is still. We can go down with the plunge of it or mount to the high beds of peat or gravel where it first secretes, which show in the photos as a crotch of soft grey between blacker, bonier knotts on the skyline. Both movements are equally natural, both (as we climb) balance each other as continuously as the emptying and filling of the hourglass.

12

Such mountains surround us like some fundamental border between the homeland and the strange land. Life springs from them, flows out and down and away to the weary plains but they remain, altering at a slow pace that enables us to make them our symbols of permanence, if not of eternity. Sheep graze them bald. Their lower slopes are trenched by prairie-buster ploughs, then blanked over with the dark trees of government. A duke or a queen commands the servants to blast a scar of a track across the mountain's face so that the rich may lurch across it in the autumn and leave the grouse dying dabbled in their own rowan-red blood . . . The mountains are neutral about all this. We gut them for their congealed metals, rive off whole masonries of limestone or slate, tread their weaknesses into running sores that will never heal while our civilisation lasts . . . They are above it all.

In the supreme photos of Paul Joyce or Fay Godwin, the massifs have just turned their backs on us; a minute earlier and we might have caught an expression but now they are as composed as corpses. Are they having us on? Surely in a moment they will signal to us – so speaking a countenance can't have gone back into its final silence? One mountain has its shoulder lifted against us; it faces always northwards, away from the peopled valleys. Another has given birth from between those pillowed thighs but

77

its offspring left for good a million years ago. Another signals only to its fellows, their brows facing each other through the clear atmosphere above the frost-fog.

> That was a way of putting it – not very satisfactory:
> A periphrastic study in a worn-out poetical fashion,
> Leaving one still with the intolerable wrestle
> With words and meanings,

as Eliot put it in 'East Coker'. How else to convey the sense that they are beings, whose company I need as much as people's?

All right – no more excuses – I went too far. I was getting carried away. I must concentrate. Take this object in front of me, page 134 of *Presences of Nature*, published by the Carlisle Museum and Art Gallery in 1982. It's a photograph by Paul Joyce called 'The Black Horse of Busha (for J.W.)' (see plate 6). Just under clouds solemn with rain two mountains brood, side by side, their flanks rounding from deep shadow on the left to pale serene sunlight on the right, their slopes plunging at length to shingled streambeds, the cleavages between them marked by lesions where turf has been flayed away by run-off, laying bare the body of the soil . . . It's no good – that sentence was written in an effort to detail exactly what was there and still it used ten human associations in sixty words. And so much was still unsaid. For those mountains look as though they are resting, they have made their colossal efforts, thrusting up from under, folding the globe's surface outwards as the fist of a baby shoves from inside its mother's belly. The range of mountains I once lived near in Ceylon was called The Knuckles. The mountain that guards Glencoe on the left as you approach across the Moor of Rannoch is Buachaille Etive Mór, 'the big shepherd of Etive'. The five elegant and high-nosed beauties arrayed just inland from Loch Duich are the Five Sisters of Kintail, and they have three Brothers nearby. In country after country the mountains stand up so saliently, signify so expressively, that it's impossible not to read them.

When I am down in the plains, seeing little beyond the next hedge or copse, I am still looking for the mountains and their

78

crags and when I see them it is as though they were already in my mind when I came into the world. My first mountain (Bennachie, 1,698 feet, in the centre of Aberdeenshire, which I first climbed when I was four) was a dream become material, although no such thing is possible. Its asymmetrical peak and abrupt squared summit where the granite strata jut out would have *had* to be a landmark on my horizon: it was what I was looking for as my eyes first opened, or so it feels. Presumably I saw it when I was a baby and a toddler, before my memory began, on our way north-westwards to the fishing village on the Moray Firth where we spent summer holidays in the Thirties, where the Three Kings stood half-buried at the far end of the beach. The journey will have been marked by the rising into sight of Bennachie, the Hill of Foudland, Knock Hill, the Bin of Cullen, the grey and the blue humps moving across each other, the glens between them opening and folding again. They were not necessary to me in any practical way; my father was not a shepherd or a gamekeeper or a vet. They were the prime signs to me that the world went on beyond my skylines. It's akin to a feeling expressed by an old friend of mine, the Gaelic poet Domhnall Macamlaidh (Donald Macaulay) from Berneray Lewis, in his poem 'Comharra Stiùiridh' ('Landmark'), although as an islander his social experience is tragic where mine is ordinary:

> Cuideachd, chan e siud m' eilean-s';
> chaidh esan fodha o chionn fhada,
> a'chuid mhór dheth,
> fo dheireas is ainneart;
> 's na chaidh fodha annam fhìn dheth,
> 'na ghrianan 's cnoc eighre
> tha e a' seòladh na mara anns am bì mi
> 'na phrìomh chomharr stiùiridh
> cunnartach, do-sheachaint, gun fhaochadh.

> And, that is not my island; it submerged long ago,
> the greater part of it, in neglect and tyranny −
> and the part that submerged in me of it, sun-bower
> and iceberg, sails the ocean I am in a primary landmark,
> dangerous, essential, demanding.

79

When I came south to live and work in England, my native upland submerged, to be replaced in the end by the highlands of Cumbria. Dow Crag and the Old Man of Coniston stand up in the north-west as we look from our bedroom window and Dow's gullies show clearly in snow, white veins on black, Great Gully and Easy Gully slanting between the buttresses. But the mountains here have not that look of having been known to me before my vision started. The difference is unmistakable when I look at Fay Godwin's photographs of 'The View from Duff-defiance, Glen Buchat' or 'Scarred Land, Glentanar' (both in Aberdeenshire). They are just plain, rounded hills, grained and marbled by heather-burning, but they give me a sense of looking into my own head, where the brain's packed folds print their pattern on the inside surface of the skull. The Cumbrian mountains give me fewer messages and far less sense that I have met and talked to people who once frequented them in 1920 or 1940 or whenever. Scotland's recent past has been fleshed out for me in all those elders. Jane Craig, my father's mother, who on her deathbed told me her memory of going to school at Portlethen, a fishing village in Kincardineshire, on a day in 1880, looking westwards at a hailstorm darkening along the flanks of the Mounth, and hoping to reach shelter before it hit the coast. Peter Craigmyle, a white-moustached farmer who ran the inn at Colquohonnie near Strathdon and who rigged ropes and sawed planks to make a swing for us on the chestnut tree beside the vegetable garden. James Coutts, an estate factor whose house, nearly a thousand feet up the side of Morven, was our holiday home for four wartime summers and who still spoke painfully and hoarsely because a Great War bullet had gone through his neck. Such people constitute a history, without it your social memory has gaps, has a whole dimension missing, and the places you look at, the dales and villages and towns, have no more depth than a theatre set. But whether or not I remain more incomer than native in Cumbria, at least this region has secreted rock. It has kept the obdurate and still character of rock in its walls and tracks and sheepfolds. It is steeply contoured so that everywhere it promises to rear into crags. In such a place climbing is *native*: the

80

mountain skylines draw us upwards as much as the sinuously enticing lines of the climbing-routes.

This comes out in the mountaineering habits of the region, for example the new sport (new to England) of going up to two thousand feet or more in the winter, with crampons, axes, and ice-screws, to climb rock routes when they're sheathed in shortlived ice and frozen snow. In spite of this the editor of *Mountain* could write recently (November/December 1985) about 'the final schism between mountaineering and rock-climbing, the adoption of a training mentality, and the elevation of standards of performance to athletic status'. Every word of this comment jars. It is full of the Latinisms of officialdom. It fixes grids on a sport whose essence is free movement. It splits off our activity from the natural world. But why argue? If there are people whose goal is measurable gymnastic excellence rather than attunement to nature and wilderness, so be it. There should be room for us both. If the wildness of certain dales and glens and coasts becomes less attractive to climbers because Extreme problems lie elsewhere, it will only help these places to become peaceful again. My own paradise of this kind is in the north-west Highlands, specifically where the rib of a colossal stone creature surfaces from the moor a few hundred yards inland from the shore, dives again briefly below its pelt of peat and tussocky heather and breaks out finally on the shingle beach where the high tides rummage the plum-coloured stones. From down here, facing landwards, you look at a raw-red face, a prime cut, as though the creature's limb had been hacked straight through its triangular cross-section.

Tempered by sea winds, each torn fibre of the Lewisian gneiss has hardened and the brittle-looking edges of its layers and cracks are tough. They are so sharp they dint their shapes into your fingerends, so secure that they encourage bold solos until you are making fingery moves forty feet above the shingle. Then you enter a zone of almost Cornish lichen – grey-green whiskers sprouting from the cheek of an aged giant. You pull through his eyebrows, up into the homeland of brown-and-olive lizards, gingerbread-coloured wild goats whose reek of rank fat can carry a mile on the breeze. Foxgloves make a wild garden among the hummocks of pink heather (and one white clump, whose site is a secret with my family).

The goal is the next nakedness of the giant rib: a face sixty feet across, one hundred and thirty high, which glares so raw-red that it looks newly-forged, and feels it. When Pete and I first climbed it and I tried to gain height along a rising diagonal, my forefinger cut itself on the left arête as I let go and I still have the shiny weal along my fingerprint. This face is oriented due west, towards the basalt ledges at the end of Skye across the water. At all times of the day it glows as though with sunset light. We had meant to climb the corner to its left, a damp cavernous place full of jammed blades and spearheads grating together. But the beautiful geometry of the grain led Pete's feet along rightwards and upwards. The section below the main crack turned out to be forward an inch from the section above, forming a perfect finger-ledge. At the right arête the rock turns the corner through more than ninety degrees, the giant rib runs up into the hill, and its periosteum is still in place, a rough hard cladding which splits just enough to make at least five excellent lines.

Down here, on the raw cross-section, we are fingering and toeing charily up the exposed marrow of the bone. Pete grips the right arête, swings boldly up, pads back left along a slab where hidden footholds accept his PA's snugly. I follow, my forefinger printing crimson on the rock's vermilion. From the slope of the belay we look out together over the village along the shore four hundred feet below: the old camping field beside the alders and ashes along the burn (whose water is so sweet that sailing vessels used to fill their casks from it); the steep quilt of pasture fields, a very few still scythed for hay, most growing rank; John's house, and Duncan's, and Alan and Heather's, and Sandy and Hilda's. Such are all the components of this place where I have summered, off and on, for thirty-four years. The patching of white houses, the occasional bluish-green of oats and sap-green of potatoes, unfurls irregularly past the sandstone pinnacle we call the Dinosaur and ends at a cottage where a small stand of trees bows and ruffles like civilisation's last flag.

82

It's now so warm that heat reflects from the rockface and we can smell our sweat. The sea has become a floor of lapis lazuli – it lets out long breaths. Down there, somewhere, a school of porpoises is surfacing to blow, rolling their glistening backs like wheel-rims out of the water and below again, browsing off the shoals of herring fry. Rousing myself from a light trance, I pull myself up the broken vertical crack above Pete's head. Just as my weight leaves a shattered step the rock bursts. The bits shower down like shrapnel. A miss or a hit? An angry shout from below is a reassuring sign of life. Soon the top pitch runs out amongst knee-deep heather.

That was Red Kite. Along the hard grey periosteum of the rib we found Elephant Dance – a name Pete never quite accepted but it seemed just right for the bulging masses of rock which crown the wall, the vast jumbo thighs and bellies, up whose blind seams you friction your unprotected way after the superb wall-climbing down below. On the thirty-first anniversary of my first touching that shore (when I came in by crab boat from the north), I soloed up the creature's next rib to the right, four hundred feet of grainy rock, relaxing slabs narrowing into vertical capped corners which reminded me rudely that the moor was now ninety feet below. I had never before even focused on this great long reef as a crag to climb. And it is only one of dozens that splay out (changing ribs to spokes) from their hub on Ruadh Mheallan, the 'broad russet top', three miles away across the water-lily lochans and the peat bogs where the village used to cut its fuel and is now doing so again.

Ruadh Mheallan is the lowest of the summits in that country. No doubt it has massively lost stature during the last 750 million years and it's now a truncated stub, finishing 2,196 feet above sea level. Nobody goes there except the occasional geologist gathering evidence for yet another theory of how the extremely old sandstone was laid down and folded. One year, on my own, I made a beeline for it with Shep breasting the heather beside me like a small boat butting into a rough sea. The Minch glittered like grey glass; Harris and North Uist were not to be seen. The sky loured, but gently, more sad than angry. When we reached the summit, I sat down on a little lawn with my back against a sandstone boulder and took out my writing-pad.

Small clouds at the same altitude as ourselves were blooming in mid-air, clotting from the water vapour. They darkened and bulked, then dropped a few filaments from their undersides until they looked like Portugese Man-of-Wars balancing in the sea before dispersing. With my pen I drew the boulders around me – buttocks and breasts and shoulders – blind totems perched on the summit table as though by an extinct tribe. And looking east to Tom na Gruagaich, and Beinn Dearg, and Baosbheinn to the north, all the great creatures petrified among their bogs and waters, I saw them as the anatomy of one being, organs linked by exposed bones and underground intestines, and I wrote the first three verses of a poem which found its continuation and its finish five months later, during the winter, when the highlands surfaced again in defiance of the cold rains and the short days.

13

From Ruadh Mheallan

The mountain's limbs take origin
From its skull-massif.
The blades of shoulders cut away,
Planing beneath the muscle-sheets
Of the multi-fibred peat.

Three miles down its spine
Twin corries hollow darkly,
Unfolding from the buried source
Where the cooled and blackened liquids
Surface and disperse.

One hand, spreadeagled sideways,
Puckers the valleys in its clutch of bone.
The western hand, relaxed and free,
Allows the sea to fill and stream
Between its joints of stone.

The originating brain has gone,
Its wild hive dead and grey.
Wolf and sea-eagle entered life
Through the round doorway of its eye
Which stared unblinking at the sky.

Now the warm-blooded thoughts have dwined,
Adders and toads alone
Infest the flesh the glacier thinned
And hoodies scutter round his mouth,
Tugging the carrion from his teeth.

But Ruadh Mheallan lies dumb,
No memories of creation
Or hopes for a millennium,
His features wrinkling only where
The anticyclone stirs his hair.

14

Peter and I never claimed or wrote up Red Kite or Elephant
Dance, or the slanting cracks so steep that Pete had to clip a sling
to one protection nut and stand in it while he reached up to place
another, or the zig-zag crack system to its left, or . . . We felt no
need to consolidate our experience into formal public words; it
had been too molten and palpable, too charged with the salt heat
of that summer coast, too purely a fierce extension of the family
times (the walking and sea-fishing and swimming) that had
always gone on in this the best of places. Two of our routes, it

turned out, had already been done and details of them are in the *Scottish Mountaineering Journal* – described, I'm glad to say, in such a muddled way that anyone who comes upon them will have to follow his own nose, his own rock-sense, and experience the crags almost as though nobody had ever been there before.

The ideal climb is this kind of venture into unknown ground, yet as hosts of us scrounge locust-like over every available yard of rock, name it and claim it and write it up in the magazines, the scope left for the ideal is cut away as irreversibly as the rain-forests of Borneo or Brazil. On our first visit to the Italian Dolomites we did manage to find our way up some untouched, or at least unguidebooked, rock and so made naked contact with this new country. We were based in the Treviso Hut near the head of the Val Canali, in the Pala Dolomites, a few tortuous miles east of San Martino di Castrozza. The week before we had been marooned in the Rifugio Rosetta above San Martino, supping minestrone and drinking the occasional oily grappa as we looked out at the Arctic desolation of the 8,000-foot plateau. A summer snowstorm had whitened the high limestone deserts, the single blue or purple flowers with their single orange butterflies were buried in wintry layers and the wheels of the funicular railway were too iced up to turn. A tactical retreat was agreed upon with our German friends. Thomas the professor, from Bremen, had been a mountain enthusiast ever since his Existentialist phase in the early Fifties when he had begun to seek out extreme experiences: a photo from that time shows him staring raptly up at thick clouds smoking over the lips of a huge cliff in Austria. Heino the wine-merchant, also from Bremen, was a novice climber brimming with zest and strength. When I was belaying him, I could hear him getting nearer down below, his great boots hammering and thudding as though he had mistaken the rock for hard snow, and was kicking steps in it. His faulty English was charming, as he well knew, and we waited happily to hear his 'I go upstairs now?' meaning 'Should I climb?'

The Rifugio Rosetta, our first ever Alpine 'hut', was of course not a hut at all, or a 'refuge' for that matter, it was a good-sized boarding-house with wooden walls inside and out, set on a tract

3. DC and Terry Gifford climbing Rivelin Needle, August 1986,
by Ian Smith

4. DC and Terry Gifford climbing Tegness Pinnacle, August 1986,
by Ian Smith

5. 'From Green Gable' by Fay Godwin

6. 'The Black Horse of Busha (for J.W.)' by Paul Joyce

of high ground like a vast infilled quarry. In the low-ceilinged dining-room we sat out the snowbound days, watching impatiently for signs that Michele Gadenz's family had begun to chop vegetables for the midday minestrone. Gadenz himself, now over seventy, was a redoubtable guide, author of many new routes just before and after the War, during which he had co-operated with the partisans in smuggling RAF men to safety through the mountain passes. He only appeared in the evenings, a broad hunched figure in breeches and a tartan shirt, hair and moustache short and dark like charred heather, eyebrows beetling over the bridge of his nose. He moved from table to table, pausing to chat, his black eyes missing nothing, as though at any moment he might give out a baritone drinking-song like the villainous innkeeper in a Verdi opera.

The Rosetta was convenient and it was bleak, dwarfed by that stone wilderness where almost nothing grows and the bones of the mountains destruct perpetually, ground and riven by ice, reducing down to brash, the drifts of it slumping into leprous grey ravines where wintry shadows lurk at midsummer noon. The only attraction of such a spot on the earth's surface is perverse and negative. It is a cemetery of ruined stone. It simulates the moon. Yet people seek it out, drawn to experience the lack of all they take for granted down in the valleys and the plains – shelter, colour, water, herbage, earth.

Two years later, staying at Campitello in the Val di Fassa, we went up in the funicular railway from the Passo Pordoi and made the stony trek to the Rifugio Forcella Pordoi. Its *padrone*, a guide called Renzo Favé, also owned the guest-house where we were staying down in Campitello. We walked in a single file, several hundred of us, pilgrims or refugees or (in the terrible post-War phrase) displaced persons, strung out along three miles of gravel and trodden slush. Low cliffs surrounded us, the texture and non-colour of derelict concrete. Here the interminable layers of the limestone rarely peaked; they were simply littered floors of bygone oceans devolved into a wasteland. At the end of the trail stood Renzo's *rifugio* – a highland pub with a crowd six deep at the bar, stretching their hands out for food and booze. Through the serving-hatch I saw Renzo himself, cheeks flushed, hair grizzled, leaning on his hands in a sink crammed with dishes, suds up to his elbows, leaning and staring downwards as though wondering if this was what he was born for. A thickset Alpine peasant with the energy and stamina of a wolverine, born to make hay and herd flocks in the upland meadows, sucked into this frenzy of drudging and money-making by the force of tourism which can turn even a desert into a commodity.

In 1980, when we retreated from the Rosetta down several thousand feet of ice-bound path, full rucksacks swaying on our shoulders, we took in provisions at San Martino – boxes of eggs, pounds of cheese, lengths of hard brown sausage, a mega-bottle of Chianti in its jacket of woven reeds – and drove round to the wooded pleasance of the Val Canali. The track up to the hut ran between a river of fuming grey water and fields whose grass grew long and a rich green on slopes running up into the zone of trees between meadow and scree, all unfenced, the slim spires of larch and spruce stepping down in crowds into the fringes of the grassland, making an irregular verge that offered sweet relief to British senses brutalised by barbed wire drawn taut from post to post along lines decreed by Enclosure acts. Beyond a rough hedge five people, aged fifteen to sixty, were scything and raking their dense crop. As I toiled past under fifty pounds of clothes and food and wine and climbing equipment, I drew in extra breath to try out my one Italian proverb in justification for walking so slowly:

'Che va piano, va sano.
Che va forte, va 'lla morte.'

Beaming and laughing, they capped the verse with another. I could hear that it rhymed but to my chagrin I did not have the Italian to understand it. Still, the good humour of the exchange helped set a tone for the days that followed in the Treviso hut, which was a hut, or at least a small house built from rough chunks of limestone, with deep wooden eaves and green shutters over unglazed windows. It was a belvedere set on a ledge a thousand feet above the valley floor, with another four thousand feet of mountain rearing opposite and above us in dream towers and

88

toothed ridges that shone gold and weathered ivory and steely grey, apparitions out of nineteenth-century romances or travellers' tales, grotesque colossi you might doodle with your pen as you fantasied your way up impossible heights.

But of course they were as actual and as known as Snowdonia or the Langdale Pikes; they had all been scaled, named, and classified in the tireless modern way. They had even been numbered and colour-coded: stripes of red and white paint and black numbers and letters painted onto rocks beside the paths. We played ourselves into this staggering new environment by climbing a well-known route, the North Face of the Punta della Disperazione, which Renzo Timillero, the short-haired, unsmiling hut *padrone*, had been the first to climb, six years before. The route was about as hard, or as comfortable, as 'D' Route on Gimmer and seven times as long. The way up the crag was marked by daubs of thick scarlet paint – a homely substitute for the British guidebooks with their minute listings of pitches, stances, holds. Five of us shared two ropes and this gregarious habit was the idiom of the place. Some yards to our left, on the south-east Buttress, an experienced leader was bringing up two climbers simultaneously, the lines of rope splaying from the krab on his chest-harness like the start of a spider's web.

The Disperazione tapers massively above a dale, the Vallon delle Mughe, which funnels down northwards into the Val Canali. The hut sits snugly in the midst of the forest girdle and from the rockfaces up there in the climbing arena you felt you could lob a stone out into the radiant and scorching air, and watch it plummet down into the chimney of the Timilleros' kitchen. Over a fortnight the path up from hut to crags became familiar but never easy. Each step took an effort like mounting a staircase with two-foot risers, balancing over boulders, zig-zagging round dense thickets of dwarf conifers, willing the open blue to appear above the mountainous skyline. But the cool of the forest shadow was a relief as we laboured. Anne identified the flowers that decorated the rocks, purple *clematis Alpinum* and pink primula, rooting in slopes so steep that we could smell the flowers without stooping. Above, the sides of the *vallon* impended so much that it was like entering a gorge, half-shaded from the brilliant Italian skyshine, and at the foot of the Disperazione a snowdrift leaked moisture like some pale beached sea-animal dying slowly.

The Disperazione, so far, had been manageable, more Scottish than English in scale, but a buttress, not a mountain. The West Ridge of the Sasso d'Ortiga felt more Alpine as we threaded our way eastwards from the Forcella delle Mughe, a col where lanky sheep were grazing, clanking their bells. We tied karabiners to our harnesses with slings and ran them along a fixed steel wire to protect ourselves on gravelly terraces above a deepening drop. The route itself was a thousand-foot crest, the spiny ridge of a Triceratops, first climbed in 1928, a little before the heyday of Extreme climbing first dawned in the Dolomites, and repeated during the War by Michele Gadenz, the piratical host of the Rosetta. Route finding up here seemed to be a matter of finding blackish passages of sound rock among unstable scoops where sockets gaped with a litter of boney scraps inside them, as though they had been the gizzards of gigantic extinct birds.

The only gripping moment occurred at the narrowest point of the spine where a colossal chock-stone (*un grande masso incastrato*) had lodged in a vee. We tiptoed round its base – we were above a two thousand-foot drop into the neighbouring *vallon*, which had been invisible till then. The thin crack (*una fessure superficiale*) which led straight upwards above this dizzy stance was steep enough to tap the spare tank of adrenalin which my system holds in readiness for Very Severe climbing. The fearless Heino must have felt the same since this was two grades harder than he had ever climbed before. As I brought him up the crack, I could hear the drumbeat of his boots – a long pause – then a great echoing skirl like an enraged tiger as he fell and the rope grooved round my ribs. A few minutes later he climbed the pitch in a splendid surge of annoyance and two years later, in the Catinaccio, he powered smoothly up something harder, the fierce split over-hang on the Piaz Crack of the Punta Emma, without an ounce of tight rope, while I eyed Wagnerian stormclouds welling over the Torri Vajolet and lightning began to ignite in fizzing explosions beyond the heavy drapes of the rain.

Above one stance on the Sasso d'Ortiga, Thomas, in his impulsive appetite for rock and still more rock, flung himself too directly at the steepest part of a wall and recoiled into mid-air as holds ran out. Neil, using a Sticht plate belaying device for the first time, held him solidly but Tom's foot had crunched into a spur. As it stiffened over a day or two, even walking became a trial. In the end, with Heino supporting him, he hobbled off down the path, leaning on a crutch Timillero had whittled out of a branch. Left to ourselves, Rob, Neil and I cast round for routes less in the old mountaineering idiom and more direct in their sallies on to exposed faces. We had noticed that grey rock was solid and yellow rock was brittle. By now Anne had bought me Timillero's guidebook, since the *padrone*'s English and our Italian were too minimal to let us tap his experience directly. A tantalising gap, for what could have been more delightful in an evening than to sit on the wooden bench that ran round the sanded ledge outside the hut, looking straight out through the branches of conifers that soared a hundred feet from root to summit, watching the moon rise over the limestone spires and hearing about good lines in the neighbourhood that had still to be climbed? But Timillero's cool eyes regarded us expressionlessly through the serving-hatch; our passion for rock and his could not have been more insulated. And this was good in the end: when we found our route on the Pala del Rifugio, we did it entirely for ourselves.

The ridge running down from the Sasso d'Ortiga into the Val Canali ends in a separated spur, the Dente (*un' elegante cuspide*). The face above the hut is seamed with routes but the jaundiced face overlooking the Vallon del Mughe seemed to have none. Its great forehead, furrowed vertically with chimney-cracks, was undercut by an area where the limestone, plagued by rising damp, had sickened to the worst colour of all, a light cheddar orange. To the right, however, before the elegant tooth leaned back into the ridge, the rock looked as though it grew chunky and sound again; at least it was a healthy grey. The boys were frankly unkeen and glowered upwards at the forbidding face. It leered back, sure of its impregnability. I ached to climb, and ached too because we had hefted all that rope and metal all that way, wading in the end through a Sargasso of bedsprings – dwarf pine whose stems locked round our legs and maddened us to swearing pitch as we struggled to reach the root of the tooth. I might have left it, and suggested we walked round to the valley face of the Dente to do a well-known route, had a groove not slanted upwards near the verge of the grey rock, beelining on a single dwarf pine. Trees encourage me – their sinewy strength, their endurance. The little four-foot tree became a goal. It also blinded me, and just as well, to any thought of what lay above it.

Rob belayed me and I set off upwards. As the groove thinned to a true *fessura superficiale*, it steepened, and the big holds that had made my fingers curl with pleasure as I looked up at them turned out to be mostly cracked through at the base and ready to part from the mother-rock. One or two, I persuaded myself, would take my weight if I performed that strange trick, like willing thin ice to bear, where you spread your weight and almost withdraw your pressure from a surface even as you exert it. But some were hair-raisingly shaky – as undermined and undermining as the gannet-shit on Mainreachan Buttress and with no written guarantee from any *Good Book*. I shouted a warning – prised off a skull-sized chunk – it whizzed down and burst a few feet down the slope from Rob, who at once resigned his belayship in protest against these murderous (or suicidal) tactics. Neil, who had been against the whole thing from the start, was forced to take over and stood there feeling as safe as a powder-monkey tending the cannon in a gunport of Nelson's *Victory*.

The dwarf pine still glistened green in the sunlight twenty feet above. By now a qualm was hollowing my gut, pressing out like a bubble into my limbs, threatening to create a void through which the brain-signals might fail to pass. It seemed unreal that my fingers and feet were still functioning, reaching when my mind told them to, clipping ropes into krabs. This odd insulation began to work for me, my fear-centre was humming all right but on its own – a phone ringing in a room at night with nobody to answer it – I balanced upwards until I could clamp my hands round that supple trunk, that sturdy little darling, thread a blue sling round it and clip in a rope. The momentum had me now, I could still have lowered safely off the tree but possibilities were flowering in the air around me, the sunlit rock was firm and wholesome, the crack opened to accept perfect hand-jams, the angle eased a little and I made myself look left along the yellowed face, safe from its infection, and then, more dauntingly, upwards, spying out ways and means. The agony returned. 'I want out of this, I'll levitate, fly off, parachute,' my fear-centre was hissing, even as my fingers selected little edges and my toes pressed down on mini-steps in the lips of the crack – hardly daring to trust them, trusting them, each fulcrum holding, and the leverage continuing to work.

Now a small platform of seared grass patched with dwarf pine glowed like an oasis above and to my right. The crack ran out in a dark sheet of slabby wall, holdless, but overhung by an eave so sharp it might offer undercling. I'd grip it, palms upwards, lean backwards a little, and friction over towards the oasis. Horrors! The eave is made of brittle laminae, in places they've dropped out like slates sliding into a raingutter. The thought of trusting my weight to them forces out a heavy sweat, which evaporates, icing me. Breaking this film, I crackle upwards, brain creaking as it sorts through useless moves, discards them, drops them through the air onto the spoil-heap down below. My fingers (mine, yes, look, they're on the ends of my hands) caress the underclings as though they were razors. They grate. I try some more, there are inches of solid here and there, shallow bumps for the feet. I pad sideways towards a bevel where the angle eases again, itching to rush for it – jump-scurry-grab – squashing that crazy urge, striving with all my concentration to keep the trembling air-bubble centred in the fluid spirit of my chest. Now homely grass is sprouting in tufts from little ledges and the second dwarf pine is holding out its sprays of needles. But its multi-stems are slender, they bend outwards, no good anchor here, I must climb on with the last few feet of rope (as Neil shouts urgently, angrily from below) until I reach twin grooves in the wall above. They're shallow, blank, *molto superficiale* – no lodgement for such nuts as I have left on my harness. With a sort of weary inured persistence

I bridge my feet on solid stone shoulders and labour with Thomas's peg-hammer, a thing I've never used before, to batter in two pitons from my tiny bunch. I lash myself close in and stand there braced, the rock radiating heat onto my back, shouting hoarsely to Neil from a mouth so dry that swallowing hurts.

To my right the unclimbed (unclimbable?) reaches of the Dente stream downwards like lava-flow suspended in mid-air. Beyond, the dream-towers of the Cima Sedole glow roseate through blue shadow on their east faces, a pale-gold dazzle on the west. The air that had crackled dangerously round me before, like ice about to give, is buoyant now, convecting upwards with a vast supporting pressure. I could stretch out on it, spread wings, grow webs from wrist to hip like a flying-fox and glide, soar, glide . . .

When Neil reached me, he rolled his eyes to signal the madness of it all, then climbed doggedly up another hundred feet to the col beside a gendarme, the most elegant tooth of all, the *totem del rifugio*. We abseiled off massive ringbolts down the dungeon-like *discesa* behind the Dente. Half an hour of torture in the man-eating bedsprings and we were showering with Anne and Rob in a waterfall which flowed straight out of the snowfield in the bed of the *vallon*.

Nothing before or since has used me more. The rest of the day felt enchanted – moving down through the forest as though on an escalator, laying down our loads at the belvedere with utter gratitude, swallowing the two-eggs-and-butter with pasta (all we could afford) and the red *vino da tavola* as though they were choice, not commonplace. I wanted nothing more. The best thing had been done. The hardness of the Dente limestone filled my body, its nervy challenges buzzed in my head. Managing the route had felt like spinning a suspension bridge in mid-air, arcing out into the void with no certainty of a solid resting-place on the far side. Now the totally relaxed fatigue was more in the brain than in the muscles because I had had to concentrate so hard, urging my conception of the route to become reality instead of leaning on a scaffold of possibility installed by previous climbers. It had been – and it remains – super-real, a three-dimensional tangible coloured image, because we had been undistracted by a guidebook which would have transmuted that cliff, that groove, that dwarf pine into human culture by naming, measuring, classifying, and describing them.

The above pages have now done this. And I have to admit that we named the line Via Fontamara, after Silone's novel, the thing from Italy that has meant most to me. And I admit, too, that I defined and classified it, in a letter to *Alpinismus* claiming the route. Perhaps it never appeared, and I would be glad about that now, since it was the fact of its being untouched that made it into such a penetrating and pure experience for us. But was it unclimbed? As I went on scrutinising Timillero's guidebook after coming back to England, I noticed with a qualm that there were several references to the Libro Rifugio Treviso, a route-book presumably, which runs to at least 255 pages. But if the Via Fontamara is recorded in it, then why has it not been transferred to the guidebook? And why did the dour Timillero say nothing about the route-book when I tried to tell him in the evening that we thought we had climbed a new route on the Dente? Perhaps my pidgin Italian signified something completely different (that I was very pleased with my new teeth?). The beauty is that none of this matters. For us it was new, and as such it afforded an experience that *found* us (in Matthew Arnold's term) in a way that differs as much from climbing an established line as *aqua vitae* does from diet-Coke.

15

Child of my culture that I am, when I go to a crag I still carry a guidebook, pick out lines according to its grading of the difficulties, and even tend to belay at the stances it suggests. Now I am adding to this terrible tendency to *colonise* the world by re-writing a climbing guide myself – the new edition of the *Fell & Rock* guide to the Buttermere area, in collaboration with Rick

Graham of Ambleside. There is a paradox here that must be faced, that each one of us can resolve in our own way. Ideally, climbing is a form of exploration. You back yourself to advance into the unknown and cope with each barely predictable difficulty that may crop up until you come to an end. This is put with salutary simplicity by Mark Wilford, a leading American rock-climber, in one of his letters to *Mountain* 'In Defence of Free Climbing': 'Whether on a 20 pitch first ascent of an Alpine spire or on the 500th ascent of a one pitch 5.9 handcrack, one of the basic questions is "Can I do it". Ensuring this question is the basic principle of starting to climb from the ground.' (*Mountain*, March/April 1986) Wilford is arguing against the techniques of current Extreme new-routers, who often abseil down a line to inspect or even improve holds, check placements for protection, and sometimes place protection in readiness for the climb. As someone incapable of working at that level – now common on the big limestone faces of Malham, Gordale, and Kilnsey, for example – I am the less entitled to an opinon of such advanced gymnastics. But Wilford's axiom applies to all levels of the sport. The moment a route has been done, the experiential possibilities for those who follow have begun to shrink. Even if holds aren't improved, permanent gear placed, or the rock cleaned, still the pristine blade of the rock has begun to blunt and dull because now we are doing it less for ourselves and more by surrogate. We know what is up there, from text and photo. We can wear down its difficulty by slotting it into our graded mental lists. We can glean advice on what moves to make on a crux. A mental or cultural ladder has been fixed up the rockface and we can step onto it when we like, to eke out our own shortcomings.

This is the penalty of belonging to an old civilisation. We can always opt out of its benefits (though we rarely do). At this point in history we have become much less complacently sure than we were before the War, say, that to civilise is to improve. In climbing terms, we civilise, or colonise, the rock by hammering in fixed gear, by rooting out saplings and bushes and scrubbing off lichen with a wire brush and by concocting those obsessional texts, the guidebooks, which by the Sixties had reached a pitch of wordiness as though their aim was to coat every square inch of the crags with a dense layer of words and numbers, like make-up on an already lovely skin. Nor is this wholly metaphorical: it has just been reported (in the *Climber*, July 1986) that all along the lower half of the Central Wall at Malham the names and grades of routes have been neatly painted on the rock where they start. So nature is denatured – dragged over into the human-social. Visit a crag today and you'll see the climbers with book in hand – in one American photo it's the *Bhagavad-Ghita* (*Mountain*, July/August 1978) but usually it's a guidebook, which they'll be consulting like electricians trying to follow a new piece of circuitry. The climbers' *Good Book* will probably say things like 'Ascend the groove for a few feet and move up to the right (good runner)' (why that last phrase? for reassurance? if the placement is good the climber will readily spot it for himself), 'then traverse back left along a sloping gangway' (it would have been more fun to spy the gangway and choose it by a decision of our own), 'cross the top of the groove, to a short corner at the end of the gangway. The corner is awkward when wet' (aren't they all?), 'and leads to a rock ledge and runner for tape' (more gratuitous advice). 'Swing up to a higher ledge; then go left to a sweep of slabs. Climb then until fine flake handholds' (if they are fine they must be plain to see) 'lead up to a ledge on the right . . .'. Eighty-seven words for ninety-five feet, a word per foot, written in the Forties by my old friend Bill Peascod and still in print, describing pitch two of his famous route Eagle Front in the guidebook we are now revising.

Bill was a miner, then a teacher of mining, and his descriptions of crags are utterly reliable. Yet to rely on them utterly is to perceive and manage and relish the thing for yourself that much less. On pitch five of Eagle Front we find the ultimate in defusing the experience: we're told that the steep wall is equipped with a 'hidden jug'. When I first climbed it, it was with Bill and the guidebook stayed in my rucksack at the toe of the crag. He said nothing about the hidden hold and so the steep wall was able to impress and fire me by its formidable leaning blankness before I stepped up onto the glacis at its foot, explored it with my hands in search of help, and felt a suddenly delicious glow (like swallowing a dram of Laphroaig) as my fingerends locked onto an acute edge.

Some guidebooks don't just defuse the hidden powers of the crags, they also patronise them and pooh-pooh the wildness which should be their inalienable quality. 'Pleasant' or 'amiable' is used for routes up to Hard Severe, although they may well be found dangerously and fiercely enjoyable by people who can't climb above Very Severe. A hillside below a crag is called 'unpleasant' because it is shaggy with aboriginal heather, studded with boulders – a tract of unadulterated nature unscathed even by the locust chewings of the sheep. And even less snooty guidebooks tend to spoon-feed, encouraging us to depend on a predigested and insipid diet. One of the most appetising climbs in Langdale, Bilberry Buttress on Raven Crag, is at present watered down by over description – but I will bite my tongue at this point rather than say more since if I quoted the words in question it would only compound the fault. It must be enough to say that if you climb the pitch unaided, you will be able to revel in a burst where you have to combine balance and muscle in just the right linkage. Follow the book and you can muscle up as routinely as if you were doing pull-ups on the lintel of the door at home.

Spoon-feeding breeds dependence, and I remember with embarrassment two occasions when depending on the book instead of applying our own perceptions to the crag had painful results. The first time we climbed Golden Slipper, above the rugged diagonal of Jack's Rake on Pavey Ark, Pete (aged fifteen) led out fifty or sixty feet of rope on the narrow wall of pitch two, then hung about, undecided, as it reared near vertical, and shouted down with an edge in his voice, 'What d'you do now?' Down below we consulted the *Good Book*, then shouted up, 'It says "A line of holds leads across to the rib on the right."' We could almost feel Pete's scepticism vibrating down the rope but he moved right, a little too far, infringed on the Extreme (5b) ground of the next route, Poker Face, and fell – a longish, bruising fall that battered his hip against the rock. We could see that it took him all his fortitude to reclimb the upper part of the wall, then follow his own eyes and his own kinetic intuition up a less rightward line to the haven of the belay ledge.

If he had climbed under his own steam at the crux, and to hell with the book, he might well have been unscathed. And he might have fallen less far if he had put on more protection. But both the *Fell & Rock* guide and Cram, Eilbeck and Roper's *Rock Climbing in the Lake District* emphasise that there is 'a decided lack of protection on that pitch'. A trap for the inexperienced! The wall is made of Pavey 'clinker', so lumpy and granular that you can almost hook your jersey onto it and hang by the fibres. When I next climbed Golden Slipper, with Andy Dight from Sheffield, he ignored the book and patiently fiddled in six small nuts on a stretch of fifty feet, fitting them like a dentist between one rough cusp and the next. He used his own eyes, not the book's – as I failed to do a few yards to the right on the crowning pitch of another Allan Austin route. Again the description advises a move to the right (what *is* this right-wing deviation on the part of a leading climber?) and when I did so instead of following my own nose straight up, I ran out of holds before I could grab the top of the wall and fell twenty feet onto a roomy ledge. Dave Steed held me, then commiserated as I gingerly worked my sprained ankle round and round before girding myself up to hobble two thousand feet down to the car.

If I seem to be blaming Austin, really I should be blaming myself. Precise moves three feet right or two feet left – six protection points or two – are matters of opinion, of taste almost. Do we like to wear out our arms (and the belayer's patience) as we prod a nut into every available cranny? or do we prefer to climb more fluently, less safely? The author's line is only a recommendation, it isn't compulsory, and the essence of climbing is not to follow the designated route like a child connecting up a dot-to-dot picture with a pencil or an adult painting by numbers but to behave as Pete Livesey, the leading climber of the Seventies, has been said to do – 'setting off across steep rock in search of whatever turns him on'.

Readers less familiar with recent developments may well have assumed that that's what happens anyway – climbers like carefree baboons, scampering across the sunlit reefs. Actually the sport is far gone into a late stage of extreme sophistication. No doubt it's luddite to fantasise that it can ever again rid itself of its machinery. How deep the sophistication has bitten can be seen in Livesey's own description of the 'first free ascent' of Central Wall on Kilnsey Crag, the black-streaked behemoth which swells out above the pasture fields as you drive up Wharfedale from Grassington. This terminology, 'first free ascent', is already significant. Nobody questions the fact that Joe Brown did *the* first ascent of the best-known route in Britain, Cenotaph Corner on Dinas y Gromlech. Yet he hammered in four or five pegs for protection, 'pulled on a sling to overcome the first hard move at twenty feet', and pulled up on a peg above the niche where the corner-crack almost closes, according to his own account in *The Hard Years* (pp 49–50, 74). Two decades later, John Syrett is considered to have 'failed' on the Kilnsey route because he used two pegs for aid in an attempt to climb it free. How finely the hairs had now begun to split comes out in Livesey's article on his own successful attempt:

> The wall steepened as it merged into the overlap, a high side pull enabling Syrett's first aid peg to be reached. I was just about to swing on it when there was a little hold above it – would it do? I climbed down a few feet for a look. The problem was to get my left hand on the hold and make a huge swing right for a flake, but the move was perfectly protected. I kept thinking – if I fall onto the peg, will it be aid?
>
> – *The Games Climbers Play*, ed. Ken Wilson, 1978, p 323

This man was doing something extraordinary, resisting gravity for one hundred and fifteen feet consecutively, at an average angle beyond the vertical. Nobody had ever done it without pulling up on slings threaded through pitons and natural eye-holes in the rock. It was cold and rainy. The horizontal breaks in the face were slippery with 'grease squeezed out of the cracks by the sheer weight of the crag'. Yet at that crucial point his concern was not so much with survival – will my arms sustain me? will the peg hold if I fall on it? – as with the criteria governing the quality of the ascent: 'if I fall onto the peg, will it be aid?' Faced with this, I hardly know whether to marvel or grieve at the distance we humans can put ourselves from the natural. Almost immersed in the elemental, dwarfed by its cavernous loom, breaking his nails on it and smearing himself with its oozings – his intellect still spins free, or wriggles, on the tapering pinpoint of his dilemma, at once semantic and ethical: if you fall onto a protection peg, is it aid? Shades of another resonant question, asked by Mrs Grigson in O'Casey's *Shadow of a Gunman*: 'Do the insurance companies pay if a man is shot after curfew?' A different kind of survival issue, the one born of utter need, the other of a situation where danger is courted (because one's life is so secure); the one decided by lawyers and businessmen for profit, the other by sports-people for fun and self-esteem. From their opposed ends of the spectrum each bears its own kind of witness to that luxuriant human capacity for breeding up distinctions out of the least promising materials. You snatch at a loop of nylon or metal to save yourself from falling – how natural! But immediately this has to be reported to the magazines, placed on a finely-calibrated scale from the free to the artificial, then aimed at week after week by people hellbent on eliminating that one little movement. And this is not at all the most far-fetched refinement of moral mathematics that the present climbing scene is scratching its head about.

The tone of debate is nicely typified in the *Climber and Rambler* (October 1985): a letter denounces 'the decline in ethics that have occurred in Cheedale over the last months'. For those who have never seen Cheedale as the Gomorrah or Vegas of the north, I should say at once that the deadly sins now rampant there include: placing a protection bolt on a new route which can be reached from the neighbouring route, 'thus reducing the seriousness of this route'; placing a bolt on a route which was 'only' 5c, judged to be a 'foul practice'; and chipping a large slot to make a hold – which the letter-writer has since filled with cement. His vehemence springs partly from his being the author of the route whose seriousness is threatened. For me the offence is more in the damaging of nature by drilling and chiselling at it – but then I've never been tempted, since I can't climb virtually blank walls, and as a climber wrote in *Mountain* (January/February 1983) on the subject of all these wicked practices, 'the challenge is too great to avoid the temptation.' This writer makes the sound historical point that all leaps in climbing standards have taken off via some form of what we now call 'frigging', such as cutting a rock-step with an axe (Professor Collie on Moss Ghyll, Sca Fell, 1892); standing on each other's shoulders, pawkily called 'combined tactics' (Herford and Sansom on Central Buttress, Sca Fell, 1914); and so on through the inter- and post-War periods. The difference today lies in the minuteness of the 'rules' that are invoked, the tetchy egotism of the disputants, and the exhaustive publicity it all receives in the several monthly magazines. As Paul Ross said to me about the easier atmosphere of the Fifties, 'Who was caring? It wasn't written up in a bloody magazine, people weren't going around shouting, "What did you put that peg in for?"'

The shouting is now deafening. A Sheffield climber wrote to a recent *Mountain* complaining about the 'cheating antics', 'bitter rivalries', and 'miserable jealousy' among 'some of the top and not so top climbers'. (January/February 1983) These antics turn out to be tortuous in the extreme. Jim Perrin felt it necessary to spend a whole article, with the menacing title 'Reactionaries', on the habit of under-grading your new hard route to make subsequent climbers think you had found it merely steady when really it had been desperate. He sees this as part of a bad British tradition, 'the perpetuation of position and preservation of information-monopolies by the creation of smokescreens, confusions, and an aura of mystery.' (*Climber and Rambler*, January 1982) The case is well argued. The sadness of it is that the language of the debate has become as dire and as devious as that of the analysts who investigate surveillance, disinformation, and other dirty tricks of the State-machine.

If we sift the magazines for the past ten years, we can gauge the composition of the seed-bed in which acrimony flourishes. Intensive effort, intricate skills are being brought to bear on very small amounts of steep rock. 'Great hatred, little room,' as Yeats wrote about his Ireland. In *Crags* (August/September 1980) Livesey wrote that 'on most modern (ie since 1970) first ascents' the climbers carry out 'pre-preparation', a suitably redundant and tongue-twisting word for the maze of fiddles that has been twined round that exhilarating and natural activity – climbing steep rock from the ground up. It seems it is now almost universal for authors of new Extreme routes to practise moves on a top rope before climbing them for real. They fall off deliberately when they get tired, then use tension from the rope to resume at their previous high point instead of downclimbing or lowering off to start afresh. They place protection gear while hanging from an abseil rope and even thread the climbing rope through a series of karabiners before actually climbing. They chip and dig out rock to manufacture holds (in profusion on some routes). They chalk holds on abseil to make them instantly recognisable when they do climb. They rest on tension while keeping their hands on the rock to pretend they're holding themselves on: 'What constitutes a hands-off rest is the subject of fierce argument.' (*High*, November 1985) Routes of less than a hundred feet are 'sieged' over several days, each day's renewal of these military activities starting not from the ground again but from the previous day's high point. Runners are placed on neighbouring routes – so near are lines to each other on our congested crags. A route is claimed when it has been not exactly climbed (ie from the ground up) but top-roped and soloed – the soloing being in name only since the climber draped a rope down the line to grab in an emergency. Practising includes 'pump-out' training – someone repeatedly climbs a route on a top rope until his arms are exhausted: this monopolises the route for hours and polishes its holds to uselessness. The whole bizarre menagerie, like something out of *Gulliver's Travels* (a cross between the military drill in Lilliput and the scholastics in Laputa?), is imaged in a photo of two English climbers in America, one dangling on a top rope, trying out runner placements, while the other stands on a ladder leaning against the outcrop and drills a hole for a bolt. (*Crags*, December/January 1981)

So much focusing on tiny features – this inch-deep hole the size of a ten-pence piece, that undercut lip as small as the knob on the lid of a butter dish! So much sweating, and dangling of metal and winching of bodies, to apply to the rockface the skills of a bank robber who crouches there for hours, eyes and mind welded to the one small patch of metal, filing and levering and drilling! If this sounds like caricature, consider that a month before I wrote this the *Climber and Rambler* (February 1986) recorded a 'brilliant' new route put up after 'a twelve month siege' – it's eighty feet high and is protected by slings threaded through holes drilled specially for the purpose; also a 'tremendous' wall, slightly shorter than the one above, protected by four bolts: 'Like it or not, it does seem this is the future of British limestone climbing.'

Can one say more than the prostitute said at the time of Oscar Wilde's trial, 'I don't care what they do as long as it's not in the street and frightens the horses'? Yet I do care when these modern technicians (most of them marvellous gymnasts) tamper with the rock, since the essence of the sport is to cope with formidable pieces of the world's surface in their natural state. The trouble is that climbing partakes to the full of modern cultural developments and it would be impossible for it to do otherwise. Extreme climbers can fall deliberately because gear has been made almost foolproof by the invention of synthetic fibres and hard alloys such as chrome-molybdenum. Ropes are unlikely to break now that they have nylon cores and sheaths. Nuts come in an array of specialised shapes and sizes that rival a dentist's tray of burrs. The most high-tech nut, the Friend, developed by Ray Jardine for use in Yosemite, is actually a machine, with moving cams controlled by wires, and they cost up to twenty-six pounds each. Such wares, fitted with lines or tapes in psychedelic colours, glitter irresistibly in the shops. Gullible novices accoutred like Christmas trees apply this hardware to routes that were put up in the Sixties or earlier by climbers carrying pebbles in their woolly hats to jam into cracks, or (as the Neolithic gave way to the Early Iron Age) nuts picked up on railway lines and reamed to take line slings. The gorgeous gear is of course advertised in the monthlies by means of colour photos featuring the great safe-crackers – the

Extreme climbers whose routes, down to their very shortest and most artificial, are recorded elsewhere in the magazines.

Self-consciousness, competition, and an obsessive professionalism are thus being maximised. So, of course, is skill. Each of us then cloaks his estrangement from the latest habits, so different from one's own, in a reasoned critique of the new. My own climbing style belongs to 1965 at the latest. Yet even Pete Livesey, who established the Seventies style by gymnastic training of particular muscles, inspection on top rope, and so on, now laments that climbing 'is being reduced at top levels from adventure to safe gymnastics' by the habits I listed above, especially wholesale bolting, resting on pre-placed protection, and failure to report these tactics when claiming first ascents. (*Climber and Rambler*, December 1984) Contrast the ethic recently reported by Martin Boysen after a visit to the sandstone climbing area in Bohemia: 'To do a new route it has to be climbed from the bottom, there is no inspection, cleaning or pre-placed protection.' (*High*, June 1986)

Is such an ethic valid or luddite? Which presumes another question, is luddism valid? The Luddites smashed the new knitting frames early in the nineteenth century because gloves could be made on them cheaper and faster, which undercut the handknitters' livelihood. They also objected on the intrinsic ground that the new gloves were shoddy: they had no selvage, the pieces were simply cut to hand-shape and so were likely to fray. But could the rapidly-growing population have been supplied with gloves made by the old method? And can the rapidly-growing ranks of climbers be supplied with new routes climbed by the old methods, given the limited amount of clean rock with natural protection-cracks and holes? It would be tactful to stop the analogy here, since taking it further might imply that the new routes are likely to be shoddy – a wanton slur on the achievement of climbers as brave and athletic as Ron Fawcett, Rob Gawthorpe and John Redhead. If they are at home on overhanging limestone, whether it rises out of a Bristol carpark, a Welsh holiday promenade, or a gorge in France, whereas I am happier if the rock is the colour of earth and lichen, sculpted in great cleavage lines, and I can share it with the ravens, peregrines, and ring-ousels, then the sport remains as various as the terrain and we can continue to explore its niceties in our own daft and individual ways.

16

The more we equip ourselves for climbing – our bodies with harnesses and nuts and slings, our minds with coded information – the less we experience the crag itself, let alone the country it's embedded in. It was a revelation to me to climb Honister Wall (above the pass between Borrowdale and Buttermere) with one hemp rope, two hemp loops, two karabiners (heavy, pre-War blacksmith's work) and no belt, no harness, no helmet. It was an experiment on the part of Bill Peascod and myself. I still wore PA's (coward!) but Bill wore his old boots with clinker nails, many of them dropping out of the rotten welts. At first I felt naked, vulnerable, a swimmer taking on a rough grey sea. In a little while, this negative feeling had turned positive with the reassuring glow of the sun warming through fog. I was perceiving the rock with all its particulars as I had not when we did the route before – the haggard weathered faces, the unstable flakes like shoulder-blades disinterred from a prehistoric midden, the clear drops of mist on the nodes of the dwarf hawthorns, the lichens like luminous grey eyes or yellow as blots of egg-yolk. The cragface seemed unnaturally near my eyes yet perfectly in focus. As I moved up, the front of me felt intimately close to the rock, touching it all over as a swimmer's body hugs the water. And nothing was incongruous, no day-glo nylon, no emerald or violet perlon, no bulbous scarlet helmets. Bill's anorak was dirty khaki, his boots black, his corduroys dark brown, his rope . . . well, rope-coloured. Nothing cried out shrilly, 'Buy me! I am the latest!' Our clothes were the colour of stones, earth, grass. We rarely paused to put on protection, because we had so little, and never to read a guidebook – we carried none since it was Bill's route anyway and he knew it as you know the shape of your own hands. We were frequenting the rock more as lizards do, or snails or voles, experiencing it direct without the incessant, fidgety resort to classifying and enumerating – 'That was at least Hard Severe – did you think that move was really 4b? – I'd better put on a No. 5 Hex here' – and all the other chattering technicalities. Our fingers grasped, our toes levered, our joints flexed and bent, our senses smelt and saw rock. Each move was a response to the unmediated features of this part of the world's surface.

Of course all climbing has something of that quality, but it is an experience which easily becomes watered down or impure. That one hour, on a poor damp day, on a route of variable quality and easily within my powers, stands out for unalloyed sensory immediacy. As Yvon Chouinard says about using as little gear as possible on ice, 'I was rewarded for walking this edge by seeing more sharply what was around me, and I felt more deeply what comes boiling up from within.' (*Mountain*, November/December 1978) Boysen implies the same in his account of climbing the unprotectable fourth pitch of Shibboleth on Buachaille Etive Mór: 'No runners relieved the tension of the climbing . . . as the rope runs out in a single sweep the sense of exposure increases terrifyingly . . . Relief follows, then admiration; such a pitch will never, thank God, be made easy by nuts or wires; it will always remain a test of nerve.' (*Hard Rock*, ed. Ken Wilson, 1975, p 32)

Without runners all that is left is the rope, and when this too is shed the person is left with nothing but the rock – impossibly dangerous for most of us on the harder routes but perfectly available to all of us anywhere according to our powers. The Colorado climber Jeff Lowe says on Michael Tobias's film *Cloudwalker*, 'The purest way, and the only real way, to be with the mountains is alone.' So it has seemed to me on Goat Crag opposite Dandle Buttress in Longsleddale, that perfect slip of pastoral land dividing the eastern fells near Kendal; on the granite glaces and towers of Lundy, especially the shaven slabs of Kistvaen near the south end; and on many of the easier crags in Buttermere, which I've swarmed all over by myself, climbing sixteen or seventeen hundred feet of rock in a few hours' happy work on Miners' Crag in Newlands, Striddle on Fleetwith Pike, and Sheepbone Buttress in Birkness Combe while checking old routes and finding new ones for the guide.

Goat in Longsleddale is a hanging wild garden facing east, the rock blackish, the ferns and hyacinth-grass dense. Almost nobody goes there: the sun leaves it before noon, the buttresses on the opposite side of the dale are the place to go because they're more continuous. The first time I went to solo a route called Black Cleft, Shep couldn't cross the beck for all his efforts. A wet spell had swollen its waterfalls, covering the boulders. Our habit is to go with him to the foot of the crag where he can park down next to the rucksacks and very likely fill them with scrabbled earth if the ground isn't level and he has to dig a 'lair'. Next time I chose the middle of a drought. Each morning for days the shrinking supply of dew in the atmosphere sparkled for an hour or so before the climbing sun evaporated it. I reached the foot of the Black Cleft while it was still bathed in its short morning. Young ferns, semi-transparent lettuce-green, fledged the rims of the chimney. They closed over behind me as I pulled up the first of the three steep stages. Rocks were as moist to the touch as the backs of frogs and my hands met cool air as they reached into the shade to find holds. A broken staircase – a tower-house deserted for centuries – a vertical rock-garden gone back into nature . . . Fronds brushed my hair, I smelt their sporous undersides, an odour between tea and avocado. Snakes of ivy clamped shattered flakes in position. The brittle, awkward rock didn't matter at all, the greenish half-light suffused me with contentment and charmed adventure – Jack must have felt like this as he climbed up his beanstalk. On the landings, between the stages, I scarcely paused to look out over the dale in the way that is usually so delightful, a hawk's-eye view, because this world of half-inside the crag, seeing stems and leaves as a beetle or a glow-worm might, had sucked me gently in.

When the cleft closed at last and I had to move out onto the sheer right-hand face to finish the climb, I was reluctant to leave that immersed passage up the mountainside as a sleeper is loth to come out of a dream or a baby to break from the amniotic harbour.

In extreme contrast, to solo the Kistvaen cliffs on Lundy, where the granite starts at the southern tip of the island's ocean-facing coast, was at first more like going down into chaos than into an element where a human could belong. I nearly spoiled the adventure by looking at the guidebook to find the 'right' go-down: 'The approach is by scrambling more or less directly down the ridge half-way between the lime kiln and the Rocket Pole'. I kept to that for a time, but presently you are on your own among groins and planes of a granite that shades from the pale pink of cod roe to brownish gold. Ramps of granite angle down to a sea where one vortex of cream foam was turning and turning, urged by the twin tides that stream down either side of the island as they do around Jura in the Inner Hebrides. Immediately to the west, zawns penetrate the rock-wall, how deeply it is hard to tell, and next to the climbing cliff the waves charge in, forced onto each other as the inlet narrows. They seethe and rise and explode, but some force is left, in a few seconds it recoils in detonations but still isn't finished, and seconds later the sea's last energy issues in an outburst of fine spume which flies backwards out of the zawn at a height of thirty feet and comes at you in wild flocks that flurry all ways in mid-air. Unsettling. Stirring. I lodge myself in a little valley of the granite and tie up the laces of my PA's, trying to accustom my head to this world where the baseline is at sixty degrees to the horizontal and the foundations of the cliff seem shaken by the sea's battering.

From then on it's steady ecstasy, padding up the slopes with fingertips clinging into the flared cracks, learning to trust the friction on the giant gauge sandpaper of the crystalline rock, tracing an unending map of fissures that link every corner of this Heaven-sent expanse. The only minor taint is that whoever first came here named the climbs after Durrell's nasty novels, Clea,

Justine, and so on, but this (like the guidebook) can be overlooked. It's a place to go as you please, letting your feet glide up and down the fault-lines, moving nearer and nearer the zawn where the air-bursts are dying down as the tide ebbs. Here a traverse with a better name, Dark Labyrinth, takes you to an eyrie overlooking the zawn. Venturing still further, at a seam where drainage from the plateau above has discoloured and weakened the granite, I pull up on a bulb of solid rock – it isn't solid at all – it starts to move with that dreadful sound of a molar grating in your jaw as the dentist extracts it. I quickly shift my hands onto something better before moving rightwards and upwards again towards the roseate tip of the buttress where the distance from the land's insidious leakings has allowed the rock to remain whole and strong.

Up above, on the broad back of the island, everything feels oddly quiet and level, cushioned with peat, grazed by long-maned ponies. Kistvaen means 'tomb of rock'; skeletons of two eight-foot people were found in a grave-chamber nearby, and this ambience of Celtic giants had seemed perfectly suited to that granite smithy where the waves hammer and hammer on the anvils of the cliff.

17

The venturing demanded by sea-cliffs feels quite different from inland climbing because you can't see the rockface before you have to start contending with gravity. You have only just parked the car, or breakfast is still a recent memory, and already you're having to find some way over the brink. The *Good Book* may encourage you with happy talk of reaching the foot of the cliff by 'scrambling down Moderate standard rock', or even admit to a 'tedious and at times mildly desperate descent'. The fact is that, from above, all brinks are points where terra-firma ends in space and there is no telling whether the drop below is manageable or sheer. From below, a small hold is the more friendly because from the moment you start to pull up on it your weight is creating friction, maximising leverage. Lower yourself onto that same hold and there is this gulp, this moment when you have to consign your body to the drop with minimal support. It grows on you, after a while the long stretchings downwards with the toes begin to feel like slow-motion dancing, and it's certainly the quickest way of limbering up the mind – of brusquely accustoming it to the day's chances.

Even when you have sussed the vertical maze, and you know how to reach this or that tidal ledge, how to avoid the coastguards' rubbish-tip and the hotel's sewage outlets, the sea-cliff still keeps, as you look up at it, a secret air. You have not been able to stare at it for an hour as you walked up the gully or across the corrie floor, identifying famous lines, eyeing up new possibilities (or impossibilities). It is the very thickness of your native land, made visible for once, defended all along one side by that mobile sea which now quakes and tilts behind you, making your ears attend to its noise in case you have miscalculated the times of the tides. When Anne and I first climbed at Bosigran, north of Land's End, we made for the huge backbone of Commando Ridge, a dinosaur with its head lolling on steep grass slopes and its tail piercing the sea seven hundred feet below. 'Very popular . . . great fun in all weathers': oh good. 'The first pitch requires a calm sea': eh? In Cornwall clear weather and a low tide do coincide sometimes but, as often as not, in the middle of the night. As we nipped round the last joint of the dinosaur tail, the tide was filling and a brisk westerly threw white water up at our heels. Anne likes to climb Very Difficult but the steep corner which is the only way out of the sea's reach felt more like Severe. She climbed it in the fluent surge that is sucked out of you by sensing that there is no other way (for eight or nine hours) to escape from the swim and churn of salt water and re-restablish yourself in your homeland of heather, dry granite, and flowers yellow as butter. The sea is so alien, so hard to live in, so far (in our waters) below blood-heat. It swarms with life but, for

111

animals formed to take in oxygen as a gas rather than dissolved in water, it is more like death – the 'cold obstruction' abhorred by Claudio in *Measure for Measure*. Once when I took a slalom canoe out into Loch Diabaig in Wester Ross, I dared to paddle between the last skerries dividing the haven from the outer sea. I saw the big slope of the ocean setting in, grey hills of water hulking up, abolishing the horizon, heaving past under me, and I felt balanced on the very fulcrum between being and not being, the above and the below.

I had never heard of that last pair of phrases or concepts until I found myself using them to epitomise my perception of a painting by Bill Peascod which hung in his sitting-room at Melbecks on the north-west slope of Skiddaw. It is a yard across and two feet high, big enough to embody the expanse of the elemental world. The upper third of the painting is made of watery ink-blues, the lower third of clay greys. Between them churns a zone of sand-browns, buffs, ochres, layered on by the palette knife in slices of acrylic. When I first took it in, in 1982, I told him how much I liked this seething stretch 'between the above and the below'. He seized on the phrase and told me it was in fact a concept in Zen Buddhism. I have always seen that painted vision of his as land and water mixed: below an overcast sky the percussion of the breakers stirs up the seabed and does away with the boundary between the waters and the earth. Bill felt he had been painting hills. In either case it is an image of the world creating itself – the original flux, from which may emerge any and every one of those shapes which we then come to think of as eternal because they outlast us.

At the very verge of the world we can inhabit naturally, the sea-cliffs stand up, and as we come to know them, whether or not by climbing them, there can exist this sense that we are looking out from life into nothingness. In Cornwall the feeling is all the stronger because out there, beyond eyeshot, the sea loses itself over the curve of the earth. The Scillies are rarely visible, the Wolf Rock lighthouse (nine miles out) epitomises with its dark, slender vertical the human effort to stand against inchoate elements. This has been felt for centuries. On September 11 1743

John Wesley preached at Sennen just after sunrise to a congregation 'consisting chiefly of old, grey-headed men'.

> We went afterwards, as far as we could go safely, towards the point of the rocks at the Land's-end. It was an awful sight! But how will these rocks melt away, when God ariseth to judgement!
>
> – *Journal*, Everyman ed., I, p 433

It's sublime, in its way, the crassness with which the true believer, powered by his vision, zooms right past the object of attention. For a moment Wesley is on the verge of reacting to what is there, a twinge of token thrill in the eighteenth-century traveller's manner, and then it's gone, and he can no longer see those blunt towers of granite glowing pale brass when the sun lights them directly, prows dividing the North Atlantic Drift, their roots in the sea, the salt spume rasping them till the crystals stand out faceted like gems: a landmark for the invaders from prehistoric Iberians to Athelstan the Saxon who finally defeated the Cornish at Boleit, the Field of Blood, a little north of Lamorna . . . All those strivings which the crag has stood for, people and elements with and against each other, are nothing in the sight of the zealot. The rocks will outlast him, will they? Very well then, his god shall outlast the rocks! But however hard he shakes his fist at the gnarled world itself, however desperately he plies the wand of belief, the rock prevails, the chapels quarried out of it are converted to garages or holiday homes, and when these revert to cairns of scree with the last crumblings of our civilisation, and there are no humans left to enlist imagined gods in the long struggle against nature, then the piled pinnacles along the coasts of west Penwith will still be raising their silhouettes against the gleaming sea.

In winter this everlasting atmosphere feels all the stronger because the swarms of people are not there, the social and the historical shrink to a scattered presence, and the bareness of things comes through as an image of the not-yet-fully-created: leaves have only just evolved (hard, smooth, and salt-resistant for the most part) but not yet corn or flowers or fruits. The light seems new, uncertain, diffused through cauls of moisture as though solidity was barely born. A bird-world, not yet a mammal-world. On the arable plateau the ploughland is a monotony of primitive brown, a rich mineral mix still empty of any sprouting. When it is windless here in midwinter, the place is more than ever like an unawakened void, the world on the second day, with a firmament dividing the waters, an evening and a morning, but little else. Is there breath in nature's body? Can the waters bring forth anything at all?

They can, they can bring forth seals. Soon after one New Year, as Anne and I followed the North Cornwall Coastal Path from Pendeen south towards Sennen, a round head gleamed up out of the sea, like water-polished rock but mobile. It turned this way and that way, looking. We hollered to it and for over an hour (or two miles of walking) it followed us off-shore, diving occasionally, coming up again for a look. We hallooed and hallooed and it did not go away until it seemed put off by the combers bursting at Whitesands Bay and went down into the sea at the same time as the sun.

A day or two later another seal bobbed like flotsam in the sea that swelled up into a zawn at Pordenack Point where Rob and I were climbing comfortably in our shirtsleeves, finding our way up little ramps and clefts and zig-zag chimneys blackened by the sea's iodine. We could have felt like 'the first that ever burst into that silent sea' had it not been for one ordinary metal nut that someone (possibly Zeke Deacon the Marine climber) had jammed into a crack for protection a generation before. Salt moisture had fused it to the rock in a blob of orange. Apart from ourselves the seal was the only other evidence that temperatures could ever rise to blood-heat or animal life take shape in the huge, twilit hollow of the cosmos.

The midwinter trance in west Penwith, if it occurs, is so momentous partly because any calm down there is a lull between cyclonic onslaughts. The energy of the wind is manic, inexhaustible. The exact point where it peaks lies on the boundary of the between and the above, the climax of the updraught. Further down the cliff it may be possible to live and climb in the wind, provided you choose a moment of slackening between gusts to lift a foot from a hold and raise it onto the next one. And on the plateau you can get used to a gale by shouting instead of speaking and leaning instead of standing. But what Yeats called 'the haystack- and roof-levelling wind, Bred on the Atlantic' becomes impossible at the cliff edge where, deflected by the two hundred-foot thickness of the granite, it accelerates upwards, tearing out clumps of sea-thrift, scouring crumbs of earth into a brown blizzard, sending the surf from the base of the cliff, where it quakes in a dense white mass like milk half-churned to butter, to blow in clots across the plateau up above. We first saw this during a late October week on Lundy, eleven miles out into the Bristol Channel, north of Hartland Point near Bideford. Force seven to force nine gales dominated us for six days on end.

We were staying in the Old Light, a great Victorian tower which had failed as a lighthouse because its head was buried so often in fog. All that week, as we rounded the base of the empty tower going anti-clockwise with the gale behind us, we were forced to run headlong. Suddenly, as you met the airstream pouring round the far side, you were stopped dead and had to force yourself forwards, head down. The froth was blowing clean across the saddle of the island, four hundred feet above sea level, in ghostly clumps like tumbleweed. One afternoon, as the gale rose to the 'sea-wind scream' described by Yeats and fumes of sulphur dioxide choked us as flames blew right out of the iron stove's little door, we all went mad to experience the wind, to drink it, eat it, embrace it. We ran down to the clifftop nearest the Old Light, between Black Crag and Pilot's Quay. You could only make headway by leaning forward, face three feet from the ground, and staggering in a long dive. At the edge normality disappeared entirely. Neil was barely recognisable, his hair racing off his head in a solid blond stream, his face squared out sideways like a rubber mask, his eyelids puffing and trembling – the grimace of the ejecting pilot in *Life* magazine's famous photos. Gravity became secondary and we could lean out over the edge, wind-supported, and peer straight down at the waves ramping below, their white limbs clambering up the cliff as though a tribe of polar bears were coming at us.

115

Two days before, we had seen a flight of curlews, flocked for winter feeding, come hurtling over the island. They should have stayed in the quiet lee of the East Sidelands, a zone of deep bracken mulch, wild rhododendrons in Asiatic luxuriance, and plinths of granite where the seals haul out to bask. The moment the updraught caught them they were forced to behave like gulls, changing course at obtuse angles, heeling to flee downwind, the leading edge of each wing sharpening to an apex as they 'bent like an iron bar slowly', in Hughes's marvellous image of the windblown blackbacked gull. How to climb when you could scarcely walk? Yet, as we abseiled cautiously down the chute of gravel and sea-thrift next to the Devil's Slide on the west coast, a sheer plane of granite that slopes four hundred feet from sea to summit, symmetrical as some great ceremonial ramp in a Maya temple, everything became less cold and easier near the tidemark, as though we had passed inside the wind and were looking out through the storm's eyes. And so we padded upwards, clumsy baboons in treble jerseys, to the horizontal break at half-height, a serrated ledge upholstered with thrift which deflates the climb a little because you can step for a moment out of the precarious world. As I stand there, waiting for Neil to come up on the rope, I chat with Norman, who's climbing the Devil's Slide route proper with Terry. Norman is fond of dry quips – you can tell when one is coming because his grizzled beard begins to twitch. In answer to the standard climber's call, 'Is that you?' – meaning 'Has the rope come tight between us?' – he's been known to answer, 'Who else would it be?' On this occasion, as the wind cuts through our woollens, I say, 'It's colder up here. That wind's finding the bone.' 'That's the trouble about climbing with poets,' he says. 'They make everything sound worse.'

Neil leads as the slab steepens, up the line called Satan's Slip. The book has told us that it's 'protected solely by a bolt'. The salt air has eroded this to nothing but Neil finds placements for six small nuts on wire, some barely sunk in the cracks but two so good that they have to be knocked out with a krab and a Cassin peg: finicky dental work in the shuddering cold, like performing an operation at sea or trying to mend a cathedral roof in winter.

To make headway upwards, fingerends must hook into little holes no bigger than a five-pence piece, better than nothing but useless for the feet, and all this delicate balancing and frictioning begins to feel weirdly furtive, as though we're tiptoeing so as not to let the wind know we're here. Gradually we near the granite bird totem to which the Slide tapers at its summit; from the south it looks like a cartoon sculpture of a cliff-dwelling bird, as though nature has contrived a memorial to the puffins which have now almost deserted the island that was named after them.

We had heard the gale scream once before, as we lay unsleeping in our frame tent on August 11 1979, at our camp in the field at Boleigh which we later learned was the very site of that last defeat of the Cornish by the Saxons in 931. Anne and I could not believe that the straight walls of the tent would stand against the demonic battering. I had laid an old telephone pole on the hem of the windward side with its metal steps sticking into the turf to prevent it rolling. Moon-shadows streamed and writhed wildly on the cloth above our heads and the whole little home-from-home was bellying and creaking like a windjammer about to founder. But it held out all night, we were saved by the slope of the field to the west where tall standing stones lean – the Pipers, where Athelstan may or may not have placed himself to observe the armies grappling. In the morning, under a sky blown by the gale into a great dome of blue glass, we went along to Sennen and stood with hundreds of others watching the sea lay on a spectacle. Beyond the horizon dozens of yachts in the Fastnet race were foundering and dismasting. Here at our feet the waves were lifting in blossom-trees of white foam. It streamed in rills off the crown of the famous climb called Demo, which starts ten feet above mid-tide and rises for another seventy. When we did it the week after, we could understand why the layer of black schorl veneered onto the granite of the final slab is fretted into shapes like the flakes of bark on a pine trunk.

On Lundy the gale began to seem as permanent as our own lungs breathing. It made communication impossible as Terry, Norman and I tried to thread our way up the climb called Cable Way, on Montague Buttress where a battleship was wrecked in

1906. For nearly twenty years they worked to salvage what they could, building a giant ladder of two-inch steel hawser with plank steps. The ruptured, rusting tendons of it still loll down the cliff. After losing my way and making an involuntary Very Severe variant that I called Bad Connection, I belayed onto a cable-end to bring the others up. The thrumming of the hawser in the gale, transmitted along the rope to my waist, was as unsettling as though the planet was shaking loose or working itself up to an earthquake.

For six days the environment was all antagonism and we went out to accept it and make the most of it. Even on the lee side, as Anne and I climbed Gannet Traverse at the north end, spiralling round the buttress below mouthed and horned gargoyles bearded with lichen, the sky sent hailshowers to rattle off our helmets and rasp the green sea dark mussel-blue. The church itself was threatening to come unstuck – the gawky, semi-derelict advertisement for defunct ideals which the wonderfully named Reverend H. G. Heaven had commanded to be built ninety years before, importing bricks and stone to an island whose main export was granite. As we walked under the east wall after a wet gale had driven us off a fine route called Ulysses Factor near the Devil's Limekiln, we saw that the clockface was shattered and fallen slates littered the grass, some driven in edgeways. What a way to go, we fantasised – your skull split by one of the Reverend Heaven's slates, as though God had reached down His hand to fell a passing atheist.

But there is no divinity in the storm, it is pure energy issuing from the maelstrom of matter, you can work with it or let it envelop you, and it was in this spirit five years later that Anne and I stood at the top of Sennen cliffs again, on the crag called in Cornish Pedn-Mên-Du. A strange south-easterly gale was blowing, in January, straight up the coast. By wave refraction this bent the sea inwards against the land and, as we watched, the waters rose in a ridge with a tossing top, the white hair blown sideways off it as it came towards us. Sixty feet below was the granite stage where you sort your gear before climbing Demo. A broad wedge has been bitten out of it, this is what focuses the

7. DC and Bill Peascod climbing Dexter Wall, Grey Crag, Birkness
Combe, June 1982, by Chris Culshaw

8. DC and Bill Peascod climbing White Ghyll Wall, Great Langdale,
August 1982, by Chris Culshaw

waves and forces them skywards. Now the foam-trees were blossoming again, improbably high up into the air, and this was going to be a big one. Shep stood well back from the edge while his humans got ready to be silly yet again. The wave hit the face of the rock-stage, burst in a white explosion, swelled on into the vee, and levitated. The gale caught the head of spume and blew it at us. Behind it Longships lighthouse disappeared. Steeply above us the air filled with grey bees, swarming, coagulating, swooping onto us, hitting me with a solid impact as I turned my shoulder against it to protect my camera, drenching me instantly to the skin.

18

In the Mediterranean the 'between' is not fought over in the harsh Atlantic way. Winds from Africa stir it white but the warmed air is more continuous with your own bloodstream, making you at home in it, and the absence of tide subdues the sea: it is going to lift no further up those rocks however many hours, or centuries, go by. The salt of it will eat and carve at the inevitable limestone that girds so much of the coast but it will always have to work at the same narrow zone, crafting it into crests as spiny as tropical fish, into systems of little pools with rims as perforated as Japanese lampstands. Moving over it is like walking on porcupines but when it rises into cliffs it is all holds, a climber's dream in which the rock, wherever you grasp it, sprouts fingerholds that might have been moulded for the purpose. On the west coast of Ithaca, facing across a dazzling channel to the Hebridean blue emptiness of Kefalonia, you can climb rock straight out of the sea. Each element impinges totally. One moment you're sliding through caressing water, the next you're holding onto frills of rock that bite into the pads of the fingertips. You pull up out of buoyancy into gravity, teetering upwards in an excruciating effort to withold your full weight for fear the serrations might draw blood. A few minutes' perching on a pulpit, like a cormorant drying out, and then the sun starts to sting and you must lower gingerly down the toothed edges and give yourself again to the fluent ease of the water.

Down there at the south end of Ithaca, where Anne and I had gone for the sake of its Homeric associations, limestone made the medium for many of our keenest experiences. In England it is my least favourite stuff because its colour is as ugly as old bones, it is uncompromisingly vertical (the split-off ends of submarine bedding-planes), it takes polish so easily that its surfaces grow as slippery as a bath with too much soap in it, and because it lacks coherent architecture. For hundreds of feet at a time it evolves no clear form, no major lines of cleavage, instead it bulks and bulges and offers only a jigsaw of little facets that slope all ways and create no ladder of possibilities, or not for the likes of me. But in Ithaca, and also in the Peloponnese where Anne and I had just been to follow her father's path as a soldier and prisoner-of-war, limestone was something else: the drums of temple columns felled by medieval earthquakes, still lying as they had fallen – a marine labyrinth at Vlykhada in the Mani, where the underground sea winds off between the pillars of the stalagmites in a trance that seems to stroke the surfaces of your brain – a floor of shingle rounded and white as alabaster eggs where we swam off the south-eastern end of Ithaca at the mouth of the ravine which holds the wellsprings of Perapigádi.

The beauty of it all was that in the deepest crevices of the rock Odyssean associations had lodged like jetsam from the Bronze Age. On a day of burning autumn, when the only flowers starting to light up the ground after the summer's scorching were the dwarf cyclamens, we set off south from Vathy to find the Fountain of Arethusa, the cave where Eumaios hid his pigs, and the bay where Odysseus landed to take Penelope's suitors by surprise. We had already been to the Grotto of the Nymphs where, according to Homer, the Naiads wove sea-purple fabric on great stone looms. We located the deep fissure in the limestone by the cypress copse like a file of dark mourners on the hillside above. Nearby, in a farm backyard whose atmosphere was blurred with dust and flies, a newly-flayed goatskin hung like a sacrifice in a glare of sunlight between the olive branches. The tarmac road south with its crumbling edges became a track of pebbles and yellow dirt. Very old olive trees, more knuckled and carbuncled by the deformities of pruning than the most grotesque elms in an English hedge, surrounded the way with their glades of ice-green leaves. The watercourses were all dry, smashed clefts choked with boulders, but now and again, through a little gate, a well showed beside a threshing-floor: a limestone parapet four-foot in diameter, a wooden lid painted Cornish blue, and the glitter of water ten feet down the shaft. Would Arethusa's fountain still be springing? We came over a ridge high above a sea fringed with the turquoise glimmer of limestone shingle under water and stepped down the hillside by a rocky path that twisted between red-berried dwarf thorn and the occasional tall flower whose leaning spires were decorated with pale pink bells. A ravine cut the hillside and the path ran under a face of dripping shale. There was a faint air of use, we poked around, and there it was, lying on a scree slope, a battered wooden sign that said in Greek and English, 'Spring of Arethusa'. This dank, collapsing bluff? How much refreshment would Eumaios' pigs have managed to suck from such a meagre oozing? Ah well . . . But there was no socket for the sign. Had it come from somewhere else? I scrambled up the scree. The rockface was split by a narrow cave that hollowed back deeply into the darkness, its natural threshold worn by feet. Half a plastic bottle hung from a string. We looked down, badly wanting the water to be there. Boulders and creviced sides just showed in the twilight. We were seeing them through water so clear and still that it was almost invisible, fifteen feet below. And so we lowered the little twentieth-century vessel down into the clarity of the ancient well and dipped ourselves drinks, perfectly pure and perhaps thirty degrees colder than the air outside.

Afterwards we sat in a nook of the ravine, eating bread and goat cheese and olives and reading the *Blue Guide* to try and glean more morsels of myth and history. 'The peasants call the neighbouring cliff Korax,' or (in Book XIII of *The Odyssey*) Raven Crag, a homely reminder of Cumbria, where every dale has one. Could it be that limestone cove a thousand feet up the hillside, its broad face and straight top barring the head of the ravine? As we watched, black silhouettes turned against the blue, cruising on the thermals – jackdaws or ravens, at this distance we couldn't tell their size. The sensation was pure *déjà vu*, as though we had space-warped out of the Ionian Islands into Yorkshire and were seeing the Cove at Malham when the huge stoop of it first shows from the road past Attermire, at the point where you look north, ready to be intimidated, and each time its louring face seems bigger, the lines of its old bolt ladders more inhospitable (yet they are now being free-climbed by the inspired young gymnasts from Leeds and Sheffield).

Just two years before, I had spent the last bright day of August at Malham with Neil. I had climbed Swingover, tried to lead it before my oil had warmed up enough, fallen off and bruised my wrist. Then climbed Scorpio and managed to lead the first pitch, muscling and bridging rather clumsily up the shattered corner. As the sun lowered into the haze, we would crown the day by climbing the first pitch of Carnage to the tree ledge, then finishing up the top pitch of Carnage Left Hand. The wall felt vertical but at least the fingerledges were sharp and good for leverage.

Neil actually likes limestone, it seems to turn him on, and he led the artificial move over the roof of the cave without a second's hesitation, putting his foot into a sling clipped into a peg and using this as easily as though it had been solid, not yawing about in mid-air. I found the dangling heave horribly laborious, like trying to lift the chair you're sitting on. It felt much harder, or I much older, than the year before when we had done it *en route* for the top pitch of Carnage itself. I lacked the composure even to stretch down from above the difficulty and unclip our sling from the piton. With the last drops of energy and willpower I made the thirty feet to the 'awkward slab', which turned out to embody all I most hate in limestone: no palpable crystals, no clean cracks, a dull sheen that suggests minimal friction. Like a spastic baboon I udge up it for a few feet, but I can't even picture the moves that might take me higher. I know I'd need to be winched up this and where's the achievement in such a manoeuvre? Why impose the weary labour of it on my long-suffering leader? 'Can't do this,' I call up. 'Better lower off.' And down I go through the yellow dusk, spinning gently like a spider on its gossamer, amongst the newly-hatched flies and the dashing and swooping martins that must have been fixing their cradles of mud to the face of the Cove for thousands of years before houses were invented, whose last broods of the season I can hear chirruping way down on Central Wall. The plumb-line of the rope is lowering almost too far out for me to reach the trees growing from the cave ledge. I swing a little, stretch and stretch, catch hold of a twig-tip and pull on it, it bends, it nearly breaks but it holds me, I play myself in along it to a branch to a bigger branch to a main limb of the tree while the sweat cools on my face, the dying light glows orange, and the first calls of the brown owls start to burble from amongst the ash trees down the dale, as softly guttural as water running under grass.

It was the luckiest of all my climbing failures, the only time I have truly shared air-space with the birds. The vision it left me with was bound to become a poem but the forming of it was unexpectedly long and arduous. I pored over photos of the crag. I jotted down snatches and glimpses of it on several sheets of paper with plenty of space between them and willed the connective tissue to grow. But the other half of the metaphor still lay buried until I saw that the Cove belonged with all those other experiences of corries and combes – Birkness high above Buttermere, the great corries on Lochnagar and Beinn Eighe, the north face of Liathach. If you stand at the mouth of a corrie with your back to it and lean backwards until you can just see the rim of the cliff at the bottom of your field of vision, the slopes at either side join onto the rim to compose a huge circular frame, a border of rock and heather, or grass and leaves, surrounding the broad blue pond of the sky: the round blue eye of the sky, with the crag as the exposed bone of the orbital ridge and the leafage as lashes. And once you have focused the rock as bone and the vegetation as its soft, ephemeral contents, this image combines with the great age of the rock, in Malham's case the limestone with its traces of earlier lives (strata, fossils, veins where waterfalls once coursed), to create a vision of a derelict giant spreadeagled across Yorkshire where he fell 500 million years ago, one arm reaching Gordale, shoulder-blades laid bare between here and the Tarn, a fist clenched at Attermire . . . So the Cove became in my poem the giant's brain-pan, the vaulted chamber of his thoughts: in his last, moribund sleep he dreams birds, 100 million years later he dreams people in his last delirium . . . In the course of all this brooding the Cove itself has come to seem less alien, less of a planet reachable only by voyagers better equipped than I and more of a station on my own journeying.

That may be why Korax on Ithaca struck me with such an uncanny look of the familiar as it loomed on the skyline of a foreign island. Whether it is an intention or merely a fantasy, it draws me strongly and I would like to get back there with all the gear, struggle up the stonefall of the ravine, and see whether Korax can be climbed. Even if I never do, it will stand above me in my mind's eye, waiting.

19

That is the frame of mind Paul Nunn seems to mean in his essay 'Climbers' when he refers to 'the sensation familiar to many climbers after travelling in an alien country. As the mountain valleys open up and the distant snows glisten, on a winter night in Scotland or in early summer in the Soviet Caucasus, one feels that one is coming home.' (*Climber and Rambler*, April 1980) He is being unashamedly romantic, and rightly so, since our cult of the wilderness, untamed nature, the far-off and hard to reach, stems directly from the sensibility of the prime Romantic artists and thinkers – from Rousseau, Wordsworth, Coleridge, Beethoven, Turner. Before their time people were most likely to perceive steepness and remoteness as ugly, frightening or plain useless. When they did begin to relish them, they still held back in an exclamatory or gushing spectator role for two generations or so before they dared to go out onto the steeps and use their own limbs to grapple with them.

Mountains and crags had generally been thought of as the world at its least congenial to us humans. The Archbishop of Dublin, writing his *De Origine Mali* in 1702, takes it for granted that 'We complain of mountains as rubbish, as not only disfiguring the face of the earth, but also to us useless and inconvenient', their only justification being that our water supplies spring from them. Even an early Swiss guidebook (1713) disparages the Alps because of their height, their perpetual snows, and their 'inconvenient and primitive' tracks (Stephen, *The Playgrounds of Europe*, pp 9–10) – precisely what we now flock there in our millions to enjoy. Two generations later, Samuel Johnson was ahead of his time in journeying deep into the Highlands and Islands yet even he saw the visiting of 'rocks and heaths' as a philosophical duty – one must know everything – and not at all as a pleasure since the 'untravelled wilderness' stood for nothing but 'the evils of dereliction', a 'wide extent of hopeless sterility', 'quickened only with one sullen power of useless vegetation': the heather which now epitomises the allure of the Highlands for countless tourists. (*Journey to the Hebrides*, 1773) Richardson, the most perceptive novelist of the time, was at one with Johnson in equating rocky mountains with poverty, and Goldsmith (so eloquent in praise of a country way of life) greatly preferred the plains of the Netherlands to the Scottish Highlands where 'hills and rocks intercept every prospect'.

Those very traditional attitudes aren't laughable, they are eminently reasonable. The steep places *are* uncomfortable, hard to live in, often barren or thin-soiled, sending down their spates of snow or boulders to crush the habitable ground below. In his *Voyage aux Pyrénées*, Taine, who was much closer to backward social conditions in western Europe than we are today, defined most lucidly the basis of the older revulsion from the highlands:

> People who had just emerged from an era of civil war and semi-barbarism were reminded by them of hunger, of long journeys on horseback in rain and snow, of inferior black bread mixed with chaff, of filthy, vermin-ridden hostelries. They were tired of barbarism, as we are tired of civilisation . . .
>
> – Plekhanov, *Unaddressed Letters*, 1957, p 32

A generation after Taine, when a Swiss Alpine guide visited Leslie Stephen in London, the man of letters was taken aback when the working-man found the view of roofs and smoking chimneys 'far finer' than the view of Mont Blanc. But as trains, tunnels, and steamboats delivered to the wild uplands more and more people with the leisure time to cultivate aesthetic pleasure as an end in itself, the habit of pleasuring ourselves amongst wildness at once took root and blossomed luxuriantly. Since then it has come to feel like a need.

Gray, the author of the 'Elegy Written in a Country Churchyard', travelled through the Lake District in 1768 and the journal that he published in 1775 is credited with helping to start the tourist boom. Thirty years before, he had had his first inkling of such an experience when he made the Grand Tour from France across the Alps into Italy and was staggered by the Grande Chartreuse: 'not a precipice, not a torrent, not a cliff, but is pregnant with religion and poetry.' (Letter of 1739) This prefigures Wordsworth and Coleridge, Keats and Byron. Yet Gray's key words still suggest the contradiction in his feelings for steeps. He is charmed, he is repelled. The crags are 'savage', 'monstrous', 'horrible', and when he makes his famous tour through Borrowdale in 1768 he is almost comically ready to imagine dangers. Gowder Buttress at Lodore, the site of many rock routes including the excellent Fool's Paradise, is perceived as 'impending terribly', 'hanging loose and nodding forwards' and best passed by quickly and silently. True, it had let fall a chunk of rock onto the road several years before but the precautions he advises weren't going to have much actual effect on anything (except morale). What Gray is expressing is a vision of civilisation just managing to keep at bay the ogreish dangers that surround it, which both fascinate and alarm. A few years later that very urbane painter Gainsborough paints the same vision in his 'Romantic Landscape with Sheep at a Spring': the two buttresses that overhang on the left are quite like Gowder in their vertical grain but we get little sense that the painter has seen these rocks. They're impressive props, suffused with pale-gold light to etherealise them and parted to show a green Eden beyond.

Writers were not yet able to make poetry directly out of the steep places – we can hardly count the florid rhetoric about the cliffs of Snowdonia in Gray's 'Bard'. This corresponds to the travellers' inability as yet to set their own feet and hands on the mountains. Gainsborough made his painting about a year before the first ascent of Mont Blanc in 1786. Most people still viewed the mountains from a distance, from their carriages, from boats on the lakes, through a Claude glass to compose the vista into a manageably pretty image. Fear of the wild uplands – albeit a 'delicious' one – still predominated because they weren't known at first hand. Even a naval veteran called Joseph Budworth, a sturdy walker who made the first recorded ascent of Harrison's Stickle in Great Langdale in 1797, 'insisted on bandaging his offside eye with his handkerchief' before allowing himself to be led by a local lad across a steep slope. (Tom Bowker, *Mountain Lakeland*, 1984, pp 203–4)

According to Budworth's local informants, ' "they never remembered foine folk aiming at et afore" '. That is, the shepherds may well have climbed the mountains even to their summits and been as unimpressed by them, for all we know, as the Swiss guide was by Mont Blanc. The first person who fused the two approaches, workmanlike and aesthetic, local and touristic, was Wordsworth, a native-born Cumbrian who climbed rock as a boy in his foragings for birds' eggs. He evokes the experience in the first piece of climbing literature in English:

> . . . In the high places, on the lonesome peaks
> Where'er, among the mountains and the winds,
> The Mother Bird had built her lodge. Though mean
> My object and inglorious, yet the end
> Was not ignoble. Oh! when I have hung
> Above the raven's nest, by knots of grass
> And half-inch fissures in the slippery rock
> But ill sustain'd, and almost, as it seem'd,
> Suspended by the blast which blew amain,
> Shouldering the naked crag . . .
>
> – *The Prelude*, 1805, I, lines 337–46

Here the local lad was at home in the places which gave the tourists kittens even at a distance. It must simply have been natural for him to go there, as it was for Jim Birkett who also started climbing 'When I first started bird nesting – as soon as I was old enough to walk, practically' and first learnt rope technique in order to get at the nests. (Bill Birkett, 'Talking with Jim Birkett', *Climber and Rambler*, August 1982) Generations of boys before Wordsworth probably did the same, but his way of turning it into poetry shows that the experience could now be claimed as valuable – fertile for your growth as a person. This was not on record before. In our time Jim Birkett, a down-to-earth man and not a poet, can say that 'if you love mountains you take an interest in everything they can give you,' and we may say that the possibility of loving mountains dawned in the 1780s:

> . . . at that time
> While on the perilous ridge I hung alone,
> With what strange utterance did the loud dry wind
> Blow through my ears! the sky seem'd not a sky
> Of earth, and with what motion mov'd the clouds!

In the famous passages that follow, about stealing a boat and skating on Ullswater, he evokes and then analyses the way in which experiences among the 'craggy Steeps' gave him his first

128

crucial inklings of those irrational states, states of 'danger or desire', which come to stand for the gamut of what life is like, how it strikes us, how we take it. His guilty depression in the days after the mountain had seemed to stride after him as he rowed in the moonlight under a 'rocky Steep' – his elation as he seemed to see the rotation of the earth in the wheeling of the 'solitary Cliffs' when he stopped skating in mid-glide: such were the moments that did most to form his image of the cosmos and himself in it.

Rousseau is often credited with first noticing, and acting upon, such perceptions and he too was brought up in mountain country. In 1728, journeying on foot to Italy from his birthplace in Geneva, he found in himself 'the strongest taste . . . for mountains especially'. His *Confessions*, started in 1766, are far from dominated by wilderness experience but where he does touch on it the feeling is acutely modern. The plains can't count as beautiful: 'I need torrents, rocks, firs, dark woods, mountains, steep roads to climb or descend, abysses beside me to make me afraid.' He knows the perversity of such experience and he revels in it: 'the amusing thing about my taste for precipitous places is that they make my head spin; and I am very fond of this giddy feeling so long as I am in safety.' So he delights in what we now call boulder-trundling, or in spending hours on a bridge with a low parapet, looking hundreds of feet down at 'the foam and the blue water, whose roaring came to me amid the screams of ravens and birds of prey which flew from rock to rock'. The convention-al literary culture to which he still half-belonged was no help to him in making sense of all this: late in life he is still saying 'at the sight of a beautiful mountain I feel moved, though I cannot say by what.' However he is unmistakably at the source of Romanticism in his openness to experiences not classed as 'useful' by society and in his persistent belief that people could only become themselves if they shook off the more elaborate social conven-tions and lived, both working and relaxing, more amongst nature. In *Emile* he extols a life where people enjoy each other's hospitality 'in the garden . . . or on the banks of a running stream, in the fresh green grass'. Lewis Mumford, most humane of social

thinkers, sees in this the germ of the picnic and the holiday –
fundamental forms of urban relief and escape:

> The rambling, the botanizing, the geologizing . . . hours spent in
> feasting around the picnic hamper or sitting lazily around an almost
> primeval campfire . . . vacations in the Tyrol climbing from
> Alpenhütte to Alpenhütte, or deep among the rocky walls of the
> Yosemite – all these delightful days were formulated by Rousseau and
> encouraged by his active example.
>
> – *The Condition of Man*, 1944, pp 297–8

From its origin this cult of the natural has had both a benign
and a darker face. Amongst nature we can both reaffirm vitality –
the energy which flows in the weather, plants, us animals – and
also admit to the allure of whatever threatens us:

> . . . the more cultivated minds of the West began to incite fear and
> mystery within themselves . . . by pitting themselves against the
> elements: going abroad in thunderstorms, with the lightning streaking
> across their path, climbing high mountains even above the snowline,
> exploring caves: in short, doing for an esthetic reason the same
> undaunted actions that the sailor, the peasant, the woodsman, or the
> miner were wont to do in the course of their works and days.
>
> – Mumford, *The Condition of Man*, p 280

Rousseau, again ahead of his time, had hinted at this when he said
to Boswell in 1764, 'There's the great matter, to have force.'
(*Boswell on the Grand Tour*, ed. F. A. Pottle, 1953, p 218) Such a
concept almost excludes ethics: any flow of impulse is exalted,
regardless of consequences. Sheer intensity of living becomes the
supreme goal. Here is the credo of those Extreme climbers in
America who are so much readier than their British counterparts
to articulate their views as a drastic philosophy. For example
Mark Wilford when he says on the *Cloudwalker* film, 'If you
knew that however stupid your actions were you weren't going
to die, the experience would be much less, like riding a
roller-coaster in Disneyland . . . I don't want to stop climbing – I
want it to end in the mountains . . . I like to operate near the edge
of what I can do, so someday, unless I'm incredibly lucky, or just
quit, I'm going to fall over that fine line.'

This pursuit of intensity through risk is already unmistakable in the first piece of climbing prose in English: a letter Coleridge wrote to Sarah Hutchinson on August 6 1802, the day after making the first recorded ascent of Sca Fell. He begins the letter by admitting that he courts danger, a 'sort of Gambling . . . not of the least criminal kind for a man who has children'. When he has to climb down a mountain, he doesn't look for a path but 'wanders on relying upon fortune'. It was this habit, pure Romanticism in its spontaneity, that led him down the rock-climb called Broad Stand, a series of ten- and fifteen-foot steps and smooth rectangular corners which rise up from the col between Sca Fell and Scafell Pikes. It is now graded Moderate and I've seen notices in Lake District shops warning walkers not to climb up it without a rope.

Coleridge's prose, like the latest American climbing writing, plunges us into the midstream of his experience, a headlong physical spate in which instant follows instant so quickly that the Latinate syntax of the time breaks into a staccato of simple clauses:

I began to suspect that I ought not to go on, but then unfortunately tho' I could with ease drop down a smooth Rock 7 feet high, I could not *climb* it, so go on I must, and on I went, the next 3 drops were not half a Foot, at least not a foot more than my own height, but every Drop increased the Palsy of my Limbs – I shook all over, Heaven knows without the least influence of Fear – and now I had only two more to drop down, to return was impossible – but of these two the first was tremendous, it was twice my own height, & the Ledge at the bottom was so exceedingly narrow, that if I dropt down upon it I must of necessity have fallen backwards & of course killed myself.

By now he was trembling too much to go on. As he writes we see how this negative state mutates into a positive one; the raised adrenalin flow fuels a high and a Romantic epiphany or visionary moment is born of it:

I lay upon my Back to rest myself, & was beginning according to my Custom to laugh at myself for a Madman, when the sight of the Crags above me on each side, & the impetuous Clouds just over them, posting so luridly & raptly northward, overawed me, I lay in a state of almost prophetic Trance & Delight – & blessed God aloud for the powers of Reason & the Will, which remaining no Danger can overpower us! O God, I exclaimed aloud – how calm, how blessed am I now, I know not how to proceed, how to return, but I am calm & fearless & confident, if this Reality were a Dream, if I were asleep, what agonies had I suffered! what screams! – When the Reason & the Will are away, what remain to us but Darkness & Dimness & a bewildering Shame, and Pain that is utterly Lord over us, or fantastic Pleasure, that draws the Soul along swimming through the air in many Shapes, even as a Flight of Starlings in a Wind.

Reinvigorated, he climbed on down to the col of Mickledore, past a rotting sheep and through the final chimney, which is so narrow that he had to slide his knapsack to one side to avoid getting stuck. (*Collected Letters*, ed. Earl Leslie Griggs, II, 1956, pp 841–2)

It's typical of Coleridge's intelligence that even while he seems to be letting emotions run riot, he can be clear with himself that the experience demanded reason – a 'calm confidence' – if it was not to get out of hand and ruin him. The point is absolutely relevant to climbing, in which physical surge and exact appraisal of the terrain have to mesh. He is also very much the Romantic in his courting of extreme experiences, as Shelley was twenty years later when he went out into the Gulf of Leghorn in a small sailing-boat as a storm blew up and was drowned, or Turner in 1842, in his rather more craftsmanly way, when he got the material for his tremendous vortical 'Snowstorm' painting by asking 'the sailors to lash me to the mast to observe it; I was lashed for four hours, and I did not expect to escape, but I felt bound to record it, if I did.' (Graham Reynolds, *Turner*, 1969, p 190) As Coleridge lost height beneath the 'enormous & more than perpendicular Precipices & *Bull's-Brows* of Sca'Fell' – a perfect description of the barrel-shaped East Buttress – a thunderstorm began to break and triggered off another epiphany: 'such Echoes! O God! what thoughts were mine! O how I wished for Health & Strength that I might wander about for a Month together in the stormiest month of the year, among these Places, so lonely &

savage & full of sounds!' And he shouted out the names of his family, exulting in the extraordinary 'distinctness & *humanness* of voice' which the mountain walls gave back. He is embracing chaos, making himself at home in it.

A month later he makes the first analysis of climbing psychology. On a day of gusting wind and rain squalls he climbed at Newlands Hause, probably with Charles and Mary Lamb, keeping so close to the edge of Moss Force that he jagged his hands on the rock. He welcomed the fierce conditions because 'I have always found this *stretched & anxious* state of mind favorable to depth of pleasurable Impression, in the resting places & *lounding* Coves' (*Collected Letters*, p 853), ie on the stances where the foregoing tensions can turn into something to be savoured. So the 'Impression', or enjoyed sensation, has become an end in itself, a state to be gone out after and got.

The aesthetics of this are pure Rousseau: like him, Coleridge puts himself in the way of dizzy feelings and delights in the force of waterfalls. On Moss Force he writes, 'What a sight it is to look down on such a Cataract! – the wheels, that circumvolve in it – the leaping & plunging forward of that Infinity of Pearls & Glass Bulbs – the continual *change* of the *Matter*, perpetual *Sameness* of the *Form*'. He is at an age of development beyond Rousseau in his ability to 'say what he is moved by'. Yet he is still some way short of Wordsworth. The scholar A. P. Rossiter – who put up the Wasdale climb called The Gargoyle that I described earlier – has shown that Coleridge melted down his Newlands experience into the poem he published a month later, called 'Hymn Before Sunrise, in the Vale of Chamouni'. He pretended that he had 'involuntarily poured forth' 'Hymn' while he was on Sca Fell but afterwards thought 'the Ideas &c disproportionate to our humble mountains' and transplanted them 'to these grander external objects' – Mont Blanc, the River Arve, the glaciers. The result in the rendering of heightened experience is pure loss. The stock bombast of the waterfall imagery in 'Hymn' – 'Unceasing thunder and eternal foam' and so on – can't compare with the original in his letter: 'in twilight one might have feelingly compared them to a vast crowd of huge white Bears, rushing,

133

one over the other, against the wind – their long white hair shattering abroad'. And when he interprets the experience all he can offer is a kind of hysterical piety, full of 'Awake, my heart' and 'Thou too, hoar Mount!' The quality of the thinking is infant-school hymn, orchestrated for an invisible choir. God is credited with making the flowers and the rainbows, one thing after another is exhorted to utter 'GOD!', and torrents and eagles, ice-falls and lightning, are enlisted in the general roll-call until 'Earth, with her thousand voices, praises GOD.' The result is neither vivid nature poetry nor convincing philosophy.

In contrast Wordsworth evokes the Alpine countryside in rich detail when he writes in 1799 about crossing the Simplon Pass ten years before:

> The immeasurable height
> Of woods decaying, never to be decay'd,
> The stationary blasts of water-falls
> And every where along the hollow rent
> Winds thwarting winds, bewilder'd and forlorn,
> The torrents shooting from the clear blue sky,
> The rocks that mutter'd close upon our ears,
> Black drizzling crags that spake by the way-side
> As if a voice were in them . . .

Description then builds to a philosophical climax, but where Coleridge was merely inspirational, Wordsworth is cogent, working with clear and valid concepts:

> Tumult and peace, the darkness and the light
> Were all like workings of one mind, the features
> Of the same face, blossoms upon one tree;
> Characters of the great Apocalypse,
> The types and symbols of Eternity,
> Of first and last, and midst, and without end.
> – *The Prelude*, VI, lines 556–572

At such points Wordsworth is taking poetry over a watershed into a new mental country. He is having a crucial experience amongst raw nature – a place which has not been brought into the scope of human meanings by cultivation or buildings or even prior myth. There is nothing social to underwrite its significance. He doesn't idealise it as Arcadia in the manner of the Classical poets or absorb it into civilisation as his Augustan forerunners had done by concocting a language based on artifice ('floating Forests paint the Waves with Green' and so on). All that guarantees the value of Wordsworth's experience is his ability to find striking words for heartfelt states of mind, and these could occur (as he emphasises himself) at the most ordinary spots among the Cumbrian mountains – beside a pool on a bare common near Penrith, for example, or in the shelter of a stone wall near Cockermouth in the company of a sheep and a blasted hawthorn. (*The Prelude*, XI, lines 302–316, 350–389)

In terms of origins the difference between the two poets is that Wordsworth climbed rock first as a boy and a youth and knew the uplands intimately over decades, whereas Coleridge climbed on just a few occasions, as a short-term resident near Keswick, almost as a tourist. There flows from them two different but kindred ways of perceiving and frequenting the steeps. Wordsworth understands them as 'local habitations' which have their own culture and entwine themselves over the years with a person's growth until they stand for his vision of life's phases and possibilities. Coleridge reacts to them as sites of heightened sensation, opportunities for ecstasy and dread and thrill. Coleridge's way can be seen as the forerunner of the climbing literature that stresses ego and the private high rather than the nature amongst which we do the experiencing. Wordsworth's way anticipates the literature that finds a source of truths and values in the organic world. The former kind includes the writers about Extreme rock who have drawn styles and attitudes from Modernism and the drug culture; the latter includes Menlove Edwards and W. H. Murray.

Between the Romantics and the moderns there lies, of course, a long trend of evolving attitudes and it is worth noticing some of the landmarks on the way. In 1825 a guidebook to the Lakes opined that Pillar Rock in Ennerdale was 'unclimbable'. By the end of the following year four local shepherds had reached its summit (Alan Hankinson, *The First Tigers*, 1984, pp 35–6) –

firstcomers in a tradition of rubbishing the 'unclimbable' guide-book label that flourishes to this day. In the 1840s two more Romantic poets, Matthew Arnold and A. H. Clough, went up Helvellyn and some members of their party tried a rock-climb on Eagle Crag, Grisedale, a steep outcrop where Jim Birkett put up the last of his routes in the summer of 1954. Between 1850 and 1875 climbs of Pillar rose from two a year to fifty, in 1857 the Alpine Club was founded. The Wetterhorn was climbed by Wills in 1854, the Matterhorn by Whymper in 1865. In America the value of wilderness, philosophised by Thoreau, was built into an institution with the founding of Yellowstone National Park in 1872. Lliwedd's west buttress was first climbed, by Stocker and Wall, in January 1883 and in June 1886 Haskett Smith climbed Napes Needle in Wasdale. These break-outs from the gullies onto the faces of the cliffs set in motion the practice of steep cragging which has never let up from that day to this. During that decade other wilderness activities started up – potholing, seacliff climbing, small-boat sailing – and between 1879 and 1893 Mummery climbed the Matterhorn by six different routes and the Grepon without a guide, on the strength of which he has been credited with 'creating modern mountaineering'. (Hankinson, *The First Tigers*, p 51) In 1890 Yosemite became part of a National Park in California and five years later the National Trust was set up, with a Cumbrian vicar as its first secretary, to 'hold places of historic interest and natural beauty for the benefit of the nation'. At the same time ski-ing was quite suddenly becoming popular in centres like Chamonix.

All this had been happening as Britain changed under the onset of the factory system. In 1790 twice as many people lived in the country as in the towns. By 1830 the opposite was the case. And the cities, growing at breakneck speed, were desperately con-gested, creating a need for space and refreshment, as did the long, enforced hours in the mills. A Lancashire weaver, John Grimshaw, epitomised the condition of millions in two lines of a song –

You musn't walk in your garden for two or three hours a-day.
For you must stand at their command, and keep your shuttles in play.
– *Ballads and Songs of Lancashire*, ed. John Harland, 1882

By the middle of the century rural depopulation was felt to be serious in outlying counties such as Dorset and Cumberland. As people drained away from the dales and the highlands, they also began to flock back for short, idyllic spells: the holiday was invented. It's in this context of growing leisure time, enjoyed at first by the upper and middle classes, that the cult of wild uplands becomes potent, in some cases almost religious.

The best (the only?) living representative of the 'Wordsworthian' tradition is W. H. Murray, a workmanlike historian and novelist as well as a major pioneer of ice and rock routes in Scotland just before and after the Second World War. His twin climbing books, *Mountaineering in Scotland* (1947) and *Undiscovered Scotland* (1951), not only chronicle the old Spartan days when gentleman-climbers referred to each other by their surnames, chopped steps with long-handled ice-axes, swam in mountain lochans before embarking on new thousand-foot routes, and drank Mummery's Blood (a mixture of rum and boiling Bovril) when they got back to the tent in a blizzard; they also seek to interpret peaks of experience in the light of an exalted metaphysical philosophy. Murray's favourite mountain, Buachaille Etive Mór, seen brilliantly moonlit in midwinter, is 'less clogged with the pollutions of mortality than is normally granted to an earthly form'. In the course of this essay, 'Evidence of Things Not Seen', the mountains all around come alive for him. He feels 'their rough honesty go straight to his heart' where it kindles 'a contentment of the same kind, if less high, as that where friendship of two men ripens until the delight of simple companionship removes the need of speech.' When the cloud-sea parts, the lochans on Rannoch Moor become 'hosts of white eyes upturned, calmly looking to the moon'.

Such anthropomorphism comes naturally to Murray, as to all Romantics. At one level it is a vein of metaphor, mined for images that will embody, by projection, the intensity of the writer's feelings among crags and peaks. So Menlove Edwards, in his essay 'End of a Climb' (1937), sees the cliffs and trees above Llanberis as animate beings:

The arms of the sun, as if driven into quick motion, lifted their beams clear of the earth, and the particles of their warmth, despairing, concentrated their last effort in a soft rose light along the western aspect of the strip of cloud. Down on the rocks a squat yew tree, clinging to the face, shivered and drew itself up. The shadows came together and lay cramped stiffly over it.

We turned our backs finally to the hills and began to chatter: setting about to make our minds easy. But behind us, fighting their slow wars, the forces of nature also shifted steadily on.

Jim Perrin, Menlove, 1985, p 317

So Murray hears 'the whole creation', including the clouds and the hills, throbbing 'with a full and new life; its music one song of honour to the beautiful', or again (after doing the first ascent of Parallel Buttress on Lochnagar), 'One heard it circle the world like a lapping tide, the wave-beat of the sea of beauty; and as we listened from our watch tower and looked out across the broad earth, our own little lives and our flush of triumph in climbing a new route became very trivial things.' So far, so conventional. The 'wave-beat of the sea of beauty' is a marvellous Romantic phrase but the 'little lives' idea, entertained as usual at sunset, is a well-worn pebble from the stream of mountain writing, to be found in Leslie Stephen's 'Sunset on Mont Blanc' (*The Playgrounds of Europe*, pp 277–8, 285), in Edwards' 'End of a Climb' (finely expressed: 'We were small to that. So many generations has man been lifting the stones, little stones, big stones, to clear a small pasture'), and in a hundred other places. At this point, however, Murray 'contradicts' himself and a strong thought comes of it:

> Yet in that same instant our climb on the granite crags, the bare summit and the lands below, were with ourselves idealized as though in a point out of time and exalted in oneness. We began to understand, a little less darkly, what it may mean to inherit the earth.

This concept of 'oneness' is from the Romantic mainstream: Wordsworth's perception in *The Prelude* that all those features of the Alps south of the Simplon were 'like workings of one mind . . . blossoms upon one tree,' or Shelley's vision in 'Adonais':

> The One remains, the many change and pass;
> Heavens's light forever shines, Earth's shadows fly;
> Life, like a dome of many-coloured glass,
> Stains the white radiance of eternity . . .

In 'Rocks and Realities' Murray draws on Keats's 'Ode to a Grecian Urn' to affirm that the deep aim of climbing is to 'win fleeting glimpses of that beauty which all men who have known it have been compelled to call truth.' Beauty, truth and oneness, throughout his two books, figure as the same. In his essay on the first ascent of Leac Mhór, the Great Slab on Garbh Bheinn in Ardgour, he writes: ' "My One Beauty is in all things." By the light of the beacon read the word on the mountain-face'. In 'Effects of Mountaineering on Men' he says that beauty, in climbing literature, goes with 'a certainty of the universal unity' or a 'premonition of an ultimate reality, the spiritual ground of things seen.'

Although my respect for Murray's understanding of the mountains (and for the whole of Scotland, especially the islands) could hardly be greater, I'd have to demur at such passages, and finally part company with them, because they lose sight of the earth itself. In 'The Undiscovered Country' he records how, squatting in a slit trench in the Libyan desert of 1942, he had an epiphany of mountains:

> I could see a great peak among fast-moving cloud, and the icy glint where its snow caught the morning sun. There were deep corries and tall crags. All of these were charged with a beauty that did not belong to *them*, but poured through them as light pours through the glass of a ruby and blue window, or as grace through a sacrament.

Shelley again! *This world* is being dislimned, blurred, conjured nearly away, and lofty chimeras take its place. Now we see them, now we don't. On the Buachaille, after being flooded with that sublime mountainscape seen by moonlight over cloud, Argyll and Lochaber visible like 'iceberg islands' and the Rannoch Wall 'pale as shadowed milk, impregnably erect', Murray still hankered after his 'ultimate reality':

> I came down from the summit filled with the acute awareness of an imminent revelation lost; a shadow that stalked at my side ever more openly among the hills. Something underlying the world we saw had been withheld. The very skies had trembled with presentiment of that reality; and we had not been worthy.

'No, no, *no*,' I want to say to him. 'You *had* been worthy of the mountain, by being up there at all. *No* world was withheld; all there was to see, you saw. The beauty *did* belong to them – it *was* them.' For isn't this the truth, which Murray, with his tremendous feeling for the steep places, should be better fitted to see than anybody: that reality is not 'ultimate' at all, it is wholly present? That Welsh rock which bulks out of the fog, its mass rooted deep in the shingle, its sea-worn faces still bearing the stress-marks of its prehistoric forging and tempering, is not a faulty copy of some ideal Rock with a capital R, which lurks somehow, somewhere, on some other plane. There is no Rock, there are only all the particular rocks that stand up out of (or lie still undisclosed in) this tangible planet which is our habitat:

> the very world which is the world
> Of all of us, the place in which, in the end,
> We find our happiness, or not at all.
>   – *The Prelude*, X, lines 726–8

The 'imminent revelation' is never 'lost'. It is there for us to see continuously, at all times, in this rock and in that: in *this* iron-dark scimitar-blade (the last pitch of Centaur on Sca Fell East Buttress) which I grip so strongly to layback up it that my finger-bones wince at its serrations; in *that* corner, indented in the mountain's brow (on Pinnacle Face, Lochnagar), a thick old piton made by some Buchan blacksmith planted in its joint, which secretes oil-black ooze as though hellbent on slithering us off; in *this* pitted rockface (Buckbarrow in Longsleddale) which looks as though shrapnel has been blasted at it to make toothed pockets for the toes; in *that* summit-pile of bone-white quartzite chunks (Spidean a Choire Leith on Liathach) which once, in 1977, so buzzed with static that Julie's hair flew outwards and each lock bristled at its tip like a lightning conductor; in *that* burnished yew bole (on the fourth stance of Overhanging Bastion, Castle Rock of Triermain) which has been so grasped and tied onto by happy, sweating hands that its bared roots splay above the rock-shelf like a stranded arthropod . . . That tree, that summit, that face, that corner, that edge – from those very ones, and their billion siblings, the world is composed. We will find nothing else, however much we yearn and hanker, and we need nothing else. Those crystals and fibres, masses and edges, great graved bulks and exquisitely chiselled details are the parts of the only world there is and the whole of that world is their sum. Nothing of it is 'withheld' (or not forever) and nothing 'underlies' it, except its core, six thousand kilometres in, where rock is three million times as dense as on the surface – and Murray does not mean that!

We can see now that a line culminated in Murray. His outlook is more or less pantheist: 'the world was full of a divine splendour . . . the whole creation had throbbed with a full and new life . . . there was nothing anywhere but He.' In the generation and a half since then it seems to have become that much harder to believe in the Θεος, which leaves only the Παν – the urgent, primitive vitality celebrated in that other branch of the Romantic ethos which specialises in heightened sensation for its own sake. Murray's highmindedness has behind it such semi-secular thinkers as Arnold, who believed that poetry was replacing religion as the medium of aspiration. The new wave of climbing writers, American West Coast based, have behind them the hedonistic or epicurean thinkers like Gautier and Walter Pater who believed in 'burning with a hard gem-like flame', in exquisite or delicious experiences which were asocial or even anti-social. Gautier praised Baudelaire for having upheld 'the absolute autonomy of art and for not admitting that poetry had any aim but itself, or any mission but to excite in the soul of the reader the sensation of beauty, in the absolute sense of the term.' (Plekhanov, *Art and Social Life*, 1957, p 157) Once the social aspect

141

of experience and the use-value of art had been played down in this way, it became the easier to turn in on oneself and explore the subconscious: the *l'art pour l'art* of Gautier is followed by the epoch of Modernism, Surrealism, and Dada. The stream of consciousness, working by free association – letting one image set off another, and another, with mimimum intervention by the reasoning mind – has been available to writers ever since and forms of it surface again and again in what may be called Extreme-rock style.

I first noticed its Joycean hallmarks in Ed Drummond's essay about climbing Great Wall on Cloggy:

> A five-foot arm suspension bridging your life inyourhandat-threefootarmIdon'thavetofalloffSolesstickonicenice. Made it, snug as a nut, my *doigt* in the peg . . . Now you're big enough to fly, jugs come lovely, hands full of rock I go up like a slow balloon, pink knees bumping after me.
>
> – *Hard Rock*, p 141

An almost subliminal sequence of instants is caught by the unpunctuated, unspaced words. For some seconds the climber's mind can't stand back from the experience, he'll only survive if he acts too fast for introspection, and this mental extreme, akin to fantasy or dreaming in which anything at all can skid, lurch, swim through your head, is caught in the extraordinary imagery: knees turn into detached balloons (as in some Modernist painting where the patches of colour have floated free from the edges of the objects); a little later 'Elephants bounce past trumpeting,' and at a crisis on pitch two consciousness splits and 'I' becomes 'he': 'Down I glide, invisible, in the lift, and slip among the staring crowd in the street. He's still up there. He must be holding on to something' – a striking symbolisation of the climber's wishing, at a bad moment, that he was somewhere else.

There is nothing else like that in *Hard Rock*, or in the contemporary British magazines, but two years earlier Drummond had published an even more extreme piece in *Ascent* (San Francisco). *Ascent*, as I know from a letter rejecting a story of mine, prefers its writing 'bizarre and innovative'. Drummond's

'Mirror Mirror' piece is certainly that. The beauty of it is that time after time the Modernist phrasing isn't forced onto the material but grows out of it, out of the almost obscene ordeal which lasted for weeks: two climbers on the 6,000-foot Troll Wall in Norway, sleeping in 'hamouacs', shitting into mid-air past each other's faces, vomiting after drinking brown water that had collected in their boots. When Drummond telescopes words and meanings into each other, it is sometimes sheer Joycean word-fun: 'Two and a half jume-hours later Hugh brooded on the haul eggs, sucking the sacred sweet, as I botched up the freeasy and awkwaid of the next pitch.' Deeper meanings begin to grow as the climb becomes mortally serious, avalanches thunder nearby, bodies deteriorate:

> A week later, his feet out like two heady cheeses in the dim pink light of the tent, Hugh has the mirror. He's checking on the stranger – the first time in twelve days, squeezing his pimples, humming some Neil Young song. For four days we've been in and out of this womb tube, harassed each time we go outside by the web of stuff bags breeding at the hole end. They are our other stomachs . . . By the time I awoke he was gone [a dream apparition] but Hugh hadn't; he was just vanishing down the hole at the other end . . . I oozed out of my pit to find lard-pale Hugh with the blue black foot, sitting stinking in a skinful of sun . . .
>
> – *The Games Climbers Play*, p 31

A sense of personality threatened has begun to lurk in the imagery, sometimes in the form of weird humour (he fears he has trench penis, dreams that the editor of *Mountain* is congratulating him on the great job he's doing for Anglo-Norwegian relations), more often in metaphors which aren't signalled by the usual 'like' or 'as though' but dropped straight into the prose-like facts: 'My fingers, cut deeply at the tips, were almost helpless. People at upstairs windows watching a road accident in the street below. My feet were dying. My silent white hands . . . upon each of my feet a dentist was at work, pulling my nails and slowly filing my toes.'

Such writing is virtually creative. Although it records an actual climb day-by-day, it moves beyond reporting into the minting of phrases that can define the most personal layers of an experience – flights-of-ideas, fantasies, irrational fears, allusions to distant areas of experience. All it lacks is the final artistic decision to depart, where necessary, from the hour-by-hour, semi-journalistic form in order to express an underlying theme. When such a thing crops up, it is too near the end to permeate the piece as a whole: 'I felt that all this was sterile. I ate food, wore out my clothes, used up my warmth, but earned nothing, made nothing . . . I had the cuttings from the Norwegian press, as precious as visas. But nowhere to get to.' For this to build into something that could be called the meaning of the piece, it would surely need to have been touched in and threaded through from an earlier stage. As it is, the extraordinary jokes and metaphors tend to function as single ornaments stitched onto the narrative rather than as a running web of meaning. Nevertheless the piece still stands as a touchstone for climbing literature by virtue of its modernity: the whole gamut of twentieth-century style is felt to be available and what this implies is that climbing is being perceived to be as complex and as integral to the person's whole self and life as any of his other activities.

Ideally, such complexity should bring together person and crag in the one complete experience. In practice the American West Coast idiom is often more aware of self than of the world around. It's fraught with instantaneity, the verbs are violent, syntax is fragmented into verbless phrases, the tense is often the present – vividly present and extremely tense, as when Tom Higgins, a brilliant exemplar of the style, writes about putting up a new 5.11 route in Tuolumne Meadows near Yosemite:

Soon, there is a brain whisper, all jumbled like bearings scattered off a shop table. 'Do. Go. Wrong foot, but do. Why have I . . . ?' The whispering is me but not me. It is like a possession. 'Just do. Fall up. Something. Try that. Do. Do.' Outside myself, I watch a foot near my shoulder. I'm catapulting over little sections, prying and foam-ing, a little crying sound bubbling out. 'Lovely horrible. Lovely horrible.' It's a veritable ricochet of thought bits, not passion, not tactic, but a precious drop of madness. 'It goes. Lovely horrible goes.

144

Bitch! Sweet bitch! Foot flake. Nail hold. Enough. Go! There! Go!'
Finally, there is a platform for most of my foot. With rest, the fire
fades and logic returns.

— 'In Thanks', *Ascent*, 1975/1976

That would be hard to better as an enactment in words of 'events
when the intricacies of each second of thought would fry the
circuits of a computer' (Greg Child, in *Mirrors in the Cliff*, p 19).
Spurts of adrenalin, stabs of realisation, the violent seesawing
between terror and elation, between repulsion at the extreme
experience and acceptance of it: this seething mixture is caught in
a prose which seems to be existing at the instant of the happening
rather than in recollection. How far style has changed from the
methodical analysis which marks Murray's most evocative
passage about hard rock moves (in his account of the second
ascent of Rubicon Wall on the Observatory Buttress of Ben
Nevis):

> The typical move, which stays in mind with all the freshness of the
> day's encounter, was that of hoisting myself up to a mantel by the
> down-press of my right palm, of lodging the left foot on that same
> mantel at hip-level, and then, without further handhold, straighten-
> ing the left leg, my sense of balance preserved by hands fluttering up
> the wall above and the right toe lifting against the wall below.

— *Mountaineering in Scotland*, p 54

Only 'fluttering' has any immediacy. Murray barely tries for this
quality. What he does remember to evoke is the lay-out of the
rockface, the looks and personalities of the other climbers, the
distant views. His account of the moves he had to make is so
precise that I'm reminded of at least five places where I've been
forced to do the same. Other Extreme climbers might recognise
Tom Higgins's fevered thought-stream but, from that passage,
they would not be able to recognise the moves he made. His sense
of anything outside his head is confined to the occasional bizarre
metaphor ('the domes standing witness, their polish gleaming
like the eyes of cold and riveted fathers') and a couple of short
asides about previous climbers.

This fiercely self-centred concentration on the moment as it happens could be seen as the inevitable style for Extreme climbing. But such an explanation would miss out one whole factor, the influence of drugs, an aid to perception which the West Coast scene shares with Coleridge. The same climber who used the image of overheated computer circuits mentions this directly in his account of the second ascent of Pacific Ocean Wall on El Capitan: 'Kim reaches us and suddenly has the grim realisation that he has forgotten our vital life support and mellowing-out formula – the grass. Darryl begins to foam at the mouth and I have to beat him over the head to stop him from chewing through Kim's rope.' ('Pacific Cruise'; *Mountain*, May/June 1978) This is so foreign to me that I can barely imagine it. My physical and mental hardihood have to be at their most stable for me to climb with enough confidence to enjoy myself and even a small whisky or a pint of beer in the hours before a climb would make me afraid that I had weakened myself. But there are more positive reasons for climbing in a normal, not a doped-up, state, and they are well put by climbers of the highest ability. John Gill is recognised to be the master of bouldering – climbing unroped on short, extremely testing passages of rock – and in 'Reflections of a Middle-aged Boulderer' he writes with benign wit about the epiphanies that can flow from a pure and unmediated experience of the rock: 'Long easy solo climbs done smoothly and continuously can arouse the sensation of weaving in and out of the rock. I've had this fascinating and drug-free experience on a number of occasions, and do not recall ever leaving a hand or foot embedded in the stony matrix.' (*Mountain*, July/August 1986) Doug Scott tackles the issue directly in his 1971 account of climbing the Salathé Wall on El Capitan. His nickname for tripping on drugs is 'the profundity trail' and what his essay evokes (without any Modernist devices) is the ecstasy he achieved from the climbing itself: 'Not for us popping a pill or drinking spiked apple cider to get eight hours of unimagined sensory splendour'. He's saying this in the teeth of the sub-culture that had grown up in Yosemite: 'Most of the acid heads, wrapped up in old blankets, were lying huddled in a heap around a burnt-out fire. A few more were reflecting by the Merced, smoking weed as the mist rose out of the river'. He allows at the end that perhaps the 'doors of perception' were not opened as wide for him as for the acid heads, yet he perceived the place with such intensity, a drop of water trickling down dusty granite, a frog hopping along a ledge two thousand-feet up the rockface, that tears welled into his eyes as he stood on a ledge after three days of climbing. Amongst crackling pinecones on the top he smelt the trees and looked out over the pink sunset snows of the High Sierra, 'guzzling in these new sensations like a greedy child, hoping this beautiful experience would never end.' (*Mountain*, May/June 1971)

Drugs aren't the necessary route to sublime visions, they're just a convenience to that end which happens to be prevalent in our society, fuelling a hectic lifestyle which has penetrated the climbing sub-culture as it has most others. As Greg Child writes in the article whose title, 'Coast to Coast on the Granite Slasher', epitomises the culture of speed in both its senses:

> . . . a hyperkinetic hotshot from the Bay Area named Zacher talked me into a free repeat of the West Face of El Cap. He talked so fast I had no chance to refuse.
>
> That's the parking lot though, a market place for partners, gear and simple amusements. People you hardly know will ask you to launch off on all manner of routes. All manner of people too. Sometimes the walls echo to the screaming matches of teams in the throes of divorce. Small issues take on strange dimensions on walls.
>
> – *Mirrors in the Cliffs*, p 24

Child himself must be very tough in mind as well as body to have kept it together all the way up those giant walls, yet in 'Pacific Cruise' he uses an imagery drawn from climbing equipment to suggest a vulnerability, an anxious awareness of how fragile sanity is, which is uncomfortably like the worry a drinker feels as he tries to retrieve a few clear images through the jittery haze of a hangover:

> Fully aware that in no time at all I'll be old and senile, my hands twisted with arthritis and the memories of youth flickering dully like a waning candle, I can lose no time at all in relating this tale. A race

147

against time: it's only a matter of moments before my brainweight pulls the teetering rurp [a protection device] that holds the memory together and unzips the entire string of flimsy aids from the present, the whole recollection of the climb falling into oblivion. Like so much suds sucked down the sink.

Such are the ironies of history. A sport which might seem to represent a high point in our happy interaction with the natural world has taken to dabbling heavily in one of the more sophisticated ways of tampering with it, of boosting and forcing it into tortuous paths. As Coleridge was spirited to Xanadu on the wings of laudanum (then lost it as the high broke down), so climbers have made the journey to Ixtlan with the help of grass, speed and acid. The evidence litters the scene in all those route names that reek of altered consciousness: Journey to Ixtlan itself, on the towering sea-cliff of Carn Gowla in north Cornwall; Acid Rock, a section of the Cheddar cliffs, which has spawned some blithe and charming names in keeping with the carefree nature of our sport, like Schizoid and Paranoid; and Cannabis and Pusher and Addiction on a limestone edge near Settle, facing the sun above a perfect pastoral village – because the crag happens to be called Pot Scar; to say nothing of Morphine, Syringe, Hypodermic, Cocaine Place, Mescalito, Magic Mushroom, Tangerine Trip, Street Legal, Living at the Speed, Bittersweet Connection, and on and on into the more shambolical and pseudophilosophical reaches of hippy culture with The Tower of Bizarre Delights, The Birth of Liquid Desire, A Separate Reality, Atomic Strawberries, Decompensator of Lhasa . . . To change the subject only a little, we may speculate that a cultural historian will find evidence of late twentieth-century morale in the willingness of climbers to affix the following names to innocent and often beautiful tracts of nature: Colostomy, Hysterectomy, Cystitis by Proxy, Rubber Panty, Sexcrime, Mass Murderer, Organ Flagellator, and When Dildos Ruled the Earth.

It would be wrong to close this account of Extreme style by dwelling on its crazy fringe. Where its powers of hallucinatory immediacy have been married with a moral sense and a love of place, it has given rise to essays of a creative wholeness, for example John Long's piece about soloing at Joshua Tree in Colorado, a desert decorated with huge abstract sculptures – single rocks so beautiful that the place is listed as a National Monument. It is Mecca for the world's best free climbers. There they can play their unbelievable games of chicken – soloing two hundred-foot routes on rockwalls at an angle of 105°. After two thousand feet of this mortal sport, Long set out to follow his mate John Bachar up a route on Intersection Rock. His near-disaster on the crux raises him to this vivid contemplation of 'last things':

I glance beneath my legs and my gut churns at the thought of a hideous free fall onto the gilded boulders. That 'little' voice is bellowing: 'Do something! Pronto!' My breathing is frenzied while my arms, trashed from the previous 2000 feet, feel like titanium beef steaks. Pinching that little wafer, I suck my feet up so as to extend my arm and jam my hand in the bottoming crack above; the crack is too shallow, will accept only a third of my hand. I'm stuck, terrified, and my whole existence is focussed down to a pinpoint which sears my everything like the torrid amber dot from a magnifying glass. Shamefully, I understand the only blasphemy: to wilfully jeopardise my own existence, which I've done, and this sickens me. I know that wasted seconds could . . . then a flash, the world stops, or is it preservation instincts booting my brain into hyper gear? In the time it takes a humming bird to wave its wings – once – I've realised my implacable desire to live, not die!; but my regrets cannot alter my situation: arms shot, legs wobbling, head ablaze. My fear has devoured itself, leaving me hollow and mortified . . .
        – 'The Only Blasphemy', *Mountain*, January/February 1982

Long's notation for momentaneous feelings is exact. The violent verbs are not the sadomasochistic swagger some climbing writers have taken over from the Spillane type of thriller, they're justified by the extremity of the state he's evoking. And he evaluates those states to reach a salutary conclusion about himself: no sooner has he risen to the tremendous 'amber dot' image than he comes out with that damning 'only blasphemy'. The episode leaves him not exhilarated but chastened. In keeping with 'hollow and mortified' he reaches an end among images that compose a glum hippy fantasy: next day he 'wandered through dark desert corridors, scouting for turtles, making garlands from wild flowers, relishing the skyscape, doing all those things a person does on borrowed time'.

Allowing for the difference between memoir and a fully-created work of art, such writing can fairly be treated as cousin to a strong family of recent poems – innovative in phrasing but less so than in Eliot's heyday, excelling at a highly physical language for states of mind, disinclined to philosophise whether ethically or metaphysically, intent on doing justice to drastic experiences beyond the rim of civilisation: 'through the sharp details which bring them so threateningly to life, they reach back, as in a dream, into a nexus of fear and sensation. Their brute world is part physical, part state of mind'. Doesn't this precisely fit the essays discussed above? Yet it is from one of the most influential critiques of poetry written in recent years: the introduction to the anthology called *The New Poetry* published by Penguin in 1962 by Al Alvarez. Alvarez himself was no mean climber: with Peter Biven, greatest of south-west climbers in the Fifties and Sixties, he put up two routes on Lundy, one of them the imposing Lucifer on Focal Buttress, and he followed Pete Crew on the second ascent of a major route on Anglesey, Gogarth, as Ian McNaught Davis relates in *Hard Rock*. Alvarez' thesis in *The New Poetry* is that poets in our time, however implicitly, write as they do because we are in the aftermath of the world wars, the death camps, the Bomb, and also of the psychoanalytic movement, which has shown us how much of the public violence lurks also in ourselves. The poet who bulks largest in the book is Ted Hughes, who has written more potently about rock than any other writer known to me, especially in the bestiary of gritstone that he weaves through the book he made with Fay Godwin in 1979, *Remains of Elmet*. Rock, not rock-climbing, is his subject but his sequence called 'Prometheus on His Crag' (in *Moortown* of the same year) matches uncannily well with the epic ordeals of climbers who bivouac on big walls night after night.

Prometheus On His Crag
Tried to recall his night's dream –

Where wrists and ankles were anchored, in safe harbour,
And two cosmic pythons, the Sea and the Sky,

Fought for the earth – a single jewel of power.
And the hammer-splayed head of the spike through his chest
Was a swallowtail butterfly, just trembling,

And neither wrist nor ankle must move –
And he dared hardly look at the butterfly,
Hardly dared breathe for the pain of joy

As it lasted and lasted –
                                    a world
Where his liver healed to being his liver.

But now he woke to a world where the sun was the sun,
Iron iron,
            sea sea,
                        sky sky,
                                    the vulture the vulture.

What strikes me is partly the physical likeness of the experiences,
partly the sense of opposed emotions inseparably fused (with 'the
pain of joy' compare Tom Higgins's reiterated 'lovely horrible'),
and partly the vision of humanity as occupying a perch tensioned
precariously above chaos.

Such a sense of things is a far cry from Murray, whose
rootedness in a long tradition of inspirational writing and
thinking enabled him to distil supportive meanings from his
experiences of wilderness and to find in the steep places 'the
ultimate reality', 'One Beauty', 'truth made manifest'. His books
and essays climb to exalted and positive conclusions where recent
writers tend to end up emptied and aimless, as Drummond does
after the Troll Wall; Long after Intersection Buttress; Rand, the
hero of James Salter's novel *Solo Faces* (1979), who has nothing to
live for after he has reached his climbing limit; or the many
big-mountain climbers who feel nonplussed at what should be a
supreme moment: the commonest sentence in their accounts of
reaching a summit is 'We felt no elation'. Murray may have felt

that he had just missed a revelation on the Buachaille but throughout his work we sense that he is at one with the steeps. In Existentialist terms, he is situated in them, not estranged from them. The 'ultimate reality' he craves to see at least belongs to a well-founded cosmos in which he is at home. The more recent writers seem to have no such access to sure foundations: when Drummond makes an Existential point in 'Mirror Mirror' he uses capital letters to mock any such certitude: 'To climb is to know the universe is All Right.' The good feeling, he implies, is fragile and can't last. We can no longer believe that the beauty of the crags 'pours through them' from some source 'underlying the world'. Rock is only itself, the sky is simply the sky and the vulture the vulture.

20

Climbing's fertility as a seed-bed for creative uses of language springs, I believe, from its essence as a sport. So much of your time on the rockface is necessarily still, contemplative, alternating with intense spells which plumb your innermost self and make fresh material available to your imagination. This is necessary in that you must focus your sharpest perception on the rock to pick holds and estimate angles and also, in extreme cases, where a discipline like meditation seems to be the only way to survive. Menlove Edwards in an essay called 'Letter from a Man' imagines a moment in the Alps when contemplating the sunset colouring the snows of the Weisshorn and the Matterhorn 'was of the greatest assistance to me: for shifting a little against the pressure of the rope loops in which I sat I was able to stare fixedly at it, and forget all else.' Here he seems to have been drawing on a desperate episode in midwinter 1935–6 when he rowed a boat, alone, from Gairloch north of Torridon across to the coast of Lewis and back again: 'Time and again I stood up, and staring fixedly at it [sunset light on the mainland coast] here and there, was able to forget all else.' (Perrin, *Menlove*, pp 319, 160) Those passages probably define a means of escape from stresses that could crush morale. But the thing has a positive face too: a rock-master of the Seventies and Eighties, Pat Littlejohn, has been described by his second, Jim Perrin, as 'staring fixedly at the piece of rock in front of him', on a new route on the Pembroke sea-cliffs, in an 'eerie, fascinating aura' of 'absolute quietude'. When Perrin asked him about it – was it like meditation? – Littlejohn described an experience on a nearby cliff when he would come down from a crux for a rest and stick his head in a hole: 'if you asked me now, I could draw you the inside of that hole in exact detail.' And his hands gestured to shape the textures of rock with the 'motions of delight' which Perrin had also seen in a craftsman-carpenter. (*Climber and Rambler*, March 1982)

Equally, if you're a climbing writer, you're hard up against, almost inside, your subject; it's inches from your nose and eyes. Behind your eyes, behind your *front* (the word still has for me the Latin connotation of 'forehead'), your mind teems, both with physical perceptions – often of tiny things: a pellet of fur and bone hawked up by a peregrine stuck to a crystal, or rust weeping from the stub hammered in by the first person to tread this way a generation before – and also with self-images. On a climb that frightens me, my self feels to me like an overheated cave; doubts of my adequacy flicker and dart like a maddened bat; not until this uncontrollable soot-black monster deigns to retreat into the deepest shadow and pretend to fold his wings in sleep can I muster my fingers, forearms, and toes, my balance and my daring, and apply this mixed bag of faculties to the leaving of this vantage-point and the moving against gravity to the next.

It's natural, then, that uncommon awareness and a habit of self-expression have been common in climbing history. A recent anthology of British mountain poetry, *Speak to the Hills* (1985), was able to list in its rock-climbing section a cluster of reputable poets (including Louis MacNeice, W. S. Graham, Patric Dickinson, James Simmons, John Fuller and Fleur Adcock). Robert Graves climbed difficult routes in Snowdonia with Mallory just before the Great War and was told by the climber-poet Geoffrey Winthrop Young that he had 'the finest natural balance' he had seen in a climber. At the height of his own enthusiasm he wrote that climbing 'made all other sports seem trivial' and in *Goodbye to All That* (1929) he records a fine physical image of the well-being that springs from it: 'I remember wondering at my body – the worn fingernails, the bruised knees, and the lump of climbing muscle that had begun to bunch above the arch of the foot, seeing it as beautiful in relation to this new purpose.' I. A. Richards, the father of modern literary criticism, loved to climb with his wife Dorothy Pilley and both wrote eloquently about it in poems and prose – in a Borrowdale climbing hut the other day I found the handwritten note of what may have been their last mountain walk in England, in the same logbook as my eldest son's record of some of his first hard routes.

The original, and most condensed, climbing poems are the names of the routes, which can be brilliant sparks of meaning when they get beyond the primitive epoch of 'D Route' or 'Route One' (and stop short of the final degeneracies listed above). Pete Livesey has coined extraordinary phrases for his routes: Dry Grasp, on Upper Falcon Crag in Borrowdale, fuses surface meaning (the need for frictiony handholds) with under-meaning (throat dried by fear); and across the dale on Goat Crag the name of his hardest climb, Footless Crow, has the surreal folk wit of phrases like 'clockwork orange' mixed with the implication (or so I read it) that a crag so steep is fitter for some maimed or hybrid bird than for us normal animals. Pat Littlejohn borrowed the inspired Joycean name Darkinbad the Brightdayler for his fearsome route up the sombre expanse of Pentire Head between Tintagel and Padstow, and Drummond's lyrical line for his best-known route on Anglesey, A Dream of White Horses, has been inventively mocked in A Nightmare of Brown Donkeys on High Tor above Matlock.

None of my own little handful of new routes has been named from poetic sources, although a limestone line near home has been called Old Man's Sleeve from a line of Eliot's in 'Little Gidding' because there is an ash on it and because by the time

Terry and I climb it, our combined ages will probably be about one hundred. But Ezra Pound was almost instrumental on one climb we did on Dow Crag. Leafing as usual through the First Ascent list at the back of the guide to get a sense of the relevant history, I noticed under 1940 (placed oddly between 1945 and 1947) a route put up by Jim Birkett and V. Veevers, called North Wall. Birkett's brief partnership with Veevers (who worked in Cumbrian forests during the war) achieved some fine things – Tophet Grooves on the Napes, F Route on Gimmer, where I had my longest leader fall and ended upside down looking into the eyes of my very inexperienced second. 'An "exposed and serious route",' I read out to Terry, 'with "doubtful rock in parts". Sounds good. What do you say?' Terry doesn't say much, being understandably (as a foreigner from Sheffield) under the in-fluence of Cram, Eilbeck, and Roper's book of selected routes: it says nothing about cold, damp, swarthy faces like this North Wall, which could only give the Lake District a bad name.

We enter Great Gully, looking for our start, and at once we're in the world of Sadak in search of the waters of oblivion. This terrific painting by John Martin, a rival of Turner's, can now be seen in Tobias and Drasdo's *The Mountain Spirit*. I had first noticed it in a tiny black and white reproduction in the *Listener* some time in the Fifties and ever since it had haunted me as a symbol of extreme exertion in pursuit of a remote goal. The mad Hebrew king, naked except for a loincloth, is doing a hard mantelshelf onto a cracked, wet ledge. An ice-white cascade pours past him. His muscles strain and twist. Dark prows rear over him. Thousands of feet above, a shaft of light splits the mountains. Exactly the feel of caving in Gaping Ghyll under Ingleborough or gullying inside Dow Crag. We reach our goal by squeezing through a green gob between two huge boulders. It's a world of submarine shade, like the demon's grotto in a pantomime. As I get high on the atmosphere, I start quoting one of Pound's *Pisan Cantos*:

The ant's a centaur in his dragon world . . .
Pull down thy vanity, I say pull down.

Learn of the green world what can be thy place
In scaled invention or true artistry . . .
But to have done instead of not doing
    this is not vanity . . .
    To have gathered from the air a live tradition
or from a fine old eye the unconquered flame
This is not vanity
    Here error is all in the not done,
    all in the diffidence that faltered.

Convinced by this, or possibly by my fondling and slapping of
the one hold hereabouts at the base of the North Wall, a creaking
black saw-blade rather like the key holds on the final wall of
Birkett's first masterpiece, Overhanging Bastion, Terry uncoils
the rope.

I tie on, grasp the blade, and stretch toes left to mini-ramps,
one-inch wide and four-inches long. They slope up leftwards to
the first reassuring feature, a facet like a paving stone tilted at
thirty degrees. Everything is green but dry: the algae have been
killed by the three glowing summer months of 1983. The
toeholds are too far to reach. I hold the blade by its left extremity,
try to extend my left leg like a telescope but it's only flesh and
bone, my trousers nearly split, and then my foot lodges, I swing
along on fingerholds, and upward flow sets in. I put on one silly
runner too near the start to be of any use. Thirty feet later I put in
two small wired nuts that fidget in their crack, then twitch out
with upward pull and whizz down towards Terry like the little
canisters in the shops of my childhood that carried change and
receipts from the counting-house to the assistants.

By now the words 'serious' and 'doubtful', especially 'doubtful', have been working on me, making fears fester. I climb in
chary slow-motion, grasping the fine rough tops of big blocks
and flakes as though they were glass on a greenhouse roof.
Nothing shifts. Nothing breaks off. I'm in a world of bulging,
grubby faces, cracks choked with silt, pieces of dark stone
jammed into each other and probably well set for the next few
centuries. Their lichenous surfaces suggest the stomachs of very
old Mediterranean tramps. And I do feel about as secure as a

stranger venturing along the waterfront in Marseilles or Naples. An 'overhung grass ledge' is promised, with poor belays and a doubtful block. 'Better to continue,' it says grimly. I long to stop, and set feet on dry solidity, but this grass is primal Cumbrian verdure, grass before climbers and before sheep. Perfect green tresses of it sprout out and down in glossy curves. What's under them? Could I crouch securely below the bristling black pelt of that overhang? There's so little guidance, no red or blue fluffs of nylon pile, no matches or filter-tips, not a scratch or a trace of sweat-polish. It's an alarming freedom, heady and keen. I embrace a tottering turret, pull round and up and along and out and up, with no great objective difficulty, until I have run out one hundred and ten feet since my last runner. A second ledge arrives, a narrow meadow, or at least an alp. The sunlit world again, or it would have been several hours ago. In the light of normality across the gully, two seasoned Lancashire climbers are ambling up the top pitches of Broadrick's Route. Above us, red shirts and grey breeches are disappearing over the skyline on Gordon and Craig's. Relief and contentment bubble through me and I chant down to Terry, 'Error is all in the not done, All in the diffidence that faltered.' He pulls up fluently, with just an exhaled 'Wow!' after that first teetering traverse. Presently we're agreeing that the whole climb felt like putting up a route and not like climbing a solid ladder of precedent. How pleasing, then, to have won a fierce pleasure in spite of the safety-net of printed words. And how absurd to have let the printed words 'serious' and 'doubtful' eat in even as much as they did. But at least we did gather a live tradition from the air as we followed the flame of Birkett's fine old eye.

Quoting poetry in that place had felt as natural as pulling upwards. Terry, a remarkable teacher of poetry, made a poem out of our climb soon afterwards and on another occasion I found myself, stirred to the quick by climbing near my limit, composing lines as I climbed, or at least as I belayed. It was the shortest day of 1984. Ed Drummond, Terry, and I were perched on the saddle of a promontory jutting west out of Holyhead Mountain on Anglesey into the Celtic Sea and looking down into Wen

Zawn – the white inlet. It's seething, the waves lift slow and bulky and burst suddenly, propelled by a force-eight gale. Rain hits our anoraks like grapeshot, pelmets of fog lour and droop on South Stack lighthouse, the airstream throws us off balance and makes breathing difficult when we face into the wind. Across the rocking water is our goal – what was our goal as we planned at home over roast chicken and red wine – the crag of quartzite that armours Wales at this point, three hundred-feet high, seamed with cracks. Ed found one of the first ways up it sixteen years ago – A Dream of White Horses. For seven months we've been exchanging poems between his home in San Francisco and mine in Cumbria. Now we're here to pluck his route from the teeth of winter but it looks madly unfeasible. We couldn't live in that maelstrom. A thread of waterfall near the start of the traverse pitch is blowing sideways and upwards. Plunging white waters bury the roots of pitch one. Ed looks and looks, saying little. Then, 'If you don't mind, I think we'll leave it. It doesn't look good. In these conditions.'

Pause. I say, 'I'm glad you've said that. Because it looks terrible to me. I'm glad you didn't feel you had to decide for it, for my sake.'

'Let's walk round and down the slope to the notch on the arête, and have a good look at the whole of the zawn.'

The nearer we creep to the sea, the less drastic is the wind, away from the focused updraught.

'Will you belay me?' says Ed. 'And I'll have a look' – now using 'look', apparently, in the Scottish climbers' sense of 'go and climb it although it's clearly impossible'. Why am I not terrified? Because there's still a stage or two of non-commitment before I have to step into the vortex? Ed climbs unhesitatingly down a groove (to reach the start of the traverse), tiptoes out along a tapering ledge, fixes a nut in a crack, and manoeuvres onto the wall, through the cascade, into the grey, fleeing world of spindrift and squall. Even the wintry twilight (at eleven in the morning) feels to be against us, subduing life. I chill and qualm as Ed places his left tiptoe on an invisible feature, poises with fingerends on other invisibilities, and clings with his right foot

158

frictioning. Seconds tick. Nimble foot-change, then a mantis's or gekko's locomotion left and upwards. Can I do that? I can't do that. But we're inside the experience now, the huge looming and sucking fear has moved beyond the rim of vision, the climb is happening, it's controlling me, its practical demands locking onto me, supplanting emotions.

After fifteen minutes' enthralled spectating as this modern rock-master moves at his ease up and down the first big crack, holding onto the rope with one hand, establishing a hanging belay where he roosts like a large orange bird, I untie from my anchor and clamber down the groove. It should feel like lowering into a bottomless ocean but no, all is possible, at our command. Ed's total competence flows along the rope. His smile of steady geniality, just visible, shows through the on-ding like a lantern. Under his guava-pink balaclava he looks like Punch, like an Andean shepherd steering his flock through a clouded pass, like the Pied Piper playing us into the hillside: contradictory symbols have begun to form.

Commitment time. From now on each perch will be precarious, spreadeagled; retreat from the razor-edge no easier than what lies ahead. As I cling to take a runner off, my fingers chill down towards the zone of incapacity, strength ebbs, command wavers. But a cat's cradle of manageability has been woven along the cliff. At the crux I shout into the wind, 'Looks difficult,' and Ed shouts back, 'Good little ledge level with your hip.' Well remembered – there it is – a rung of possibility in the midst of nothingness. I press more blood out of my congealing fingerends, brachiate to the slim vantage-point (four inches by one and a quarter), and try to will the next stage. I don't want to move, to take my left foot off terra-firma and trust my compulsively curling fingers yet again. I must. I pull up a foot or two, lock my arms bent at right angles, shimmy my feet, and it's happening – I'm in balance – the abyss of nothing, of non-possibility, has firmed over and turned material. I reach for a protruding rim of quartz, it's rough below its film of wet, in ten seconds I'm stretching for the krab on the soaked yellow sling that hangs from a fang of rock below Ed's feet. I clip on, plant my feet, lean backwards at my ease, and chat happily on the flush of adrenalin.

As the wind poured its moisture and the winter day gloomed darker and darker, Ed decided against finishing the route by the overhangs, where the climbing is less hard but a slip could leave you hanging above an implacable sea-cave. We climbed homewards up pitch two of Joe Brown's route Wen, the first way to be discovered up this cliff, a near-vertical ladder of chunky black holds as convenient as an old-fashioned route in the Dolomites. Up on the skyline something was looking down at us, a family of heads poised on a ledge, great green brains, exposed most tenderly as though they lived in an air and country so benign they had no need of skulls, yet here they grew, these bulging tumps of sea-thrift, worried by windstream and our red rope fretting at their stems. As Ed pulled over onto their ledge and his silhouette merged with theirs, he fused with a brain, vanished into it – annihilated to a green thought, no doubt, and as I followed ten minutes later and made it into earshot, I shouted up to him, 'Brains, they are – you vanished into a brain!' And he laughed back down, 'Oh *no*! I'd hoped that they were breasts and I was suckling up to them!'

From that moment, and the earlier sight of his pink balaclava through the spindrift, a four-page sequence grew outwards on various lines, until it started with a seal who had been swimming next to the broken water when we arrived – the one being dense with blood in all that wan dilution, all that waning towards zero, who had steadied there for quarter of an hour, focusing his eyes of a loving Labrador on our eccentric antics, solidarising with his fellow-mammals that some freak wave had tossed onto this stark slab where there was no couching-place – and ended with a view of what it had taken to manage the climb in the thick of all that instability.

Living the Dream

Ed traverses, steadily diminishing
In slow reverse zoom, withdrawing himself
From our nervous cameraderie – perching
On this eyrie notched between the forever
Collapsing earth-fall smelling of blood and fat
(Generations of fulmars brooding, regurgitating)
And the ocean's tilting and breaking.
He traverses, creating our zone
Of survival, negotiating
The boundaries of this corridor
Between land's end and the sea's shattering,
Testing his chain of the possible
As he works along it, weighing
Its superfine links, cold-forged
By the wind's hammer, tempered slowly
Under the salty drainings
Of the spume's condensing, framing
A basketwork of safety along the face
(Adamant alloy wedges, lissome rope)
Until his Punch-smile, widening,
Signals 'Come' and he plays us
Over into his niche where home is
For a time, where Holyhead Mountain
Opens the stone lips of its haven.

This is the shortest day. The lighthouse
Projects its miniature sunset into the fog.

The seals have all gone under the sea.
The climbers have all gone home from the hill.

To climb A Dream of White Horses with one of its authors had the fascination of a time-warp. For nine years I had been looking at Leo Dickinson's photo of the first ascent in *Hard Rock* – the striated shield of foam-white rock, the spindrift ghosting straight up out of the surf and reaching out twin arms to wet the climbers' dangling ropes. That image had become literally a memory of my own and it gave it another layer of reality to know that cells within cells of further, more involved images of the place were housed in the hive of Ed's head, a few yards from my own. It resonated specially for him too, signalling his return (perhaps for good) to Europe, reminding him of when he reclimbed it with his son Howarth a few years before.

Climbing history is a tiny twig on the whole cultural tree, no doubt, but it still forms a delicately continuous trace back into the past. How had earlier climbers found those lines which had once been only a web of potentiality, hidden in the rockface, but were now meshed into the culture via all those words and names and photographs and paintings? What had it been like to push out into the steep unknown when ropes were short and weak and there was so little protection gear that a fall would be likely to injure or kill you? How lonely had the crags and mountains felt when rock-climbers were few (today there are more than fifty thousand) and the lack of cars meant that it took extra determination to get far into the dales (today 120,000 people walk over the summit of Ingleborough each year)?

Wanting to get as near such experiences as possible, and also to naturalise myself a little more in this second homeland, Cumbria, I phoned Jim Birkett several times in the autumn of 1981, asking to interview him about his climbing career a generation ago. He had answered in the shortest possible speeches, 'We had some fun', 'People don't want to know about us', sentences like that, before his final 'No – I won't bother.' His self-contained lack of desire for limelight is well known and I completely respect that: it was his life, why project or mediate it? But I still wanted to reach back into history. 'W. Peascod' was the other name that cropped up all through the guidebooks' First Ascent lists, from 1938 to 1952, and 'W. Peascod' had recently proved that he was still alive by writing a funny, scathing letter to the *Climber and Rambler* satirising the notion of tourist equipment in the mountains – noticeboards, turnstiles, slot-machines . . . On March 13 1982 I wrote to the address against his name in the phonebook and on March 18 he replied: 'I would be pleased to take part in your project and would, in fact, be most interested in repeating some of the climbs with you.'

His most famous route is Eagle Front, five hundred feet of exploration up and across and again up the face of the biggest mountain cliff in England (equal with the main face of Sca Fell), a whole country of rocky spurs festooned with ferns and hyacinth grass, gullies black with perpetual drainage cleaving slantways between towering buttresses that stand out stark and grizzled above the floor of the big corrie, Birkness Combe. Bill first climbed it on June 23 1940 with his regular partner, Bert Beck, an English teacher. His second ascent of it was also the second by anybody, in the summer of 1948, partnered by a fellow miner from Workington, George Rushworth. Since then he had lived for twenty-eight years in Australia, climbing nothing harder than Hard Severe, and in 1972 he had suffered a massive coronary. Now, re-settled in his native county, he had resumed hard climbing but he had also spent a quarter of a century living with the expectation that he would never again reclimb his own classic routes. In *Journey After Dawn* he records that he expected, with me, to do no more than 'visit somewhere gentle and pleasing . . . in the sun'. But the drought of April 1982, and the radiant sunshine on April 19, encouraged me to try for the Big One while the Eagle was, for once, not shaking the water from its feathers.

We arrive at the toe of the crag. Bill slaps the rock and shouts out, 'Well, old girl – I'm back!' 'Ack-ack-ack' echoes from Grey Crag, across the bowl of mountains. 'Bert was a great cairn builder,' he says, looking keenly round for the piled stones, but they can't be seen. Bill adorns himself with a selection of wired and hexagonal nuts from my harness and leads off upwards, finding clean ribs among the little wild gardens of heather and hyacinth grass, its blades seared dull copper by the winter frosts. He is a short and chunky figure with a broad chest, slightly bowed legs with massive calves, a miner's hefty shoulders, and thick knuckly hands. I begin to recognise the surprised chuckles with which he greets each chance for a runner placement, a sound between 'Aah' and 'Wow'. He and Bert Beck usually climbed with two rope loops each, two karabiners (one a screw-gate, vintage 1939), a thick hemp rope, and boots nailed round the welts with clinkers or Tricounis. As their standards of difficulty rose they took more and more to climbing dry rock in Woolworths pumps, which they called 'rubbers'. After the War more krabs became available, from ex-Commando stock, and they also took to using parachute cord for slings – 'eighth-weight nylon,' which Bill doubts would have held a leader fall.

The crag steepens and begins to exact our best efforts. We're now weaving across the face like parasites in the pelt of a bear. The rock is awkward, resistant, grained the 'wrong' way – footholds slope steeply, you have to step up on friction again and again and find little keys for the fingers, about one per crux, letterbox-slots, natural triangular chips, and the occasional sharp pocket. The cliff is bearded with leaves and tussocks, its back to the sun. Its rambling bulk, the maze of dead-ends, 'obvious black corners', and growthy terraces, the torrent of scree down its northern flank remind me of the Mainreachan Buttress – not as loose or as high but so inhospitable compared with the burnished architecture of Gimmer or Bosigran. Corrugated brows frown. Pocked faces stare stonily. I get the hang of it and pull pleasurably up steep scoops, stride along glaces, and chatter down to Bill, inviting him to marvel at the decadence of us moderns with our fancy metal toys to fit every weakness of the rock. As he picks his way up, he exclaims, sighs, chuckles, all in a spirit of wondering respect for his own young hardihood: 'I don't know, I must have had the hide of a . . .' A wilderness of rock now rears and shears away on every side. Stance five is a bevel of rock running along an exposed face. What a place to have been the first person ever to reach, with no sure foreknowledge of the way out or up! There is nothing to belay on but pitons: three of them, one of each main kind, are arrayed like museum exhibits along the crack behind the bevel, the oldest frail with rust. 'I had brought a six-inch nail from the pit at Workington to belay on,' says Bill when he joins me, 'what we called a dog-spike. We'd no hammer. I banged it in with a stone. Later I got a slater's hammer and made it down to use for a peg-hammer.'

I probe along the ancient dirt beside the pegs and there's the nail – a little stub of rust. I show him but he's sceptical. 'It was square,' he insists, 'blacksmith-made, wrought iron.' I probe some more and reveal the square cross-section of the fine old relic. Bill leans past me and with his pawkiest laugh inserts a No. 1 Friend in a flake crack beyond the pegs. 'That completes the series.'

A little later the summit crack yields to joyous thrusts upwards with the feet and hands. It's a great, salient feature, the only detail visible from the dale-bottom, a *grande fessura* formed by the slow, millennial tearing-away of the Eagle's beak from his skull. 'That's what we were making for,' says Bill as we stand below it. 'It was the goal and reason for the climb. We'd done the Girdle the fortnight before to get the hang of the layout but the climb itself was completely new. We'd seen the crack from down by Gatesgarth and we *had* to climb it.' The stance, in sunshine at last, is a soft balcony of winter-yellowed grass. Bill's eyes are shining, his face is richly mantled with well-being. 'When he'd done it, we just sat here, Bert and me. We didn't say a word. We were so . . . used – full – happy – contented – knackered.' With characteristic style he calls the balcony a 'belvedere' and relishes its goodness after the sombre labyrinth below. We shake hands and look round the great amphitheatre of the combe, littered with boulders, thinly peopled with Herdwick sheep, no people at all, as peacefully empty as it was forty-two years before, when there wasn't even a path from above Gatesgarth across the fellside below High Crag (where Bill put up the first hard routes).

'How did you *know* your second ascent of the Front was the second ever?' I ask him.

'We knew everybody, literally everybody, who was climbing in the area. Remember that with the petrol rationing, and my lack of a car, we were all very confined to our particular haunts. That's why I did so little in the way of new routes anywhere else. Jim Birkett's situation was just the same.'

Recapping and re-screening continues as we contour round to Grey Crag to climb what he clearly feels to be one of his small gems, Fortiter. 'When you said to me,' he now confides, '"Will we make it Eagle Front today? It'll never be so dry again," I had a mental battle. But I had to agree. I'd never thought for a moment that I would ever be here again.' Later, at our sacks below the Eagle's toe, he thrusts his fingers into the dense grass, still searching for Bert Beck's cairn, and at last lays bare the remains of it, two flat foundation stones. 'You see? Bert always made them well.' He puts a chunk of rock on top of them. 'That's for Bert.'

Fortiter had been climbed, on July 12 1941, in a burst of activity that included Suaviter, nearby on Grey Crag; Dexter Wall, the wonderfully sheer face near the summit, one of Bill's hardest pitches and the only one he tried first on a top rope (we repeated it on a sweltering day at Whitsun) (see plate 7); and Y Gully on Haystacks a mile up the dale. The idea was to get in as many good new things as possible before Bert went off to the War. All their friends were volunteering. 'We wanted to get into the RAF and kill Nazis. I was filling coal in the two-foot seam, but I didn't say clearly what my work was so I got past the first medical. But at the second one the doctor asked me exactly what it was I did and I had to tell him, face-worker. So he told me to piss off out of it and stop wasting his time.' Later he recalls, moved and with a shake in his voice, the good mates and acquaintances who were killed. Gordon Connor, also a Workington miner, one of twins, who was on the first ascent of Far East Buttress and the Girdle Traverse of Eagle, was killed after three months as a tail-gunner in a Lancaster bomber; and Sid Thompson (who led the first ascent of a tough Very Severe on Gimmer), shot down in a Mosquito flying out of Brussels in March 1945. Bert Beck survived, but the gap torn through the community is clear from the list of First Ascents in Buttermere – only seven minor items between autumn 1941 and August 1945, the month of Hiroshima and Nagasaki.

Exploration then came back to the crags in a spate of discovery: Buckstone How near Honister Pass; the opening up of Eagle, Borrowdale; the big four on the eastern slopes of the Newlands valley, Grey, Red, Waterfall, and Miners'; and Dale Head near the pass where the Newlands path climbs over to Borrowdale and Honister. All were untouched until the Workington climbers opened them up, all seamed and ribbed with imposing routes. During the next ten weeks we climb nineteen of his routes, including the never-recorded Girdle of Miners' Crag (one thousand feet) and his first two routes, done with the Connor twins just before and after the start of the War, on a steeply domed outcrop called Round How (high up behind Green Crag), where we also put up two new routes, calling them Tuning Fork and Tambourine after the rather vibrant flakes which we have to trust with our weight.

Mostly we concentrate on Newlands and Buckstone How. 'Really,' says Bill on one occasion, 'we were looking for another Castle Rock of Triermain, and I think we found it.' To my mind they didn't. The majestic leaning sheerness of the Castle is something else again. Buckstone is a trove of splintered blades jammed into the mountain, disintegrating slowly out of it, like bales and bales of some layered material, charred newsprint or shattered car-bodies, which has been seized and bent and burst and burnt and tattered. Its awkward vertical grain lets in draining from the wet fellside above and poses endless teethy problems. You have to pinch edges too blunt for the purpose, lay away on arêtes likewise, and step up on slim spikes which seem to hold only because your weight thrusts them a little deeper into the soil. From below it looks a wreck. Peascod and Beck, with their unfailing appetite and taste for untouched rock, realised that an array of steep lines could be traced through this beetling maze.

Sinister Grooves was their first. They followed their noses up the weakness pointing to the first stance and then (on a cold, gusty day in February 1946) backed off, 'well pleased with our reconaissance'. Within the month they had climbed it to the top. We repeated it on another shuddering day – May, but more like March at this height, eleven hundred feet above sea level. 'I *love* this rock,' says Bill as he leads off up pitch one. I press into a niche between two ribs, trying to conserve body-heat and remembering his words on the Girdle of Miners' Crag as he abseiled off a shaky pinnacle into a holly tree, 'We must have had a perverse taste in rock in those days' – said with relish, of course. Now he pulls steadily through a notch in bristling overhangs and looks down, circling thumb and forefinger in a French chef's gesture of delight. I join him and stare up at the big groove, invisible from below, which had made them feel that here was a route and a half: '*The* Groove, Bert has called it ever since. I told him there was a good hold at fifteen feet and he said to himself (not to me: Bert never complained), "What do I do for holds *before* the good hold?"'

The good hold is now smothered in the fibrous remains of a nylon sling secured there by a jammed knot – another nice item of climbing archaeology. Lodging my left toe on a tiny blade, I scan the featureless walls that bound the cleft. People must have bad dreams about places like this – rearing and smooth-sided, no way up, a chasm below. Bill is looking up, chuckling, enjoying my impasse, occasionally repeating his nostrum about 'turning to use the right wall'. How do you turn when the least twist would slip your foot off its minimal vantage? I udge my right buttock harder into the corner, commit myself to chimneying (but really the facing walls flare too much), shove my right foot into the corner as though to make it crack and part, and place my right palm down the left wall. Charily I push on it, I rise a bit, my left foot stretches way out to a small pocket, it holds, I rise some more, swivel precariously towards the promised convenience of the right wall, raise my right foot to a little sloping ledge, going up now sir, it keeps happening, the top's within reach, it's a jug-handle of a hold, I pull over and out into wuthering gusts of wet wind.

When Bill comes up, he chimneys in majestic security, his spine planted against one face, rejecting my squalid cower into the supposed security of the cleft. Above, we groove steeply upwards for another hundred feet, our feet frictioning on vertical edges sticking out from the throats of the chimneys, green and narrow like reptiles' tongues, the broad blades and shares of the slate barring out the rain. When we get back to Bill's house on the north-west slope of Skiddaw, he rings Bert Beck at Workington to tell him about the day's delights.

'How did you find The Groove?' I can hear Bert asking.

'Desperate,' said Bill.

'And how did *he* find it?'

'Not easy.'

'Good,' says Bert.

Although Bill takes a wicked pleasure in the hardness of The Groove, he obviously feels that Cleopatra, at the other end of Buckstone, was his *pièce de résistance*. It was climbed, not in 1949 as the book says, but on May 18 1951. Peascod and Beck had explored the crag by walking directly up the steep slate scree from the Matterhorn Boulder, next to the roadside parking place, which they used for practice. The walk in from Honister summit is easier but 'Bert's old tourer couldn't get up the steep bits unless all the passengers got out and pushed.' A brown-streaked, holdless-looking wall declares Cleopatra's quality: I never got round to asking Bill whether they chose the name because the naked rock there has a 'tawny front', 'with Phoebus' amorous pinches black, And wrinkled deep in time.' When they were making the Girdle in the winter of 1948, they spied a line of two-inch ledges and finger-pockets corrugating across the wall from a birch-tree ledge on the right. Three years later, when Bert had given up hard climbing, Bill went up there with a new partner, Brian Blake, traversed the wall from left to right, then abseiled off the birch. The angle of the rock above looked very high, the holds fragile, and 'In those days we couldn't afford to fall. With a bow-line round your waist, it's excruciating even for the second man to hang suspended – try it yourself with a rope over the bough of a tree. And we didn't trust the thick old hawsers. A hawser-laid rope could break – we knew of cases. Another thing, we couldn't put on many runners when there were only line slings. If the rope went through, say, four of those, even if they were in line, it was impossible to drag it through against the friction.'

The two men then explored the upper pitches over two days and on the third day went up to string it all together: 'We climbed the exact edge of the wall above the first set of overhangs and stepped left under the steep area – and there was the crux.' (He still breathes in deeply, recalling it.) 'Getting up that bloody groove! We knew there must be a way. That pinnacle that crowns the arête – it had to be good – it just had to be. So Brian got up on the second little pedestal below it, without any delay – we were mad, daft! – I stood on his shoulders, then his head, "combined tactics", as they say, and I grabbed the pinnacle, and it was good.'

Bill told me all this after we had climbed the route. At the time, I stood up on the second pedestal, lodged my fingers in the first and deepest of two rough pockets like the insides of geodes, fiddled a wired nut dentally into the second pocket, gained enough height to scan the pinnacle top and like the look of it, but how to reach it? Back down to the pedestal for a think, then lean away left to suss the neighbour groove – rough enough but very steep and with nothing I'd call holds. I try to step left into it but at once that Extreme feeling sets in; I'd need to levitate to get up it. I step back onto the pedestal, muster my energies, swing my left foot as high as it will go, into the big pocket, grasp the arête and try to layback, it goes, my foot stays rooted, I rise, shift my hands higher and reach for the top, it's positive and angular, I pull up happily, find a series of reasonable footholds leading away up leftwards above the serried overhangs, and waltz across on them, the Buckstone exposure giving a birdlike freedom of the air.

In my excitement I've neglected to put a sling round that lovely pinnacle top. I find just one more runner in the next hundred feet and run out most of the rope before anchoring without much confidence on two vibrating spikes. The whole crag is unsettlingly musical, slivers of slate on the old quarry-spoil down below clink like sheep-bells though there is nothing moving there, and it occurs to me that the Peascod/Beck route-names reverberate like bells: Suaviter, Fortiter, Dexter, Honister, Sinister. Bill's Tyrolean hat with its Austrian and Cumbrian climbing club badges comes into sight below the crux. He calls up from the pedestal, 'Can you climb across that little wall to your left, so you're above me? If I come off here, I don't want a swing.' I do that but have to leave a sling to protect myself. The zigs in the rope now threaten to nullify our manoeuvre. 'Bill,' I roar down, 'can you untie? I'll pull the rope right up through the runners and drop it straight down to you.' It reaches him nicely but a long loop of slack lodges firmly behind the pinnacle. As this dawns on us, I see his face stretch in its pawkiest smile and he says, 'I will not look this gift in the mouth – this one is from God . . .' When he climbs, he pulls up on the virtually fixed rope – a nice piece of combined tactics again, outwitting the crag's defences and compensating for my thoughtlessness.

Cleopatra was one of a series of names based on what he called 'ladies of reputation' – Jezebel, Cleopatra, Delilah, Eve (and with Neil and me he put up a short hard route on Round How which we called Salome: after all, it was just next to Tambourine). The latter three, all masterpieces of Lakeland rock, were climbed with Brian Blake, who was running a youth centre in Maryport and had been living in a caravan in Borrowdale. Eve was found almost by chance, unlike the bigger gems on Eagle and Buckstone which were stalked and closed in on over weeks or months. They had gone to Shepherd's Crag to climb Ardus, then just five years old, but it was occupied. Bill spied the line of Eve, in particular the airy slanting traverse that crowns it, and said, 'Let's do that.' His diary claims, proudly underlined, 'This is the first ascent of the North Buttress.' They called it Eve because it was evening and the barmaid at the Scafell Hotel, where they did their drinking, was called Eve. 'Thin, she was,' Bill says, as we sit there having a pint after Cleopatra, 'and a hard nut, a real tough character, and a good friend.' To celebrate putting up Cleopatra Brian Blake had suggested that they went right along the line of liqueurs in the Lounge Bar. 'My head was ballooning before we'd finished.' We're now sitting in the back bar, to which climbers and walkers are directed these days. 'There used to be a photograph of me here,' Bill recalls, 'but it's gone, I see – I don't suppose anyone knew who it was.' There are some climbing photos, a fine sequence of a gentleman in a Tyrolean hat on a hemp rope, stepping round an exposed rock nose. 'That's Westmorland, on the North Climb on Pillar. He's in his nineties now. He lived in Keswick.' This was the Westmorland who put up the route named after him on Dove Crag, Ullswater, in the autumn of 1910. Bill's knowledge and memory are so complete that, though he is only sixty-two, to talk to him is to reach down through historical layers to the roots of modern climbing.

The ambience of the Scafell has got to him now and he muses on the difference it would have made if climbing could have been his career, not just his ruling passion:

> I would never have left England. But there was no money in it then. None of this great range of gear. No tele-climbs. I had come onto the scene long before Brown and the Rock & Ice, remember. Birkett and I – the quarryman and the miner – *we* were the first of the working-class climbers. I tried registering as a guide. The man who ran this hotel, if his guests wanted an outing, he put them on to me and I took them out on the crags. But there was no money in it, just payment in kind – I stayed here and got free board. My then wife might have put up with climbing better if it had been my income. As it was, it was a tremendous struggle to get away each weekend, and when the car or bike or bus drove off with me aboard, I felt the pressure lift in my head . . . Everything seemed to be coming to an end just then – it was a real climacteric. Arthur Dolphin was killed. Hargreaves was killed. Bert stopped hard climbing. Birkett did only one more new route of any note – Kestrel Wall over in Grizedale . . .

Bill's awareness of his past and origin is edged by a powerful sense of the effort it took to hew a way out of the Clifton pit near Workington, away east into the Cumbrian mountains, and up the steep, loose, unknown rock. 'In the pit you were nothing – always would be nothing. But on the crags you were the master.' He has the miner's painfully ambivalent view of the life underground, recognition of the human achievement in winning a life down there mixed with hatred of its more awful qualities. His father, with whom he worked at the face for years, was killed when coal fell on him and broke his neck. Bill's vision of that 'monstrous soul-destroying existence' was expressed, in the end, in paintings he made when he had become a full-time artist in Australia and he deliberately burned the surface of oil paintings to make tarry scabs and drippings which stood for the darkness of the mines (his own interpretation. An Australian critic took those images to suggest Hiroshima).

When we were half-way along the sheer traverses and shaggy gullies of the Miners' Girdle, I looked down Newlands and remarked on how suitable the name of the crag was. Below and across it was all mining: an old track, clearly not a hillwalkers' path, rising in green hairpins past holes with rusty spoil at their mouths; a scar slicing deeply across the dale-bottom, following a weakness where metal salts must have bubbled up through the faulting; and other remnants of the lead and copper workings which had gone on there since the thirteenth century and been heavily invested in by the Tudor monarchy to supply ore to six furnaces near Keswick, reached their final closure not long after the Great War. But the miners commemorated in the crag's name are Peascod and Rushworth: '*We* called it that. It was our secret egotism – George and I. These crags were all just Eel Crags. But we thought, we've found them, we've climbed them, why shouldn't we name them?'

The turn to the mountains, from that harshly worked-over coastal plain of west Cumbria, had come literally overnight. Bill had followed his father into the pit at fourteen and was filling coal at the face when he was eighteen: 'It was a time of black depression for me.' One day in 1937, cycling home after the night shift, he said to himself, it's too fine to stop at home. After a bath in the tin tub he turned his bicycle round and rode off east, fifteen miles into the mountains round Crummock Water and Buttermere:

I'd never been there – never thought of going there. I still remember the horses and carts in the valley bottom, the sounds rising up clearly, the gentle mist behind the mountains. It was then that I really saw rock for the first time, and once I'd seen it – well, then I was burning and thirsting to climb.

The personal surge which set in at that time expressed itself in many of his routes, and though they are often distinguished by delicate wall traverses (the bottom pitches of Cleopatra, Delilah, and Border Buttress, Black Wall on pitch four of Honister Wall, the top pitch of Jezebel), which have the texture of his more atmospheric and Turneresque paintings, there are also equally characteristic pitches where you have to muscle your way into the grain of the ground and forge upwards by sheer animal thrusts. On dirty, broken terrain Bill loves to mine and quarry and always has done. Bert Beck's humorous and graphic article on their first ascent of Y Gully on Haystacks says that when the rock was especially bad, Bill gave an 'instant demonstration by plucking forth sundry lumps of it and hurling them from him . . . the more he "quarried", the more determined he appeared to become.' (*Fell & Rock Climbing Club Journal*, 1942, p 114) This first came home to me on our 'dress rehearsal' for our climb up Y Gully – a sally up a Peascod/Rushworth route called Alcove Ridge on Grey Buttress, Newlands, on a drenching morning in July.

The 'difficult start' is so sodden and filthy that I can barely get off the ground, the ground being a spongy green slope which floors the crag's steamy ante-room or alcove. Above hangs a forsaken garden – a gutter congested with turfy tussocks, ferns with a drop of water on each frond-tip, the unstable earth saturated. My left PA skids out of nooks on a greasy rockface, my fingers burrow under the crag's rotting upholstery, feeling for roughness, sharpness, dryness – not finding them. Breathing heavily, my arms weighted like a deep-sea diver's by wet jersey and sweaty tracksuit, I let technique slough off me and shove my knees into the plant life, feeling like a corm trying to root, or possibly to evolve, against the barely stilled lapse of the earth-fall. Ponderous movement upwards . . . No runners . . . This is the most unmodern and basic pitch I've ever climbed – what Neil and I call black-pudding climbing. The belay rowan is dead, of course; its slippery, barked stems poke out of the soil like a deer's skeleton. I start to dig with my broddling tool (meant for getting jammed nuts out of cracks) and shower Bill with brown loam as I dissect slivers of buried stone, peering into the crag's black sinuses, feeling into them like a barbarous surgeon. Finally I

174

fiddle two small hexes into bottomless cracks and pull them together with a sling in a semblance of a secure anchor.

When Bill surfaces out of the greenery below, grinning knowingly, I remember that there are techniques even for such a pitch. My brutalities were unnecessary. He has jammed his back against one wall, his feet against the opposing one, and chimneyed upwards in stately style. In a few minutes we make it into the world of rock and air via a delicate traverse on damp, mossy knobs. The rock is excellent, rough-edged and pockety, the line a real one, zigging and zagging up a face which had seemed a jumble of mountainous by-products but turns out to be a slim buttress in its own right. But mining is not quite over: to improve stance two, Bill wrenches off a stretch of turf the size of a hearthrug and when he flings it down into the ante-room, it explodes and then bounces down the hillside in flurries of black soil.

Two weeks later, under a sky of burning blue, we stepped into the dank shadow of Y Gully. Bill hadn't been back there for forty-one years and had never dreamed that he would. The attractions of the place are specialised: the current guide uses expressions like 'unpopular', 'evil', 'rock very poor' and Bill himself wondered if he enjoyed gully-climbing because he 'just liked playing in muck'. Certainly the lower part of Y Gully is a gut layered in slime, the few clean bits are unclimbable overhangs smoothed by water. We tiptoe upwards on wet snouts and the delving begins. It goes on for six hours. We test handholds by banging them with our fists, then pick them off and throw them well clear. They whizz in mid-air like Catherine wheels. Chris, who is climbing with us and taking the photos, fantasises that salmon will presently come leaping up the mossy steps and shelves. A barrier overhangs twenty degrees past the vertical and we have to traverse out and back on clumps of sphagnum moss, sinking our fingers in it, groping for solidity. The banks of the gully are an avalanche of flowers – meadowsweet, yellow saxifrage, alpine lady's-mantle. Now the gut sucks us in. Committed, we peer upwards to the vent on the skyline two hundred feet above, tresses and tatters of heather silhouetted

175

against the radiance of the normal world waiting for us. More fantasies, of being a foetus, head engaged, looking down between its mother's legs, urging to be born.

The 'holds' in the gully bottom are like taps: when you pull on them, a thin stream of water pours or trickles. But at last the gut gathers itself into a solid constriction, the 'inverted funnel' that crowns it: a hundred feet of Very Severe rock. Time to chimney (I've learned that at last): back against a perpendicular wall striped with moss, feet on moist bevelled ledges, eyes looking longingly up at a twenty-foot cracked blade which may or may not support a layback and then a turn inwards to face the rock and climb upwards normally. You have to commit yourself to becoming a strut of bone and flesh braced between the walls. The gristle in the lumbar region grinds against rock. You don't want to sit there in mid-air and crane left for a runner placement – you've got no option – you dig and scrape with the broddler and release a smell of old iron and rotting meat, as though the slit in the joint at the back of the chimney is tainted with sheep-oozings (there is a smashed carcase on the scree at the foot).

Still you rise. The quest for drier, sharper edges forces you out from the impending chockstones in the back of the chimney till you feel like a pilot who has just ejected, sitting in mid-air, the narrow oblong window of the gully's open side blazing at you with its purple and brown images of Striddle Crag and Fleetwith Pike across the dale. Trust that undercut flake above your feet, pull on it with just half your weight, stand on it, eel round leftwards through ninety degrees with the help of a half-inch ledge carved out with the broddler, then bridge and mantel and udge a final forty feet onto a heathery shelf swamped in earth by some recent spate and tie onto tottering rowan saplings with your last two slings. Buttermere and Crummock Water beyond it stretch towards the sun in dazzling expanses; beyond Grasmoor the blue humps of Scotland show through the haze across the Solway. Above us the gully has narrowed to a yard-wide gutter of stone and we burrow upwards through jungly heather that has never been cut or burnt, grabbing it, hauling on it, ploughing through it, swimming in it, almost engulfing and ingesting it in a primitive passion upwards to the full sunlight where we can sit in a mild trance and let our adrenalin level sink to normal again.

That complete involvement with the earth's undersides and surfaces is the key to Bill's climbing and to much of his other living. He split and dug it as a miner; balanced and stretched and pulled across and up it as a climber; and as a painter he recreated its grain and the texture of the light and rain and snow that rasp across it, working it into the forms that our fingers latch onto as we resist gravity. His fundamental impulse upwards is figured in paintings where the ridge lifts, lifts to a skyline accented with a crest of cream or white like snow or looms just visible through grey showers.

> When I talk to beginners about landscape, in my classes, I tell them to forget the foreground – concentrate on the shape and edge of the mountain – the skyline. The foreground is a minor affair – people's own imagination can fill in the details . . .
>
> I recently met a leading Japanese climber, an Everest man [at the BMC conference in Buxton, where Bill's wife Etsu was interpreting]. And he was agreeing that what mattered absolutely was the urge upwards towards the ridge. Everything that goes before, down below, is nothing compared to that.

He is serious about what he means but also light and easy.

> I quite believe this claptrap they say about the two great influences on my work being mining and climbing. I built up this thick texture – you could climb up some of my paintings . . .

He hooks his fingers in the air, palms facing the listener.

> I built them up with PVA glue and rock-dust – sand and cement.
>
> When I was a Sunday afternoon painter, I only wanted to do pleasant things – watercolour, pen-and-ink drawings. I went to classes in my middle teens – because of the shifts, I could only manage two evenings a month. It was some time before I realised that to do anything much you need to develop *commitment*.
>
> I used sometimes to draw some climbers, standing there on a face, with their gear. Awful! They looked completely artificial [he had recently, in a review of *Ascent*, compared American drawings of climbers very unfavourably with colour photos]. At that time

painting took second place to climbing. When I went to Australia, I did less climbing and painting took over. It's always been like that with me – the one works in relation to the other, but never at the same time . . .

He gestures with his two hands like claws swivelling, the fingertips of each hand near the others but not interlocking.

Through it all what stands out is the tactile experience. *That* has been the source of my happiness. That's the thing, isn't it? You do something because you *must*.

23

In the middle of summer 1984 I met Bill in Borrowdale to clean and climb a new line he had spotted on one of the 'new' small crags above the Troutdale carpark. It had been named Beth's Crag, after the daughter of Colin Downer, a powerful climber from Keswick who had been active in the digging-out and cleaning of Great End Crag nearby and has recently given the same drastic treatment to Bleak How in the mouth of Langstrath further up Borrowdale. We dearly wanted to bag this line. There is so little rock left untouched in this heavily frequented part of the world that a new route at a standard we could manage (up to Hard Very Severe) would be a rare find.

When climbers clean a crag to make it more manageable, less vegetated and cluttered with loose rock and earth, they call it 'gardening'. A euphemism. Nothing is helped to grow. Growth is expunged. Ivy tods and small yews and rowans are liable to be cut away with axes, even powersaws. Sods of grass and heather are rooted out, lichens and mosses scoured away with a wire brush. The boles of trees are scarred by abseil ropes. Resinous conifers occasionally catch fire when nicotine addicts stub out their cigarettes on them and they smoulder until too little is left to survive (the pine on stance two of Brown Crag Wall on

Shepherd's Crag). Climbers' feet wear away the soil on a ledge, their ropes and slings erode the bark, until the tree, however tough, dies slowly and stays standing as a tottering monument (the holly on stance three of Holly Tree Traverse on Raven Crag, Great Langdale). Trees that are climbed habitually, as part of a route, lose bark and branches until they start to die from the top (the yew on pitch three of North Crag Eliminate on the Castle Rock of Triermain: the top is now reduced to a naked spearhead and I've known a climber mask it with his helmet in case he fell back onto it and castrated himself). My personal list of murdered trees is a long one and I can't even claim to have kept my own hands clean.

Here at Beth's Crag, between the branches of the oaks and sycamores, a series of outcrops a hundred feet high loom in the half-light like hulls of sunken ships encrusted with growths. The wood is ankle-deep in humus, the rich slithery soil has crept into terraces which almost look like paths, but nobody seems to come here, there is no reason to, the walkers make for the clean-swept skylines of Cat Bells and High Spy, following green trods between the bracken, leaving these little woods to grow and decay and grow in their own deciduous rhythms.

On the outcrops many faces and ribs show palely clean, like faces newly shaved of mature beard. The moss and turf which coated these north-facing crags with their perpetual draining of moisture from above, fed by Borrowdale's teeming rains (its gauge records the highest rainfall in England), have been stripped down to bedrock by the Merry Men of Keswick and the ground below them is ankle-deep in fresh brown soil, like a garden newly dug in spring.

'Our' route lies at the right-hand end of Beth's Crag. A feature like a vertical canal nine inches deep and two feet across cuts upwards above a little wild garden of saplings and hyacinth-grass. There seem to be cracks in the twin corner-joints of the 'canal' but they're clogged with scrappy vegetation. It's a Heaven-sent natural line. The sides of the canal converge high up in the cleaner reaches of the rockface and this exaggerates the perspective and makes everything look loftier, like the

179

escarpment 'somewhere in Africa' at the start of the Johnny Weissmuller Tarzan films.

Bill declares himself disgusted by the mucky state of this fine route. He's brought a builder's hammer, a dandelion extractor, and a wire brush. While he readies himself to tear into the sapling platform at the foot, I scramble round the end of the outcrop and pull upwards through a jungle of heather and blaeberry which has never been culled or burnt – festoons of it cascade down slopes so steep that everything, boulders and dead trees and beds of earth drifted with the leaves of many autumns, looks permanently on the verge of avalanching.

It is all beautiful: fairy woodlands created by Mervyn Peake for a film of *The Wind in the Willows*. Ferns spring from the ground in green fountains, fronded mosses upholster the boulders so thickly that you must wade through their velvety clinging, not caring how often you stumble and go in knee-deep. Cars on the road below sound remote, out there in the twentieth century. Where is Bill? Where is the crag? Pointed or scalloped leaves lattice the air, veil the distances. At last I identify the crag top and toboggan down towards it in a welter of ropes and tools and harness until the verge of the drop makes further progress dangerous. 'Bill!' I roar into the leafage. 'Bill?'

Crashing and clumping sounds. 'Hullo? Dave? You sound quite near.'

I uncoil the rope, pass one end of it round a small sturdy oak on the lip of the outcrop, pay it out, then throw both ends out and down. The whole length of it runs out and Bill confirms that it has nearly reached the foot. For the next three hours I work my way slowly down the 'canal', controlling descent with my figure-of-eight descendeur, tying it off to hang in perfect suspension while I clean a five-foot section, sliding down some more to reach the next stretch of crack.

Bill is mining away heartily. Indignant shouts rise up: 'There's an awful lot of rubbish here.' Whole tussocks of hyacinth-grass fling off into the air, tangle with the twigs of trees, and hurtle off down the slope. Branches go flying, small boulders, pieces of turf as big as bathmats. Eighty feet above I dig at knots and mats of fibrous soil that choke the cracks. Few plants manage to mature here, evidently: some heathers, mostly wiry stems with little foliage, some blades of fescue grass. What muffles the sharp edges craved by our climbers' fingers is mainly compacted earth and rootlet, like coir fenders on an old fishing boat. The prongs of the extractor tear into them, break them down to crumbs, the drifts of it build up between my thighs and stomach and the rockface until the bulk is inconvenient and I lean back and let it pour down onto Bill's head. Dust like cocoa builds up thickly on the little ledges and steps and I have to blow them clean, puffing and puffing till my head swims. In the sultry afternoon, sweat steams from under the pressure-cooker of my helmet and wasps come moseying round, drawn by my meaty smell.

It's marvellous to see the features of the rock start to come out clear, like printing a photo and seeing the lineaments of the image emerge, first ghostly, then distinct, on the blank surface of the photographic paper. It is natural to think of the revealed rock as perfect, but it's not: the left-hand joint, on which I'm concentrating, is blocked from time to time by flakes of stone like neolithic arrow-heads. They must have been splintered off from time to time by natural processes – shifts in the cliff mass, the expansion of water into ice, the prising of tough roots. Now I ask Bill for the builder's hammer and he sends it up tied to a loop of the rope so that I can pike out these splinters with the grating sound of teeth being extracted from a jaw.

'There is no such thing as a ruined stone,' says Hugh MacDiarmid in his profound meditation on geology, *On a Raised Beach*. Not true – I spend hundreds of hours each year among 'ruined stones'. Nature breaks down all the time (to build up something else: the pulverised rock refines, its minerals go to compose the soils) and this makes it easy, amongst this clutter of starved plants and shattered rocks, to think of ourselves as improving on nature – getting the route sheer and clean-cut, solid where there had been instability, visible where it had been obscured.

By four in the afternoon I've joined Bill amongst the heaps of earth and foliage at the foot, ankles aching, chipped knuckles ingrained with dirt, and we're looking up at the face, well-pleased with its soaring architecture. Then we climb it, finding it strenuously steep but with sharp ribs for our feet to bridge on and deep cracks for the fingers which will only improve as the dusting of soil washes off. The finish is superb, left haunch lodged against a prow, right foot braced against the opposite side of the canal, nothing but air below this little span of leg. We graded it Very Severe/4c and some months later we called it Stingray: Bill had found out that Ray McHaffie, ubiquitous veteran of Borrowdale climbing, had bespoken the name Sting for it (had he too been troubled by wasps?) when he saw the line some years before and it would have been grabby to foist in a brand-new name of our own.

Should we have created the route at all? Throughout the afternoon my head had chattered with argument: 'I'm killing plants. But still, it's only a few dozen scrawny heathers, a few dandelions and blades of grass. Nobody has ever seen them, or ever would. From a hundred yards away – where nobody ever goes either – nothing will seem to have been altered. Why, nature itself destructs continuously, the wood up there is a shambles of dead trees and branches, saplings dying from lack of light keel over and rub sores in the bark of healthy trees, the rock has split to smithereens in many places, the bits of it dribble down onto the rubbish-heap below. And anyway, each year I climb thousands of feet of crag which would have been a mass of fungi and detritus had not the pioneers cleaned them out and brushed them down. The finest Lakeland climb put up between the Wars, The Crack on Gimmer, was so dirty when MacPhee and Reynolds first climbed it, in late spring 1928, that 'showers of moss and lichen dust' filled their eyes and MacPhee suggested that it would be best in dry weather to climb it wearing goggles. (*Hard Rock*, p 78) Now it is as clean as a whetted knife. Is it right for me to benefit from the cleansing of nature by my predecessors? But I do, so why jib at my own small manicurings?'

So much rationalisation and special pleading! We had lusted after the route. No qualms of mine were going to inhibit me from doing whatever it took to create it. Yet I know, or believe, that we should leave nature alone, if at all possible (already the qualifications are creeping in). And I do try to – although I poison snails and slugs in our garden, hundreds every year, sprinkling the blue-green pellets of metaldehyde so that they feast on them and drown in their own excessive mucus. Should I not leave them alone – and let the beans and peas and spinach be eaten to death the moment they sprout? In any case such poisoning could well be thought less wanton than to go into one of the few half-acres of wilderness left in Cumbria and carve and strip and scour it into yet another 'recreational facility' for us insatiable humans.

For one thing, given the nerve, a climber can often make the route without stripping the rock. In 1980, at Exmansworthy near Hartland Point in north Devon, a climber called Andy Brazier put up a ninety-foot Extreme pitch without cleaning out the cracks for protection points – true, this looked so dangerous that some of his companions refused to watch. (*Crags*, December/ January 1981) For another thing, the fact that few people frequent that little craggy wood in Borrowdale is an argument for leaving it alone, not for despoiling it. A myriad of such places hide themselves in the crannies of the continents. Without even having to see them we know they are there, waterfalls bridged by fallen trees, dells knee-deep in the humus accumulated since the last Ice Age, the swamps in the Andes where giant coots heap up their nests so deep that heat generates spontaneously in the mattress of flag and sedge and warms the eggs against the freezing nights . . . But even that has been filmed, and have the giant coots recovered yet from their fright at being surveilled for days on end by a television film crew? No doubt the BBC were careful and humane and built their hides as unobtrusively as possible, but nature has a right to be left intact. We ought to hold back from those fastnesses and leave the spores and larvae, mammals and tubers, to live out their own lives – preying on each other, feeding each other, but immune at least from invasion by the species that wipes out dozens of other species every year – killing 500 million butterflies annually in Taiwan alone to make ornaments from them (*Observer*, January 26 1986), or helicoptering two huge blocks of rock off the Matterhorn and sending them to exhibitions in Colorado and Utah (*Climber and Rambler*, December 1984).

24

Against Looting

Leave the mahogany where it is!
Leave the mahogany trees in Borneo
Where the orangs embrace them gently.
Leave the geodes where they are!
Great egg-wombs toothed with crystal,
Leave them in the Brazilian darkness.
Leave the edelweiss where it is!
Its foliage woven of frost,
Leave it to root on the bergs of the Dolomites.
Leave the ambergris where it is!
Leave it, oily and fragrant,
In the gut of the sperm whale.
Leave the scorpions where they are!
Leave them to sting in the mating battle
Under the rocks of Atlas.
Leave the white-lipped amethyst where it is!
Glistening arachnid sculptured in quartz,
Leave it to lurk in Mexico's granite caves.
Leave the urchins where they are!
Slow sunbursts spined with rays,
Leave them to graze on the skerries.
Leave the eggs of the osprey where they are!
Leave them to hatch
High on a resinous bower in the pines of Garten.
Leave the tortoises where they are!
Leave them to warm their shells in Lombardy.
Leave the orcas to wrestle with the squids,
                                        leave them:

Leave the snail-gatherers of Papua
Grooming each other beside their waterfalls,
                              leave them, leave them:
Leave them in memory of the slaves
Stowed in the holds like carcases,
In memory of the elephants fettered and swaying
In a concrete hangar, of the gorilla
Counting the links of his chain
Over and over and over, and leave them
For the sake of the children
That they may never laugh at a prisoner
Or try to buy a life with a coin.

25

The original inhabitants of the crags are the animals. How could
they take to us immigrants, with our loud chatter in alien
tongues, our lurid dress, the filth and junk we litter about, our
whining music and late-night parties? If only we respected the
older traditions of the place . . . But we are getting used to each
other in some ways. The peregrines serve territorial notice by
buzzing us but (unlike the terns) they never actually attack. We
avoid their crags, and many sea-cliffs, in the breeding season
when they are naturally jumpy and possessive. When Bill and I
were reclimbing as many as possible of his routes, we kept off
Falconer's Crack (the first line ever climbed on Eagle, Borrowdale) until September 8 to avoid disturbing the peregrines. The
second stance is on or in their eyrie, nesting twigs snap under
your feet and a few red and white rings with little numbers show
that their diet includes the occasional homing pigeon. The
climbers of Bill's wave (the Thirties to the Fifties) acknowledged
their fellow occupants of the crags in the names they gave their
routes. The right wall of Gillercombe Buttress, standing above the
moors between Honister and Green Gable, is all birds: Peregrine

Way and Tiercel Wall and Eyrie and Raven's Groove, the last one named by Jim Birkett, who became so expert in cliff-dwelling birdlife that he was asked by the RSPB to mark peregrines' eggs with green dye to make them valueless to egg thieves. He is also cited many times in the standard monograph, Derek Ratcliffe's *The Peregrine Falcon* (1980).

That is the acme of the mutual relation that should hold between humans and other animals as we climb. We are sharing, rather than invading, a habitat, to satisfy an appetite for exertion and attainment almost as imperious as the birds' and the mammals' for food and security to reproduce. To thrive in it we take on their ways. Our eyries are the stances where we accumulate our temporary nests of rope. We spool back the millennia of evolution when we crouch and grip with all four sets of digits (especially the East German climbers, who climb barefoot). We crawl with chests and bellies to the rock to negotiate a shelf pitch with a roof – sometimes called a stomach traverse – or brachiate outwards to the lip of the roof with the locomotion, not of a gibbon, since we don't dare do it fast, but at least of a sloth, hefty, deliberate, with strong hooked hands.

But we can never fly. Icarus on Eagle, Borrowdale, was well named. We can almost feel the feathers sprouting from our arms as we perch looking out into air, but no, the slopes and faces across the dale can only be reached laboriously, by trods or tracks. The crystal walkways through space are only a fantasy. We cannot get into that sheer untethered freedom of take-off or swoop, air streaming past our eyelids, unless we give in to the thing our whole efforts are bent on avoiding – falling. Our safety gear is so elaborate that we rarely harm ourselves fatally. Few climbers have been killed in mid-climb. The well-known deaths (Tom Patey, Laurie Holliwell, Keith Darbishire, Peter Biven, Tony Wilmott, John Cunningham) have occurred while abseiling or setting up abseils, as a result of a freak wave, or during solos. The commonest crag deaths happen to the sheep, who would be much less at risk had we not bred them top-heavy, neat hooves and legs supporting that gross stack of wool, and pastured them on uplands at the very limit of the habitable.

These days every climbing crag in Cumbria has its corpse, exuding that dreadful smell of metallic rot until the foxes and crows have chewed off every morsel and the bones and wool begin to meld with the scree. The sheep follows a grassy rake, nibbling its way outwards from the easier pasture until there is a long drop below it. A last green bite tempts it, it goes for it, grazes it to its roots, and by now it is in a dead-end too narrow to turn round in. On Dow Crag we found a panicky Herdwick on Easy Terrace – if only it had had a guidebook it could have found the way off comfortably – and we had to rig a harness of slings round it and drag and herd it onto safer ground. On Round How, among the little tarns and rocky knolls south of Honister, Bill, Neil, and I had just put up Salome when we came upon a sheep cragfast on a heathery ledge. The others waded off uphill to fix a belay and I closed in on the sheep. It rushed past me, on the outside, careering dangerously close to the hundred-foot drop. I swung round, went for it again, again it barged past my half-hearted tackle with the force of an All Black forward. Its brute panic was getting to me, it was all headlong impulse where I was all aversion, I would have to become as physical as it. Next time it charged I stepped outwards to the edge to deflect it inwards, then threw myself at it and pinned it to the inner wall. It convulsed, heaving its weight against my thighs, I sank my fingers in the wool of its back, struggled a long sling round its head and forelegs and began to half-shove, half-goad it up the heathery gullies between the last of the rocks, my nose filled with its choking smell of oily rope and urine, while the others took in the rope and kept me firm.

It was a good espisode, a necessary piece of work which went a little way to repay the debt we owe the hill-farmers and their flocks who graft a living out of the rough country where we can take our ease – where we can do so all the more easily because they and their predecessors have long since established the paths and drove-roads which thread the uplands. That same year, between Middlefell Buttress and Raven Crag in Langdale, Terry and I noticed a sheep cragfast on a tall narrow pier of rock that separates the two climbing cliffs. Here was a quandary. We could top rope down to it but wouldn't it panic and plunge suicidally once we were sharing its precarious perch? We climbed for three or four hours, suffused with June sunshine, a little overcast by the unresolved dilemma and our town-bred lack of craft to cope with it. Hour after hour querulous bleating echoed along the rockface. I gave the animal a last guilty look as we took up our rucksacks for the walk down. Almost at once we met a National Park ranger who asked us if we could reach the sheep and lower it down to him. It had been there for eight days and the farmer had decided it was time to set up a rescue.

So we roped down for him,
Hovering peregrine above him,
And as my feet reached rock
He panicked with his last energy,
Turned in his own length and
Sprang – already airborne –
Heeling into the void –
Cartwheeling belly upwards,
Landing on his back, volleying
Helpless as an avalanche
Or its victim, a brown bale now
Bouncing boulder to boulder
Corpse-heavy down the gully
While I hung there, wincing
At each killing thump
As though I were hitting him.

When we reached the bottom
He was standing, stunned,
Struggling when the Ranger felt him,
Fingering firm legs, worrying
In case the scarlet blood-streak
At his nostril was more than a cut.
His black alien pupil-slots
And acid-yellow irises
Levelled indifferently
At the fuss and flurry
Of our self-conscious concern.

And when the Ranger shouldered him
Like a saint in a picture,
He settled himself wearily
For the steep slog downwards
To the dogs and the dipping-trough,
The clipping-shears, the jostle
For tasteless, baled winter-feed
Around the iron manger.

– from 'Cragfast'

The following day I phoned the Ranger to find out whether the sheep was still doing well. It was, and he promised me a pint the next time I came up to Langdale.

People like to think that the Herdwick sheep, with their wiry, warm-brown wool and short, broad muzzles, were brought in by the Vikings. More probably they have been bred by generations of Cumbrian hill-farmers to survive in wet, cool country and keep their footing on steep slopes. At any rate they were introduced, not truly native, and as farmed animals they are dependent on humans for baled fodder, vitamin licks or cakes of concentrate that can now be dropped from helicopters onto the winter snowfields, and shearing to rid them of the dense surplus fleece at the start of summer. I have only once seen a perfectly wild animal beleaguered, up a blind alley, among the crags. On the south end of Farleton Fell, a couple of miles from home, a long berg of limestone separates our part of south Cumbria from Lunesdale. The last exposed stratum has separated into segments, vertebrae, great gappy molars, turtle domes, elephants' backsides cleaving and hollowing into grey intestines – a herd petrified in a frieze, commemorating the warm times between the last Ice Ages when musk ox and woolly rhino grazed from here across to Yorkshire. These monoliths look like animals set free from Henry Moore's studio, and other animals inhabit them. Up there, one day, Shep came nose to nose with a fox, which sprinted madly off while he paid no attention whatsoever, having been bred to haul nets for the fishermen in Hudson's Bay but not to hunt. In winter the hares, great middle-distance runners, bound effortlessly uphill, turn in a burst of white powder when

189

dangerous noises reach them (the hollow bang of a shotgun, farm dogs barking), and whisk off between the outcrops. Twice I have seen an albino carrion-crow and once an albino buzzard, flapping steadily over, unaware that they look like ghoulish negatives of their species.

Frequent any country for long enough and you will have these strange encounters. One morning as I was making the first pull up the brow of a monolith, fingertips feeling for dimples in the hammered pewter of its crown, footsoles slick with late winter moisture struggling to stay lodged on little puckered incuts, a flash of burnished yellow crossed my vision. I pulled over and saw, heading for the cranny between the halves of a Moore knife-edge two-piece, the dumpy backside of a badger, its hair soiled yellow like an old man's moustache discoloured by a lifetime's smoking. Its snout locked into the far end of the crevice and there it stayed, immobile. I at once went round to the east face of the crag, to give the badger a chance to get away, and spent a quarter of an hour on favourite problems. But when I came back the animal was still there, tranced by fear. I approached it gingerly, remembering tales of its bite that crunches the bones of your leg to smithereens. I stroked the coarse hair of its back, smelt its sweaty odour, and was sad to see its small black eyes dulled with resignation. It was at bay in its own terrain. So I left it, hoping the glaze was not the look of sickness – by evening it had gone.

Henry Moore's bone forms, his vision of animal and human likenesses jutting up everywhere out of the world's stony matrix, come home to me constantly among weathered limestone and gritstone. 'My' boulders on Farleton Fell are equivalent in detail after detail to the elephant skull which Julian Huxley gave him in 1968, which he etched repeatedly for two years. (W. J. Strachan, *Henry Moore: Animals*, 1983, pp 115ff) The valley between the lobes at the back of the cranium, moulding between steep shoulders, exactly simulates the curved tops where I fight to gain traction with my palms, or perhaps a fist-jam in the hollow, and eel over onto the top. Below the lobes the great skull caverns into a network of sinuses, archways, flakes sticking their tongues out of holes. You can see it as a model one-tenth the size of the Farleton boulders, imitating those places where rising damp and the chiselling of ice into the bedding planes have fashioned an area for the toes to stick thankfully in while the hands grapple with the convexities above. Or you can see it as a tiny minature of the labyrinth which mines two thousand feet below the summit of Ingleborough, ten miles to the south-east: 'tunnels regressions dark depths,' as Moore jotted beside his main skull etching.

Bone and limestone are bound to be similar to each other: calcium makes them so. But the Yorkshire rock that Moore's work seems to spring most directly from is that great tribe of gritstones which have come to rest at Brimham, above Nidderdale, twenty-five miles north-west of Moore's old home at Castleford. The likenesses are precise. The 'Two Piece Points: Skull' (1969) which he got from the elephant skull has just the smoothed-off forehead with a beak dividing the air under it which crowns the first tor at Brimham beyond the carpark. The Birch Tree Wall, up whose front a superb Very Severe route twists subtly, has been rasped by the ice into horizontal striations, exquisite pickings-out and fine sandy weaknesses, which are identical with the side-to-side gougings Moore has worked into the faces he most wanted to leave rough, offsetting the proud and inscrutable sleekness of the upper areas, in sculptures such as 'Atom Piece' (1964–5), or the 'Reclining Figure' on the grass at the Scottish National Gallery of Modern Art, which looks as though it will outlast Edinburgh Castle. The raised knees of this monumental thing bulk backwards towards its breast with a nearing and then a not-touching which simulates all those tantalising gaps between gritstone boulders that lure you to jump, for example Pigott's Stride on Low Man at Almscliff near Leeds, which I mention because I actually managed to get across it.

Moore's sculptures tell me what the crags and boulders tell me. That our bodies are worlds, their interiors never seen but the self is in there, hard to reach yet as material as the grains of rock or the fibres of roots – a fundamental truth which Wordsworth distils in a single line of 'Tintern Abbey': 'All thinking things, all objects of all thought'. That we at least partake of rock's strength in the taper and torque of our bones' shanks, the arch of the pelvis, the vaulting of the skull. That the strong parts of the world are less sensitive, less mobile, than its quick but at least they endure. My skull will outlast, for days or decades, the self that pulsed inside its glossy helmet for seventy or eighty years, as the rocks have outlasted the pulpy tissues of the animals and plants that swarmed over them in the tropical epochs or even went into their making, contributing shells and little castings of themselves to the seabeds that hardened into Cambrian limestone.

We have inhabited the cliffs themselves for a hundred years more or less (I'm writing this a few weeks before the centenary celebrations of the ascent of Napes Needle above Wasdale). We flicker over their surfaces like the shadows of the pallid and alpine swifts who make their momentary glyphs on the faces of the limestone at Buis les Baronnies in Haute Provence or the Piz di Ciavazes above the Val di Fassa in the Dolomites. These light-black shadows, skimming a flake as you pull up it by lodging your fingertips in a solution channel and smearing your footsoles on the rock's heated shield, are disconcerting: was there something there? or did the brain hiccup and confuse itself? In a minute, when you're safe again, you look round for the original of the shadow – nothing – dazzling air above the metallic sheen of the ilex two hundred feet below, or the resinous tassles of the pinetrees. But here it comes again – no illusion (the real thing is always more wonderful than the illusion) – a swift, the ultimate aerobat, hunting along the rockface, spidering on the invisible strands of its airways, scissoring to turn inwards – how can those blade-wings achieve the least leverage or buoyancy on thin air at nine thousand feet? The impetus is everything, and the eyes in the streamlined brow, and the balancing and tilting on a fulcrum as fine as its own bones. Quick as a hair flicking subliminally in the gate of a film-projector, the bird is away careering round the profile of the buttress and you climb on more joyfully because for these hours you are able to share the swift's space – almost.

We had first seen them as they swarmed in their hundreds in

front of the sun-coloured towers of the Cima della Madonna above San Martino, the whole air peopled with flickering black exclamation marks as though all the languages of Europe, all its feelings and thoughts, had clustered into one orgy of communication. The swifts, swallows, and martins, especially the swifts, have legs that are little more than attachments for the feet, they are fated purely to fly and must build nests high up from which they can launch instantly. So walls – in the climber's sense, not the builder's – are their original habitat. I saw this first on the lower forty feet of Malham Cove's main wall, just above the terrace where any walker can move across above a short drop. One September day the air chirruped shrilly. Anne, Rob, and I looked up, and there, just under sharp eyelids of limestone, the martins had moulded their cups of mud. The ends of old climbing bolts punctuated the rockface beside them, the occasional bleached and frayed loop of nylon was threaded through a natural eyelet, but only a handful of climbers were capable of free-climbing there at that time (it's crowded now) and the first autumn we noticed them, the birds were raising their second or third broods in perfect peace. The following year, when we went back to see them, the chirrupping chorus was a mania of high notes and the air straight above our heads, where the prehistoric waterfall had divided the brink of the Cove, was as crowded with silhouettes of birds as a spring pond with tadpoles. On the face a light-brown shape looped in and out and in again, fleet and arrowy, wings tapering. It flew into the cliff, disappeared, re-emerged. Bits of caked mud pattered down around us. In the poem I wrote about this display of sheer raptorial potency, the kestrel ravaging the nursery of birds is seen as menacing: from the martins' viewpoint, a war-mask staring in, shuttering out the white light, its dagger-tongue reddening between the double butcher's-hook of that tearing beak. I sided with the victims. It is so hard not to wish values onto nature. Yet the kestrel was feeding as necessarily – as rightly – as sparrows or blue-tits pecking greenfly off a rose. We empathise with the threatened martins (pretty little blue-birds) but a dearth of fresh meat would be as bad a threat to the hawk.

The fact is that I know what it is to feel threatened on a crag myself. In Trowbarrow Quarry two miles west of home, the owners, Tarmac Ltd, had been worried about liability for injuries to climbers using an unstable area of the limestone. So they blasted it away – and so provided us with a superb ninety-foot wall, at eighty-five degrees, seamed by three major cracks and a web of finer ones and studded all over with delicate holds, fossil stems of marine water-lilies. If you arrive there before anyone else, or leave last, a horde of jackdaws takes off, like shadows broken loose from their originals, or recolonises each sill on the upper crag like harbingers of an original tribe readying themselves to move back in when the quarrying and climbing peoples have left for good.

Once as I climbed Jean Jeannie at Trowbarrow Quarry and felt, as usual, rather dwarfed and vulnerable on the nearly vertical face, the cliff susurrated on a rising note, a seething hiss like nothing else I had heard except once when a chorus of adders threatened us from a cairn amongst wild grassland in the Vercors, west of Grenoble. For a moment my reason wavered, the weirdness seemed levelled at me, coming nearer and nearer. Jackdaw chicks – what else? There must have been nests in there. My smell and shadow would have frightened them worse, and more reasonably, than their chittering did me. But might not a parent bird have launched from deep inside the crack, hit me in the face, and knocked me off backwards? In fact I've never heard of such a case.

The fear working in us needs no actual grounds. In an essay about climbing on the Pinnacles in California (*Ascent*, 1980, p 210), Tom Higgins evokes his repulsion from the animals harbouring in a big open-book corner in the Balconies area: 'It is a horror of horrors. The dihedral is weeping black ooze. Whines, buzzes, bleats, and chirps emanate from it, sounds we cannot associate with any familiar life form . . . Thank God we won't have to insert any limb into its dark, humming recesses.' Really it was the ooze that endangered him, plus the difficulty of the rock (the route had never been free-climbed before), and not the lurking animals. He was displacing the fearsomeness of the crag onto the

194

bats – the scapebats. 'Finally, I'm obliged to stick a hand into the crack, lie back a bit, and otherwise become far too intimate with dark, damp places. Whirr . . . bip . . . bip . . . bip . . . eeeooo . . . All the fearful sounds begin, and as I peer into the crack I see tucked-up limbs and fuzzy ears. God, I've got to get out of here!' Perhaps Higgins always hated bats, but now his hang-up was being magnified by the danger of the climb, 'this minefield of wobbly rock and shaky bolts', and the animals conveniently incarnated it so he could hate them instead of realising his own fear and perhaps being unmanned by it.

The neurosis involved, which few of us seem to be free of, shows through in the excessiveness of a further animal image near the end of the essay: 'We feel like children who have just touched a tarantula and gotten away without a bite – that slow, devilish black rambler, so beautiful and frightening all at once.' Of course if poisonous spiders had actually inhabited that crag (as they did the fabulous tropical scarp of Roraima, climbed by MacInnes and his merry masochists in 1973), then the fear would have been rational, not neurotic. This is the meaning given to an encounter with a big bat or flying fox in Jeff Long's novel *Angels of Light*:

> John Dog inserted his hand into a fist-size hole on the third afternoon [of a climb on Half Dome, Yosemite], only to be bitten by a startled foxbat. Without a second thought he did the most intelligent, cold-blooded thing possible: he dipped his hand back into the hole, grabbed the bat by one dry wing, and brained it against the wall. Then he dropped the feather-light carcase to Tinkerbell, who gingerly stuffed it into the top of their red haul bag. That night, several hundred feet higher, the two climbers scrutinised the brown creature and tried to decide if it might have been rabid. Finally, unable to decide, John Dog tossed the body away. A butterfly that had lost its color, it sailed crookedly into the night.
>
> – *Ascent*, 1984, p 74

Are climbers ever savaged by wild beasts on Californian cliffs? Mostly, to judge by the literature, they encounter nothing more carnivorous than frogs and mice (see *Mirrors in the Cliffs*, pp 23, 82–4). Renato Casarotto was plagued by a rat that ate slings on

Mount Watkins but he was not scathed himself (*Mountain*, January/February 1984). Long would seem to have set up that striking moment in his novel to put as rational a gloss as possible on the abhorrence that we secrete like bile when, in a situation that is already steep and scary, we come hard up against an alien species and can't get away from it. A bizarre case of this happened to Rob and me on Doorpost, which climbs diagonally, then steeply, then comfortably up the middle of Bosigran Main Face. As I reached the roomy gallery of the second stance, a sound from the grotto at the back made me actually start, and enhanced my sense of the drop behind me – a grating breath, between the deterrent hiss of a goose or a swan and the sound a conger makes, as though it were spewing molten bone, when it's dragged inboard on a fishing-line. From the deep gloom at the back a herring gull was glaring out at me. Its beak had grown out at the base into nobbles and blebs of diseased bone. Had it taken refuge here, outcast from its own species, unable to mate or fish, and therefore at risk from predators? As we eyed each other I could feel my shock turning into the antagonism that arises as someone with a deformity stares at you, daring you to pity him. I tied on and brought Rob up, and though I warned him as he came within earshot that there was a sick bird in there, he too started as he focused on it. Next day, when we reached that same point, climbing the neighbouring Doorway with Tom Metscher, it cost us some mental or moral effort to use the stance again. The pariah, silent now, was still squatting there in the dark.

The tortured pathology of that beak, the bat's twisted rubber caricature of a human face, the jackdaw's frost-blue eyes, as fixed as a lizard's – we don't want to know these appetites and panics, not that close up. They are too other. Animal life is all very well, if it's a yellow Labrador as warm as cushions, attuned to our least whims, willing to drink in our cuddles or cower under our scolds; if it's a squirrel or a roedeer given the Disney treatment, coy and compliant with the saucer eyes and curving lashes of a novice in a Fifties beauty contest; or a rabbit in Alison Uttley, taking tea off lettuce-leaf plates in a converted cottage under the roots of an oak. But the real thing is utterly other, its dead-weight

bruisingly heavy, its eyes as unfeeling as gemstones, the unpre-
dictable stab of its beak or fang. Its gape reeks of unknown
chemicals, its pelt or plumage crawls with parasites. From the
shady mouth of its den the one message vibrates on the airwaves:
'Mine. Me. Here. You. No. Go.'

Their otherness reacts on our neuroses as sensitively as the
beetle-scratchings of a Geiger counter registering radioactivity.
Why do we (some of us) abhor spiders, or worms or harmless
snakes? Neil has never been conditioned to shy away from
nature. The first time he saw an earthworm in the garden, when
he was crawling along the path, aged fifteen months, he began to
cry. We reassured him, handled the worm, returned it to the
flowerbed. The next time he saw one, a year later, he picked it up
with interest and began to lift it towards his mouth as though it
was a noodle. So the fears die back into the subconscious, but in
there, still, the Things twitch and scurry, too galvanic for
comfort, too good at clinging to smooth surfaces and disappearing into crevices. On an outcrop of Torridonian sandstone I once
felt my nose and mouth netted by strong elastic spider-web as I
pulled upwards. If I had been at one with nature, I would have
backed off and downclimbed, or traversed, calmly, and found a
new line up the bulging layers of the face. As it was I clawed the
strands off my face with my left hand and was then mortified to
see the spider with its black and white legs and tapering egg body
scuttle away for dear life from its ruined masterpiece. There
should be a word – speciesism? – for this tendency to make
enemies of creatures who have never done us any actual harm.

Bill Peascod would have had little patience with such scruples.
He was no philistine but he had a characteristically hard-nosed
though playful habit of regarding me as an over-sensitive
intellectual. His own intellectualism was workmanlike and
profound. On one occasion, as we picked our way across the
clinking slither of the slate heaps between Honister Pass and
Buckstone How, he spoke continuously for a quarter of an hour
about a concept he had found fundamental to mining – the
pressure arch. Summarising four years later can only weaken
his vision but his gist, I believe, was that a miner as he works

underground, hinges his life on his sense of where the pressure arch is. It is not a veritable curve of the rock or the coal, it is his notion of the section where the crucial stresses apply. If he cuts too far back from it, the face will not fall away readily enough. If he cuts too forward of it, the roof will fall in behind him.

The concept seized me and stayed with me as a symbol that should work in any area of experience – in politics, for example, where a revolutionary leadership might lag behind the doings of the ordinary people on the streets or, alternatively, might become so obsessed with a radical ideal that they lost touch with the rank and file behind them. There is even a link between the local form of the pressure arch in a single Cumbrian mine (or was – they are all closed now) and the structure of the Lake District as a whole. Arthur Trueman showed that the rock strata of the region are 'domed upwards', sandstone upon mountain limestone upon slate. The radial drainage system (recognised by Wordsworth in his *Description of the Scenery of the Lakes*) evolved accordingly, 'rivers flowing outwards in nearly every direction from the centre of the dome more or less as the rain streams outwards from the top of an umbrella.' (A. E. Trueman, *Geology and Scenery in England and Wales*, 1971, pp 244–7) The two notions are very different: the pressure arch is more conceptual, it can never be seen, whereas the rock dome of prehistoric Cumbria was once there and was never seen only because there were as yet no eyes. But the notions are also akin: each is a form of the curve of the world.

In the winter of 1983–4 Bill felt that the beat of his heart had become irregular again, and he went to Carlisle for an ECG. It was reassuring, but the poem I wrote for him at that time, called 'Pressure Arches', in which every image tries to mean, simultaneously, a winter storm, the explosive work of mining, and a heart under stress, ending with an image of injury:

> Hail-shocks hammered and beat
> On the hunched hill-shoulders.
> By sunset their whitened brows
> Redden again like blood through bandages.

During those seasons of 1981 to 1984, established in Cumbria again, Bill's painting and climbing had been fusing more completely than ever before. He was painting incessantly: delicately-layered images of slopes and rising edges and sky-lines, in which the formidable mass of a mountain or a buttress clarifies itself out of the nothing-mist below. He was now reversing a trend towards an almost abstract impressionism – although when Etsu first visited Buttermere with him on a trip home during the Seventies she had already been able to say to him, 'This is what you've been painting all these years.' (*Journey After Dawn*, p 118) Now, as he got back into steep and difficult places which he had believed he would never revisit, he reconnected his earlier and his later life and produced many paintings as explicit likenesses of particular fells, Ullock north of Skiddaw, Hobcarton up Newlands, Eagle Crag raising its great whale skull out of the dark backward of Birkness Combe.

On an airy stance, or back again at the foot of the crag, he often said, laughing at himself, 'What's an old man like me doing in a place like this?' (see plate 8) What he meant was, 'I can still do it!' When I asked him about some other, not necessarily older veteran, he would say, 'He's past it,' then add, '*I* won't go gentle into that good night.' And he did not. On May 17 1985 he was climbing with Don Whillans and Jim Birkett's son Bill on Cloggy – Clogwyn dur Arddu, *the* Welsh crag – which all his life he had greatly wanted to visit. Whillans led the first pitch of Great Slab, Bill followed. Just before he reached the stance, he said, 'Don – I feel dizzy.' He started to keel over. The two others between them lowered him to the ground and with the help of an experienced diver who happened to be there, they worked for an hour to resuscitate him. But he had died – he had been in his element to the last.

We had been due to climb the following weekend and had climbed at Honister in wintry drizzle four weeks before, a route of his own, The Garden Path, on a crag with a strong vertical grain called Yew Knotts. I had made a poem from our experience (we had already done the detailed planning for a book of his paintings twinned with my poems) and when I sent him a copy he suggested a Cumbrian word in place of the Scots 'tyauve' (strive) in the final line.

26

In the Toils of Yew Knotts

Slicing the airstream with its upright knives,
The rockface barely admits our alien lives.
We must accept its nature, twine and crawl
Like honeysuckle up the garden wall,
Bleed on its dogrose thorns, and sink our fists
In sodden moss that numbs us to the wrists.
A green slot narrows: now we hoist ourselves
Upwards out of the ledge's tussocked shelves
And snake like ivy fingering into cracks,
Holding the rock apart with knees and backs,
Turning its colours, smeared with browns and greens,
Blue-black as ravens, grey as peregrines.
A sloth might flourish here, a large-brained bat
At ease on overhangs we gibber at –
A suctioning gekko – a slug whose muscled foot
Cleaves close as stone embedded in a root . . .
An earthy sinus gapes, I palm its stones
As surgeons try the integrity of bones.
They quake and give. My earthworm snout recoils,
Then slithers off to inhabit denser soils
Sinewed with rowan roots and spined with slate
Where groove and buttress, rib and jut create
A wind-driven mountain-mill whose chutes and wynds
Pour down cold brash as the giant quernstones grind.
This is the life – earth in the scalp, the nose,
Gravel like nails driven in between the toes,
Blood on the knuckles, bird-lime in the hair,
Rain in the armpits, lichen everywhere –
Better to tyauve like this than age in an armchair.

27

After Bill's burial in Bassenthwaite, under the north-west flank of Skiddaw, I stood talking with Don Whillans and Peter Greenwood and arranged to reclimb their route, the Raven Traverse, Thirlmere, in mid-August. Between the late winter of 1952 and the spring of 1956, Peter, who was one of the Bradford Lads (a loose grouping, not a club), had climbed with most of the rock masters of the time (Dolphin, Whillans, Paul Ross) and had put up twenty-eight new routes in Cumberland. In so doing he had brought the sport through into the Extreme age via Sword of Damocles on the Langdale front of Bow Fell and Thirlmere Eliminate on the Castle Rock of Triermain. His climbing style had been extraordinarily free and fearless. He put up Angels' Highway (splendid name) on impulse and on sight – one hundred and twenty feet of Hard Very Severe climbing, straight up the Castle Rock with no resting place and just one sling for protection on a creaky flake. He was at the crest of the wave after Bill Peascod's and they had never met. One day in the summer of 1956 he said to Whillans, 'I'm giving up climbing.'

'You silly bugger.'

'Well – d'you want my gear?'

'Oh aye.'

This abrupt departure from the scene (to get married and to find a steady job) helped turn him into a mystery man. The more I had noticed his name against what became (with Birkett's) some of my favourite routes – Obituary Grooves on Black Crag, Funeral Way on Lower Falcon, Vesper on Shepherd's, and many more – the more I wanted to know about him. People would say 'He disappeared . . . he got rich, then lost it all,' and other legends of the kind. All the time his name was in the phone book. When I rang him in November 1984 and suggested a meeting, to talk and perhaps to repeat his routes, he readily agreed – at least to talk.

On a December day when the sun seemed hardly to get above the earth and clouds, rocks, and tree-trunks all looked the one dingy colour, we walked up to Lower Falcon above Derwent-water and he cast a curious eye over the undercut, angular pull-and-stride-and-swing which is the start, not only of Funeral Way, his final route, but also of all climbing on a crag where thirty-one routes now go, none below Very Severe. A sharp gem to have crowned your career but too hard for the start of a comeback, although the dripping moisture would probably have bothered him less than it would me: 'We were never turned back by much, however wet it was. We'd come all that way, so we had to have something to show for the hours and hours on the road.' So we went along to Shepherd's and climbed Little Chamonix, the most spectacular easy route in the Lakes. Peter strolled up it with unhesitating placements of his hands and feet – his first climb for nearly three decades. He had driven past the crags and mountains many times since he retired from climbing and said he had never regretted his decision or wanted to begin again but one reminiscence gave a poignant glimpse of how much rock had meant to him: 'When I gave up, I bought some pegs, and an ice-axe, and a peg-hammer, and a krab, to hang on the wall of our new house. I had never owned a piton till I stopped climbing.'

Three weeks later, when January had turned the wet to rime and snow lay like granulated sugar on drifts of dead oak leaves, we met at Armathwaite on the banks of the River Eden, along with his sons Paul and Shane. They had often asked their father to take them out climbing and he had always said no. Now the four of us climbed enthusiastically: Kingfisher, Glenwillie Grooves, Flasherman, the graph rising from Very Difficult to Severe to Mild Very Severe, angling upwards (hopefully) towards Angels' Highway, which I might dare to lead, and Hell's Groove (Sca Fell) and Sword of Damocles, where I might have to enlist the leadership of Pete and Neil. Standing on the fine-sand beach below the weirdly sculpted terra-cotta wall where the Carlisle climbers temper their fingers to a special steely hardness, Peter signalled his comeback in earnest by putting on a pair of Spanish climbing-boots with the new high-friction rubber and a new harness, whose tapes and buckles he cursed heartily. He believes in the simplest of climbing styles, a naked encounter between person and crag, climbing from the bottom up with no high-tech frigging and a minimum of equipment.

In March, with the winter's last cold rainfall still squelching out of the turf, I met him with Bill Peascod and Mike McKenzie (joint author of a fine route on Esk Buttress, Gargoyle Direct) at Raw Head in Langdale. Our combined ages came to 223. We limbered up for the season on Mamba and Centipede, east of the main face of Raven Crag, and then, with Peter, I climbed Mendes, zig-zagging from one acute hold to another up the steep lower face of Middlefell Buttress. 'You came up that good and fast,' I said at the top.

'I had to,' he answered – abrupt and undemonstrative in what I recognised as his idiom.

A few weeks later, when the sodden frustrations of 1985 were still in the future (but Bill had already opined to me that 'we were in for a bad year'), Peter and Bill went to Newlands on a wettish day and Peter fell off Grey Slab. He had finished the hard climbing on pitch three when his feet skidded and he broke his ankle when he hit rock on the way down.

> 'It was daft really – the falls I had were all in the damp. There was Deer Bield, of course [see below] . . . And on Central Buttress on Sca Fell I went up the layback and my fingers were so near – inches from the flake top – I put my right foot out onto the wall and it skidded right off the little hold – I fell right down, hit The Oval, and broke my wrist. Freddy Williams, who was seconding, said, "I'm not leading back down there!" So I had to, broken wrist an' all.'

At Bill's funeral on May 22 Peter's leg was in plaster but by August 4 he was able to limp up to Shepherd's with me and climb Ardus in good style, on a day when its delicate and unprotectable final wall was secreting moisture in dark trickles. Perhaps, in two weeks' time, we would be able to climb the Raven Traverse when Don Whillans came back from the Dolomites. On August 18, just after arriving in England, Don died in his sleep.

The extraordinary and tragic sequence was not yet at an end.

But the glum skies parted now, late-September sunshine lit up the first yellow patches on the birch leaves, the brambles were black but tasteless after the wet weeks without sun. On Peter's fifty-fourth birthday we made it at last – we reclimbed a route of his, the Far East Traverse on the Raven outcrops in Langdale. He had put it up on a 'fine, calm winter's day' in 1952, with Harold Drasdo and Dennis Gray. They just pushed out the line, hoping it would continue. Thirty-three years later we basked in summer-like warmth that made my fingers slip as though buttered when I set off rightwards from the crag's western edge, strayed too high to avoid a blank vertical groove, and found myself faced with forty feet of traversing against the grain of the rock. Placing a nut behind a shaky fang, I teetered sideways, sweating. Black mini-steps, rims for side-pulls on fingerends, little vertical shelves that end in mid-air and force me to invent a grip in which I cup my fingers under a shelf and pinch it before laying-away rightwards from it – the pinch-cling-lay-under? This is nearly beyond me, enforcing a concentration that tries nerves as much as muscles. At last I'm striding across a steep gutter and sinking my arms behind a big flake of pale-orange Langdale rock before embracing the grey-satin trunk of a holly with utter gratitude.

'I've news for you,' I yelled to Peter when he came into sight around the far arête, and when I explained my epic he said, 'It'll be too hard for me, then.' But he tracked unerringly downwards where I had risen and in ten minutes he was tying onto a holly twenty feet below my own. Pitch five of the Traverse down-climbs pitch two of Arthur Dolphin's route, Nineveh, and Peter led this in his eagerness to find the place where he had nearly cratered on the second ascent of that route. A turf ledge fell away complete and he had almost hit the ground before springing ten feet back up on the elasticity of the rope. To his delight the mark is still to be seen, a slaty ledge unnaturally smoother and darker than the much more weathered neighbouring rock. After three hundred feet of excellent climbing, as long as Gimmer Crack and two-thirds of it good-value Very Severe, we sun ourselves amongst the bleached grass on the crag top while Peter enthuses – 'one of the best routes in the valley' – and defends the Far East

Buttress against the old charge that it's 'the boozer's crag' – ten minutes away from two good pubs. But his satisfaction is clouded:

> 'In the old days you just went up it like that, on sight. Whatever you looked at, you could do it. But now – half a million fags and fifty thousand pints later . . . I can rely on natural technique still, but the strength and the drive, they're not there . . . You're lucky perhaps, starting late – you've still your enthusiasm.'

For four weeks more the Indian summer mellowed through the Borrowdale woodlands and if it had not been for the silent rusting of the bracken it would have seemed as though time had stilled and we could move at will from 1985 to 1955 and back again. In mid-October we climbed up through the trees at the head of Troutdale and found Black Crag at its blackest, gleaming like fresh tar under the big eave on the north buttress, which was first climbed by Peter, as part of the Girdle he put up with Paul Ross and Dennis English. On my harness I hang a Teacher's bar towel from the selection Peter's been getting me from his local and a pair of socks to put on over my PA's in case friction sinks to zero. I ask him what kind he used to use and he says, 'Other people's. We used to raid the drying rooms.' He has been anticipating the delights of the traverse under the eave 'on big holds'. But as I stride and stride along the glacis, splitting my trousers which were already indecent, there is nothing for the hands but a series of shaky plaques with half-inch tops, like slates on an aging roof. All along I can see my fear barrier getting nearer: a soaking stripe as shiny-black as liquorice. At its verge I balance on twin thorns of rock and stare across the 'barrier' at a wet but level ledge beyond it that has become my goal. What's the stepping-stone? Only a rim four inches long and less than an inch broad, barely tilted inwards. The joint under the eave, previously closed, has relented slightly. I stick my fingerends in, palm upwards, and brace my knuckles downwards against the glacis. The tiny rim has become the hinge of my world: it can lean me inwards to the security of continued contact with terra-firma, it can cant me outwards into mid-air, birchtree tops and wood-pigeons and the thirty-two-feet per second accelerating plunge. I lean along, my right foot edges on the mini-hold, my left foot smears on slick black slate, my hands tense, my right foot goes for the good step, my left touches the mini-hold, thanks it briefly, and then I'm reaching for some semi-detached flakes on the edge of the earth-filled gully while elation brims and soaks through me like the sunlight.

Before I made the moves I'd given the usual silly shout of the nervous leader, 'Mind the rope now!' and Peter, ever literal and brusque, had shouted back, 'I'm minding it all the time!' The crux for him, in 1955, had been on pitch two:

> 'When I led the pitch, I climbed past a huge flake. And as I used the edge of it, it moved! So I told Paul I was getting rid of it and I got above it and pushed it off with my foot. Christ, what a crash! Paul thought the whole crag was coming down. It went all the way down to the valley – the trees were only small then and I could see the rock bouncing right the way down. Robin Scott [the first man to use Alsatians on mountain rescue] was picnicking beside the stream and he said bits finished up beside him.'

Perhaps the trauma with that tottering pinnacle was still in Peter as he called to me from the steep slab beside the still undarkened scar of it, 'You don't half get me into some terrible places.' When I reached the pegs on the stance shared with The Coffin and The Shroud (Peter's black humour started the tradition of funerary names in this part of the dale), he had called out, half-jokingly, 'Could you abseil from them?' – in case we had to retreat – and at the foot of the crag he remarked, 'You're a rotten bugger, dragging me into this when I could be in the garden, or fishing.' On trying cruxes every climber must have felt this but other things were ganging up on Peter now. Shortly before I met him he had been working on building sites and was hard and fit. Now he'd been inactive for four months and had put on twenty pounds.

On the last day of our Indian summer, October 27, when the hayfields round Rosthwaite were green again after the last mowing of the year, we climbed the tall black slanting cleft of his route Libido, on Castle Crag in Borrowdale, named by its co-author, Chris Drake, who 'knew about words like that'.

'He'd a gingery-blond beard – not so comon in those days. And you'd come into the Carlisle Club hut at Rosthwaite and find him reading Marcus Aurelius or summat.'

'What did he do?'

'Not a right lot. He was in the Keswick pencil mill for a while and he brought them out on strike . . . He was drowned in Windermere, years ago, and he'd said to us, two years before, "I'm going to vanish after drowning on Windermere." '

Peter's anecdotes, uttered quickly with amused flashes of his very bright brown eyes, give glimpses of a sub-culture whose members were almost piratical in their living rough, their free-and-easy manners, their bursts of aggression, even their nicknames for each other, which included 'Death' and 'the Pale Man'. Peter's reminiscing about them teems with quirky and drastic images of character. Recalling Whillans's arrest for drunken driving, which was reported in the national press, he says, 'It took six policemen to stop him. He'd been weaving along, but when they stopped him he laid one out. In the end they had him handcuffed to the seat, so he tore the seat out. That was his instant reaction. It was a climber's reaction. He wouldn't be stopped. That's what it took to do his climbs. He'd keep going, whatever . . .' Shades of Rousseau's 'There's the great matter, to have force.' When I tell him that Paul Ross said to me that he hammered pegs into an unclimbed face on Gimmer 'to provoke the Langdalians', Peter says, 'Bless him! He was a *daft* bugger. It was a joke to him – fun – he just loved the gymnastics of it.' About Bill Aughton, a second of Ross's, he recalls that 'he used to wear a top hat and keep a massive box of matches under it. He'd whip it off if he met a lady and offer her a light. He's bald as a bladder now' (because of the matches?). As we stand on the triangle of grass where the roads meet under Raven, Thirlmere, before going up to take some photographs, he remembers happy days with Peter Whitwell, the Pale Man, who was his second on Angels' Highway and the Direct Finish to North Crag Buttress on Shepherd's: 'We had a fight here – I don't know what about, we'd gone to do a new route with Paul. Luckily for me he wasn't trying, so I just got him in an arm-lock and held on.' But his favourite second was clearly Freddy Williams, whose name is not in any guidebook.

After holding Peter on his famous fall during the second ascent of Deer Bield Buttress in Far Easedale, 'Freddy came up no bother. There never was. He'd never lead a thing – he was too lazy. He used to hitchhike lying down. When we were on anything hard he'd whistle a special tune – a tango – to spur me on.' In *Hard Rock* Harold Drasdo honours that ascent as 'one of the most astonishing leads on record' and 'the effort of a lifetime'. In Peter's account the difficulty comes out with doubled force. A week or so before, in June 1951, Dolphin had put up the route – a long-standing and famous goal for the climbers of that wave – and he had described it in a note he left in Peter's jacket in the Old Dungeon Ghyll without saying a word. Now it was drizzling and the head of the Buttress was in cloud. A loose block fell and cut their rope in two so they had to discard twenty or thirty feet of it and carry on with it drastically curtailed. Nobody today climbs such a route in those conditions but the post-War climbers pulled a pair of socks over their 'rubbers' and got on with it.

What we should have done is what you do today and said "Bugger this." On the overhanging corner [the first crux, and of a technical grade as hard as anything then climbed in Britain] I'd my legs stretched out across the walls. My socks were worn out by now, I couldn't get a grip, I needed to get up and I needed to get down. This solution came to me. Take off the dirty wet sock, hold it in my teeth, take off the plimsoll, hold it in my teeth, take off the sock, hold it in my teeth, put on the plimsoll, put on the sock on top. Which I managed to do. And I did the same procedure a few moves later with the other one . . . On the second crux a block had come out and formed a gangway with a roof on it. Somehow you had to get a hold on this shiny, slippery roof to reach up to these good holds above. The more I tried the more my bloody hands were slipping off until I was going "Pfftt" and passing down the crag. No problem, Freddy held me all right. I collected my wits and said, "Are you going to have a go, Fred?"

"Am I hell!"

At his second shot Peter climbed the crux by wedging a knee under the roof to free his hands for the holds above, and he used this trick again to gain height at the top of the ferocious leaning crack that opens Hell's Groove on Sca Fell East Buttress, which rebuffed me when I tried to lead it with Neil in 1986.

A month after Libido, when the rock had turned wet for the winter, I met Freddy Williams, now a professional artist, at the first-ever reunion of the Bradford Lads – the group who, between them, had put up the bulk of the routes that had come to mean most to me. He was a perfectly charming, sardonic, yet gentle figure, his complexion a ghastly papery pale-yellow, his eyes hollowed out by arthritis and a heart condition. 'Last year I was saying, "When I climb again". Now I'm saying, "When I walk again".' A week later he sent me some information on a postcard of one of his own drawings of Whitby: grey pencil, meticulously detailed, olde-worlde Whitby for the tourist market. In February I heard from an art-dealer in Silverdale that he had died. These men (and women – Dolphin's ex-fiancée was there too), with their delight in physical struggle, their defiance of gravity, their tingling reminiscences of a prime just thirty years before – what was happening to them all? And to Jim Birkett, who was walking with difficulty after an operation on his knee?

Time had set off again, making moves which they could not reverse. In the course of the coldest late winter and early spring for sixty years, Peter and I climbed Bill Peascod's Groove One on Buckstone How, to check it for the guidebook, while the cars parked at Honister Pass shuddered in the gale. Then we retreated down to Lodore where we climbed a mossy direct start to Gowder Buttress (quite hard, and not in the guidebook) and abseiled off while hail flicked against the bare grey ash branches. Up at the Pass Peter had said, 'I suppose you've still your enthusiasm? I have to work it up each time. As you must have noticed.' As we warmed ourselves with soup at Grange, I said (knowing that he was perfectly candid and without false pride), 'Do you not fancy doing your own old routes?' and he replied, 'I never did, to tell you the truth.'

During the June heatwave he went fishing on the River Avon in Scotland (not far down the glen from the famous Shelterstone Crag, where Bill Brooker and his mates had loved to climb) along with Jack Bradley, his second on Necropolis (Raven, Thirlmere) thirty-three years before. When he got back, he listened with relish to my descriptions of grappling with his fierce twins on Sca Fell East, Hell's Groove and Pegasus, and then he said in his terse and final way, 'Now you know why I won't be able to repeat my routes.'

28

The Veterans

They were the natural climbers,
Working in the grain of the rock,
Short men with hefty calves and precise hands,
Small enough for me to identify with,
Old enough to be the kind of brother
Who tunnels through to manhood maybe a decade
Before oneself, grows hair in the crutch
And bloodies the knuckles half a generation
Before I learned not to blush, before
I left Kincorth behind me and the horizon
Of my world moved southwards
Nearly as far as Watford.

Two Norths count for me:
North of the Mounth, where the Wells of Dee,
Invisibly translucent, send their impulse
Through seventy miles of granite to the sea;
North of the Ribble, where the monochrome
Of Cumbria's hay and pasture fields
Is gentle enough to make me call it 'home'.

There is a vacancy in Bassenthwaite,
A hollow place on the flank of Skiddaw.
Now another has gone, from Penmaenmawr.
When will the black-coats call at Little Langdale?

A stone fist hammers the breastbone –
Meant to resuscitate? or to crush?

The hands that placed the second stone
On the cairn at the Eagle's foot,
The eyes that followed the lift
Of the exposed rib, ready to paint or climb it,
The feet that plodded heavily up the combe
High above Gatesgarth, ski'd down scree
With a boy's abandon – they are all sucked down
Into the eating earth ('to every airt a limb')
Where they will come again in the human profile
Seen on the crag through cloud or twilight,
The mumbling voice in the ghyll,
The clink of slatefall under Buckstone
Which makes you turn, thinking to see their faces . . .

I will lift my eyes to the hills
Which these men felt as a sculptor feels
A seamed and muscled torso
To find his vision's traces
(Now keen, now muddied)
Graved across the rockface.

My foot he'd not let slide,
And he was safe with me.
But when his heart failed him
There was nothing they could do
But lower him onto the earth.

He is beyond sunsmite.
Unshakable Don, who held him
On that ultimate stance,
Has followed him down now.
Now we will never trace
The raven's way together.

211

Jim can mark the peregrine
With his eyes only but
His river's hands still flex
When Harlot Face and Haste Not
Rear in his mindsight, milestones
Round the boundaries of his homeland.

Peter can still remember
Everything but fear,
Taking the direct line always,
Making his wicked jokes,
Planning to 'blow up Napes Needle'
(Only the gentlefolk believed him).

Their sons' sons and mine
Will meet on a stance or a summit.
Their eyes will expand for a moment
When our names are mentioned
Before their lines separate,
Climbing on beyond us.

Glossary

Belay	(verb) to anchor oneself to a stance, hence to be in charge of the other climber's safety; (noun) a ledge or other perch suitable for tying onto
Cassin peg	a type of piton (*qv*)
chimney	a vertical or near-vertical groove in a rockface with parallel sides
crux	the hardest point on a pitch or section of a climb
Extreme	the hardest category of rock-climb, divided into one to eight, eight being the hardest so far
karabiner	a snap-link through which the rope runs (krab)
pendule	a swing across the cliff-face (often involuntary)
perlon	a type of woven nylon
piton	a hard steel peg for hammering into a crack, with an eyelet to which a sling or karabiner can be attached, to act as either an anchor or a running belay
protection nut	usually a wedge-shaped piece of alloy, fixed to a loop of perlon or wire, wedged into a crack and clipped to the rope by a karabiner
runner	protection consisting either of a nut (see above) or a taped sling
Sticht plate	a disc of metal with two slots through which the ropes pass; the climber, anchored to the stance, fastens the plate to his harness and can then hold a fall by letting the running rope jam in the slots